Malcolm Mann
Steve Taylore-Knowles

B1+

Student's Book

Contents

Unit	Topic (T)	Reading	Grammar 1 (G)	Vocabulary (V)
1 Family Ties PAGE 6	people and relationships	scanning for specific information	tense review: present (simple and continuous)	key topic vocabulary, word formation (prefixes), phrasal verbs with *up*, metaphors (people)
2 The Open Road PAGE 14	transport	scanning for specific information	tense review: past (simple and continuous)	key topic vocabulary, confusable words, collocations (transport)
Revision Units 1–2 • PAGE 22				
3 Killing Time PAGE 24	free time activities, hobbies	recognising discourse markers	tense review: present perfect (simple and continuous)	key topic vocabulary, idioms (time), phrasal verbs with *down*, metaphors (time)
4 Work Wonders PAGE 32	occupations	scanning for specific information	tense review: past perfect (simple and continuous)	key topic vocabulary, word formation (suffixes), confusable words
Revision Units 3–4 • PAGE 40				
5 The Global Village PAGE 42	the media, communications	scanning for specific information	the passive	key topic vocabulary, phrasal verbs with *on*, idioms (the media)
6 Come Rain or Shine PAGE 50	the weather	understanding main concepts	the future (1): *will, going to*, present (simple and continuous)	key topic vocabulary, collocations (weather), confusable words
Revision Units 5–6 • PAGE 58				
7 A Matter of Taste PAGE 60	food and drink	grammatical referencing	reported speech	key topic vocabulary, phrasal verbs with *out*, collocations (cooking)
8 Out and About PAGE 68	travel and tourism	text type and function	full infinitives (with to) and *-ing* forms after verbs	key topic vocabulary, word formation (irregular forms), metaphors (life)
Revision Units 7–8 • PAGE 76				

Listening	Speaking	Use of English	Writing
predicting, Soundbite: /ɪ/ and /iː/	talking about family	stative verbs, word patterns	selecting correct register, informal letter/email
identifying location, Soundbite: /æ/ and /e/	comparing	*would*, *used to*, *be used to*, word patterns	presenting an argument, essay
understanding attitude, Soundbite: /ʌ/	making suggestions	articles, synonyms	awareness of target reader, informal letter/email
listening for specific information, Soundbite: silent letters (1)	expressing uncertainty	comparatives and superlatives	layout and text structure, report
listening for gist, Soundbite: /ɜː/	talking about experiences	countable and uncountable nouns, homonyms	using descriptive language, story
listening for specific information, Soundbite: weak forms (1)	speculating	question tags, connectors	selecting appropriate style, article
identifying roles, Soundbite: /k/, /g/ and /ŋ/	agreeing and disagreeing	indirect questions, prepositions	using prompts, formal letter/email
listening for specific information, Soundbite: /s/ and /z/	giving examples	*prefer*, *would rather*, *had better*, parts of speech	expressing opinion, review

Unit	Topic	Reading	Grammar 1	Vocabulary
9 Lab Report PAGE 78	science and technology	scanning for specific information	conditionals (1): zero, first, second	key topic vocabulary, collocations, phrasal verbs with *off*
10 Let Me Entertain You PAGE 86	entertainment	distinguishing fact and opinion	modals (1)	key topic vocabulary, confusable words, collocations (entertainment)
Revision Units 9–10 • **PAGE 94**				
11 The Learning Curve PAGE 96	education	lexical referencing	relative clauses	key topic vocabulary, phrasal verbs with *over*, metaphors (the mind)
12 Fighting Fit PAGE 104	health and fitness	scanning for specific information	result clauses: *so, such, too, enough*	key topic vocabulary, collocations: *make / do*, metaphors (problems)
Revision Units 11–12 • **PAGE 112**				
13 Art Attack PAGE 114	the arts and music	understanding main points	the causative	key topic vocabulary, word formation (suffixes), metaphors (description)
14 Game, Set and Match PAGE 122	sport	understanding text structure	modals (2): modal perfect	key topic vocabulary, collocations, phrasal verbs with other particles
Revision Units 13–14 • **PAGE 130**				
15 Up in Smoke PAGE 132	the environment	grammatical referencing	the future (2): future perfect (simple and continuous), future continuous	key topic vocabulary, confusable words, metaphors (ideas)
16 On the Run PAGE 140	crime	scanning for specific information	conditionals (2): third	key topic vocabulary, word formation (irregular forms), word patterns
Revision Units 15–16 • **PAGE 148**				

Writing database • PAGE 150
Writing planners 1–16 • PAGE 155
Word pattern database • PAGE 163
Phrasal verb database • PAGE 164
Speaking database • PAGE 165
Grammar database • PAGE 166
Webquests • PAGE 198

Listening	Speaking	Use of English	Writing
listening for specific information, Soundbite: /s/ and /ʃ/	talking about hopes	unless, in case, as long as, word patterns	paragraphing, informal letter/email
predicting, Soundbite: /ə/	expressing attitude and opinion	parts of speech, word formation: prefixes	cohesion, essay
predicting, Soundbite: stress (1)	prioritising	relative pronouns and prepositions, word patterns	selecting correct register, informal letter/email
listening for gist, Soundbite: /ɑː/, /ɔː/ and /uː/	discourse management	infinitives of purpose, word patterns	awareness of purpose, report
identifying relationships, Soundbite: silent letters (2)	talking about interests	gradable and ungradable adjectives and adverbs, synonyms	making recommendations, review
listening for specific information, Soundbite: stress (2)	comparing	the unreal past, common mistakes	selecting correct register, article
understanding purpose, Soundbite: /ɒ/ and /əʊ/	expressing attitude and opinion	transferred negation, word formation	using prompts, formal letter/email
listening for specific information, Soundbite: weak forms (2)	seeking clarification	wishes and regrets, parts of speech	paragraphing, story

1

Family Ties

🛈 Start thinking!

Do you have a large or small family?
How many of you live together?
How many cousins/uncles/aunts do you have?

📖 Reading

1 🎧 **1.01** Read the post and comments on a social networking site. Whose family sounds most like yours?

2 Read the post and comments again, and decide if the following statements are true (T), false (F) or not stated (N).

1 Jenny has a very large family. _____
2 Gokhan has brothers and sisters. _____
3 Masha is younger than her sister. _____
4 Pete regularly stays with his biological father. _____
5 Alicia wants to meet her biological parents. _____
6 Alex's biological father lives in Greece. _____

3 Write a word or short phrase from the comments to the post to answer each question.

1 Who says that they have a pet?
   _____
2 Why doesn't Angie live with her father?
   _____
3 What's Alex's sister like?
   _____
4 When does Pete stay with his real dad?
   _____
5 What do some of Gokhan's friends do?
   _____
6 What is Masha also doing right now?
   _____

www.myfamily.com

Jenny
Hi all my MyFace friends around the world! We're doing a project at school on families at the moment and I need your help. Do you have a large or small family? Who do you live with? Do you all get on? I'd love to know what your family's like! Comments please!

👍 17 people like this.

Gokhan
Hi from Ankara, Turkey! Jenny, my family's quite small because I'm an only child. In the flat where we live, there's just me and my mum and dad. But my grandparents (my mum's parents) live in the flat upstairs, and my dad's parents live nearby too, so it's not too lonely! To be honest, I sometimes wish I had a brother or sister to play with, but at least I have a bedroom to myself! Some of my friends have to share a room with their brother or sister. I wouldn't like that!

Masha
We're doing a project on families at school at the moment too, Jenny! I live with my parents and my older sister, Natalia, in Novosibirsk in Siberia, Russia. Natalia and I love each other (of course!), but we don't always get on. She's always complaining that I play my music too loud! I often get annoyed with her, though, because she borrows my things without asking! (Natalia, if you're reading this, I want that magazine back!)

Pete
Hello from California, USA! My family's a bit complicated. My parents are divorced, and I live with my mum and my stepfather. My dad also remarried after the divorce, and I spend almost every weekend with him and his wife (my stepmum). I've got a stepsister called Angie. That's my stepfather Alan's daughter from a previous marriage, but she's older and works in New York, so she doesn't live with us. I've also now got a half brother because my dad and my stepmum have just had a baby! I told you it was complicated! It's great, though. We all get on really well. My parents are still good friends, and my stepfather and stepmother like each other too. It's actually a really loving family, and I'm really grateful for that.

Alicia
Hi, Jenny! My parents adopted me just after I was born, and I live with them and my brother and sister and our dog, Cassie. Even though I'm adopted and my brother and sister aren't, our parents treat us all the same. I totally feel part of the family, and don't want or need to find my biological parents. As far as I'm concerned, my mum and dad are my real parents! (By the way, I live in Lublin, Poland.)

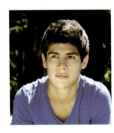

Alex
Hi from Australia! I'm Greek-Australian, so most of my family live on the other side of the world. Here in Brisbane, there's me, my mum and my younger sister, Georgia. Georgia's a bit spoilt, to be honest. Anything she asks for, my mum gives it to her! The rest of my mum's family all live in Greece. That's more than 15,000km away! I've got three aunts, two grandparents and loads of cousins there, and I've never met any of them in person. My mum keeps in touch with them by phone and email, and I've spoken to them (of course!), but it would be lovely to meet them. I'm sure I will, one day!

WORD BOX

4 Use words or phrases from the post and comments to complete the sentences. You've been given the first letter to help you.

1. It would be fun to have a brother, instead of being an o_____ c_____ .
2. Lisa gets what she wants. She's becoming very selfish and I think she's a bit s_____ .
3. My parents are d_____ and I see my dad every weekend at his house.
4. My mum met a man last year and she r_____ .
5. My dad married Sarah's mum last month so Sarah's my s_____ .
6. It's important to grow up as part of a l_____ family.
7. I didn't know you were a_____ . Do you want to find your real parents?
8. Kevin and I have the same mother but different fathers, so he's my h_____ b_____ .

Have your say!

- What do you think are the advantages and disadvantages of being an only child?
- Is it better to share a room with a brother or sister, or have your own room? Why?

1 G Grammar clinic

Present tense review

👁 Look at *Grammar database* pages 166–168 before you do the exercises.

1 Read these sentences and phrases from the comments to the post on pages 6 and 7. Match each one with an explanation.

1 That's more than 15,000km away! _____
2 Natalia and I love each other (of course!), but we don't always get on. _____
3 I spend almost every weekend with him and his wife … _____
4 We're doing a project on families at school at the moment … _____
5 She's always complaining that I play my music too loud! _____

a This is a regular habit.
b This is an annoying habit.
c This is a temporary situation.
d This is a general, scientific truth.
e This is a feeling or situation, not an action.

2 Circle the correct tense in each sentence.

1 Our family **goes/is going** on holiday to Spain every year.
2 Did you say you **stay/are staying** with friends until your house is ready?
3 My sister doesn't have a car because she **doesn't drive/is not driving**.
4 People **live/are living** in many different kinds of family.
5 Brothers and sisters often **argue/are arguing** about unimportant things.

3 Complete the sentences using the correct form of the verbs in the box. You may need to use a negative form.

try • go • learn • see • live • like

1 My brother and I _____ to the local secondary school.
2 We _____ here until the new house is ready.
3 I _____ French for my trip to Paris next month.
4 My grandparents _____ milkshakes, but I do!
5 'Wait a second. I _____ to find my keys.'
6 We _____ our cousins every Christmas.

4 Use the notes to make complete sentences.

1 My brother/always/complain about/me to my parents.
2 In our house,/we/always/eat dinner together/and I/like it.
3 My stepsister/play/the piano and she/know/hundreds of songs.
4 I/think/Mum/have a shower. She/usually/have a shower at this time.
5 My relationship with my sister/get/better.
6 I/not believe/everything my brother/tell/me.

5 Read Jenny's comment about her own family. Find six mistakes with verb tenses and correct them. Use contractions (*you're*, etc) where you can.

Jenny
Thanks for all your comments! You all have really interesting families! Masha, you do a project on families too, so I thought I'd tell you about my family. There are five of us in my family – my mum and dad, me, my older brother, Alex and my younger sister, Lizzie. My mum's being a newsreader on TV and my dad works in an office (I'm not really knowing what he does!). I'm generally getting on very well with Lizzie and Alex, but they're always playing tricks on me, and that's very annoying! I've also got two sets of grandparents, and they often come to visit us. In fact, Grandma Mollie and Grandpa Doug stay with us at the moment, which is nice. I'm loving my family!

Vocabulary builder

Adjectives to describe people

1 Match the words in the box with the correct definitions.

selfish • popular • sensitive • arrogant • pessimistic
amusing • ambitious • considerate • generous
optimistic • modest

If you are …

1 _____ , you want to be very successful.
2 _____ , you think the future is going to be bad.
3 _____ , you have lots of friends.
4 _____ , people think you are funny.
5 _____ , you share what you have with other people.
6 _____ , you get upset very easily.
7 _____ , you think the future is going to be good.
8 _____ , you only care about yourself.
9 _____ , you care about other people's feelings.
10 _____ , you don't like to talk about your achievements.
11 _____ , you think you are better than other people.

Word formation: prefixes

2 Complete the sentences with the correct negative form of the word in bold. Use *in*, *un*, *im*, *dis*, *il* or *ir*.

1 I'm sure Nigel didn't mean to be _____ when he spoke to you this morning. **kind**
2 A lot of people think it is _____ to visit without calling first. **polite**
3 Nadine thinks she's _____ , but I think she's quite pretty. **attractive**
4 Don't be _____ ! Let your sister play with you and your friends! **fair**
5 I think it's very _____ of you to lie to your brother like that. **honest**
6 My mum is _____ of being rude to anyone. **capable**
7 Jenny is in trouble after doing something _____ . **legal**
8 Don't include any _____ points in your description. **relevant**

Phrasal verbs with *up*

3 Phrasal verbs with *up* often have meanings connected to making things appear or things suddenly appearing. Match the phrasal verbs in the box with the definitions.

makes up • turns up • comes up
thinks up • brings up

1 If a person _____ , they arrive unexpectedly.
2 If a problem _____ , it appears unexpectedly.
3 If a person _____ an idea, they have it before anyone else.
4 If a person _____ a story, they create it.
5 If a person _____ a subject, they mention it in a conversation.

Magic metaphors

4 When we talk about *people*, we sometimes use words or phrases that have a connection with *temperature*. Complete the sentences with the words from the box.

warm • cool • icy • hot-tempered
cold-hearted

1 I thought John was very _____ when he said he didn't care about people who don't have enough money.
2 My grandfather was a very _____ , kind man who would do anything for anybody.
3 Our head teacher is quite _____ and gets very angry about unimportant things.
4 Tony is really _____ . He doesn't let anything worry him.
5 When I asked Mrs Brown how old she was, she didn't answer me; she just gave me a(n) _____ look instead!

Listening

1 You are going to listen to five people talking about members of their family. Before you listen, read the questions and talk about what each person might say in these situations.

2 🎧 **1.02** You will now hear five people talking about members of their family. For questions 1–5, choose the best answer (A, B or C).

1. You hear John talking to his friend. Why is his dad angry?
   - A because John was late home
   - B because John was not studying
   - C because John broke something

2. You hear this woman speaking on the radio. What job does her sister do?
   - A doctor
   - B teacher
   - C architect

3. You hear this conversation on a bus. Who does the boy miss?
   - A his father
   - B his brother
   - C his uncle

4. You hear this teenager speaking on the phone. Why is she upset?
   - A because her sister uses her things
   - B because her sister goes out a lot
   - C because her sister is always annoyed

5. You hear your friend on the phone inviting you to a family party. Whose birthday is it?
   - A her cousin's
   - B her brother's
   - C her mother's

Soundbite /ɪ/ and /iː/

 1.03 Listen to someone saying 10 words. Look at the list of words and write down the number of each word you hear. What is the secret 10-digit number?

0 bit **2** pill **4** seat **6** mill **8** still
1 meal **3** steal **5** sit **7** beat **9** peel

Now write down your secret number. Say the words and ask your partner to find your secret number! If they can, score a point!

Speaking

1 Read what Julie says about her family.

'There are five of us in my family. There's me, my two sisters, my mum and my dad. I go to the local comprehensive and I'm in the first year. I'm the eldest. My dad runs a shop and my mum's a lawyer. My ambition is to be a lawyer, like my mum, when I grow up.'

2 Choose the most natural way of expressing each idea. *(Useful Phrases)*

1. a 'There are three of us in my family.'
   b 'My family consists of three members.'
2. a 'I go to the second year of the Second High School of my town.'
   b 'I'm in the second year at my local secondary school.'
3. a 'I have one sister and one brother and I am older than them.'
   b 'I've got a sister and a brother and I'm the eldest.'

3 In pairs, ask and answer the questions. Try to say as much as you can. Use the phrases below to help you.
- Do you come from a large family?
- Are you still at school?
- What do your parents do?
- Would you like to do the same job as they do?

> My family's quite small/large. There's me, …

> Yes, I'm only 14, so I'm still at school. I go to …

> My father's a … and my mother works as a …

👁 Look at *Speaking database - Giving personal information* on page 165.

Use of English

Stative verbs

👁 Look at *Grammar database* pages 167–168 before you do the exercises.

1 Circle the correct tense in each sentence.
1. I *think/am thinking* that your family is the most important thing in life.
2. My mum *can see/is seeing* my maths teacher tomorrow.
3. Elaine *isn't looking/doesn't look* like her sister at all.
4. The Robinson family *owns/is owning* a lot of the land around here.
5. Living with all your cousins *sounds/is sounding* like chaos to me!
6. You look unhappy. What *are you thinking/do you think* about?

Word patterns

2 Complete the sentences using the correct form of the verbs in the box.

look • accuse • deal • blame • care

1. My sister is always _____ me for her problems.
2. It's hard to _____ with people who won't listen to you.
3. Mum _____ me of lying, but it was my brother's fault, really!
4. I try to _____ about the feelings of the other members of my family.
5. Auntie Pat usually _____ after us when my mum's at work.

3 For questions 1–10, read the text below and decide which answer (A, B, C or D) best fits each gap. There is an example at the beginning (0).

Babysitting

Babysitting is a good (0) __way__ for teenagers to earn some extra spending money, and it can teach you some valuable skills too. Looking (1) _____ young children – even for a few hours – isn't always easy. Problems (2) _____ up, and kids don't always do what they're told, especially when they know their parents are away. At times (3) _____ that, you have to stay calm – and that's an important lesson to learn. You mustn't let the situation (4) _____ out of control. However badly the kids behave, don't let them (5) _____ you – and don't get depressed! It's not your (6) _____ that they're misbehaving, but it is your responsibility to solve the problem. (7) _____ a solution to problems like this is an extremely important skill, so where better to begin than trying to get noisy kids to go to bed? The question is, how do you deal (8) _____ a problem like that? The secret is to be calm, but firm. Don't start shouting and (9) _____ them of destroying your evening. Just keep repeating in a calm, firm voice what you want them to do. It takes a bit of practice, but it (10) _____ work in the end! Good luck!

0	A path	B road	C way	D route
1	A about	B to	C for	D after
2	A appear	B come	C go	D get
3	A like	B such	C as	D similar
4	A turn	B go	C get	D come
5	A argue	B complain	C mind	D annoy
6	A fault	B blame	C cause	D reason
7	A Doing	B Finding	C Making	D Getting
8	A over	B about	C of	D with
9	A accusing	B attacking	C criticising	D blaming
10	A makes	B does	C is	D has

Writing

An informal letter/email

👁 Look at *Writing database - informal letters/emails* on page 154 before you do the exercises.

1 Read this writing task. Why should your letter be informal?

> Your cousin, who lives abroad, has recently written you a letter. In it, she asked you to tell her all the family news she has missed. Write a letter, telling her what she wants to know.

Write a **letter** of between **120** and **180** words in an appropriate style.

2 Match the formal language with the informal language.

formal language	informal language
1 Dear Mr Smith / Dear Sir/Madam,	a Let me tell you about …!
2 I hope you are well.	b Tell me …
3 I am writing to inform you …	c All my love,
4 In addition, …	d Can't wait to hear all your news!
5 I wonder if you could tell me …	e Dear Tina,
6 I look forward to hearing from you.	f Oh, and another thing!
7 Yours sincerely, / Yours faithfully,	g Hope everything's okay.

Working model

3 Read the answer to the writing task.

Dear Tina,

It was great to hear from you! Hope everything's okay. Have you started your exams yet? Good luck!

Anyway, you asked me to tell you all the family news. Well, a lot's happened since you were here. The big news is that Uncle Tom got married! Can you believe it? His wife is lovely – she's a doctor and she's really beautiful. We all went to the wedding and had a wonderful time. Grandad danced! It was so much fun.

Oh, and another thing! Dad's got a new job. Do you know the old shopping centre in town? They've built new shops there and Dad applied for a job as a manager and he got it! He's really excited. He starts next week.

One last thing. Do you remember Fluffy, the cat? Well, we can't find her anywhere. We've got no idea where she's gone. It's a bit sad, really. We all miss her. We're hoping she'll come back soon.

We all miss you too. Everybody sends their love. Can't wait to see you in the summer.

All my love,

Martin

4 Find these informal words and phrases in the letter.

Anyway, …
All my love,
Well, …
It was great to hear from you!
One last thing.
Oh, and another thing!
Dear Tina,

5 Decide if the statements are true (T) or false (F).
In informal writing,
1 we always use complete sentences. ☐
2 we use exclamation marks (!). ☐
3 we use contractions (*it's*, *we're*, etc). ☐
4 we write as if we are talking to the person. ☐
5 we use everyday vocabulary. ☐

Ready to write!

6 Look at this writing task. Who are you writing to and why?

> You are staying with your pen friend in England. Write a letter to your brother, Dean, telling him all about the family you are staying with.

Write a **letter** of between **120** and **180** words in an appropriate style. Do not write any addresses.

7 Make a plan of your answer. Use your imagination.

- How are you going to start your letter?
  a Dear Dean,
  b Dear Brother,
  c Dear Mr Jones,
- What's the name of the family you are staying with?
- Which town are you staying in?
- Do you like it? Why?
- Who are the members of the family?
- What are they like?
- What do they do?
- What do you want to ask your brother about home?
- How many paragraphs do you need?
- How can you end your letter?
- How can you sign your letter?

Now complete *Writing Planner 1* on page 155.

Now write!

8 You are now ready to write your letter. Use informal language and a conversational tone.

Check it out!

9 Check your work. Tick (✓) what you have done.

- I have started and finished the letter in the correct way. ☐
- I have used informal language. ☐
- I have told my brother about the members of the family. ☐
- I have used a friendly, conversational tone. ☐
- I have used paragraphs. ☐
- I have checked my spelling and my grammar. ☐
- My letter is between 120 and 180 words long. ☐

◀ Look Back

Can you answer these questions? If you can't remember, look through the unit for the answers.
1 What do we call someone who doesn't have any brothers or sisters?
2 What tense do we use to talk about general truths?
3 How would you describe somebody who gets upset easily?
4 What's the negative form of 'honest'?
5 What have you learned about stative verbs?

2

The Open Road

Start thinking!

How fast do you think a horse can run?
Do you know who invented the aeroplane?
Do you know when people first landed on the Moon?

Reading

1 🎧 **1.04 Read this extract from an encyclopaedia.** As you read, check your answers to the questions opposite.

TRANSPORT (noun):
the activity or process of moving things or people from one place to another

Early humans dreamed of going faster and further than they could on foot. They probably first achieved this in northern countries before 3000 BC (before Christ) using skis. The wheel was invented around 3500 BC, but carts were very slow without roads. So for many centuries the fastest and most popular means of transport was the horse, which can run at about fifty-five kilometres an hour. This record for speed was unbroken until the end of the eighteenth century when the hot-air balloon and the railway both began to develop.

The hot-air balloon made its first free flight in 1783. Two Frenchmen, the Montgolfier brothers, were working as papermakers when they had the idea for the balloon. A fire heated the air, making the balloon rise. During the first flight, the two passengers were admiring the view when they suddenly saw smoke! The balloon was burning but, luckily, they managed to put the fire out and land safely.

The railway developed gradually from carts on tracks. The first vehicle with an engine to run on tracks was developed in 1803 by an Englishman, Richard Trevithick. In 1804, he took the first passengers, although they didn't have to buy a ticket. Unfortunately, they were travelling in the train when it began to fall off the tracks and Trevithick realised that the tracks were not strong enough to take the weight of the train. The passengers escaped unharmed, but it was another example of how dangerous the development of transport can be.

Perhaps unexpectedly, the bicycle didn't appear until around 1840 when a Scotsman, Kirkpatrick Macmillan, created the first one to have pedals. People rode bicycles without pedals before then, but they were slow and not very popular. It took around 140 years for Macmillan's design to develop into modern mountain bikes.

2 Complete the sentences by writing a number in each gap. Look at the article again, but don't read it in detail.
1 People first skied around _____ BC.
2 People first travelled by rail in _____.
3 Bicycles with pedals didn't exist before _____.
4 Mountain bikes developed around _____.

3 Read the text again. For questions 1–5, choose the answer (A, B, C or D) which you think fits best according to the text.
1 The wheel didn't lead to fast means of transport because
  A people could already travel fast.
  B they invented it after skis.
  C good roads didn't exist.
  D people preferred to use horses.
2 The passengers discovered the fire
  A while they were checking the balloon.
  B while they were in the air.
  C before they left the ground.
  D after they landed on the ground.
3 The invention of the train
  A came as a complete surprise.
  B grew out of things that came before.
  C took longer than anyone expected.
  D didn't make Trevithick much money.
4 The writer is surprised by the fact that
  A the inventor of the bicycle was Scottish.
  B nobody had invented the bicycle earlier.
  C Macmillan's bicycle had pedals.
  D we waited over a century for the mountain bike.
5 What can we say about the aeroplane?
  A It had a great effect on people's attitudes.
  B It wasn't as popular as the car was.
  C It came to the Wright brothers in a dream.
  D People didn't want to allow it at first.

The twentieth century saw the development of many other means of transport, including the hydrofoil and the hovercraft. The petrol-driven car (invented in 1885 in Germany) completely changed the way people thought about transport, and so did the aeroplane. People have always dreamed of flying. One day, in 1903, that dream became a reality. Two American brothers, Wilbur and Orville Wright, managed to make a short flight in their aircraft, the Flyer. From there, a huge industry grew that allowed, and still allows, people to visit the whole world, easily and cheaply.

The challenge for the twenty-first century is transport in space. Since the first Moon landing in 1969, technology has developed to give us the space shuttle (1981) and even the space tourist (2002). The future of transport will probably be as exciting as its past.

WORD BOX

4 Match the words from the text in the box with the correct definitions.

cart • tracks • hydrofoil • vehicle
pedal • hovercraft

1 This is a kind of fast ship that partly lifts out of the water.
2 This is a general word for a car, a bus, etc.
3 This floats on a cushion of air on land or on water.
4 Trains travel on two of these, made of metal.
5 This has four wheels and might be pulled by a horse.
6 You put your foot on this on a bicycle.

Have your say!

- Which form of transport has had the biggest influence on our lives?
- Explain what difference your chosen form of transport has made.

G Grammar clinic

Past tense review

👁 Look at *Grammar database* pages 168–170 before you do the exercises.

1 Read the sentences and phrases from the text on pages 14 and 15. Match each one to an explanation.

1 The hot-air balloon made its first free flight in 1783.
2 … the two passengers were admiring the view when they suddenly saw smoke!
3 People rode bicycles without pedals …
4 … the fastest means of transport was the horse …

a This describes a repeated action in the past that doesn't happen now.
b This describes a past state.
c This describes an action in progress when another action happened.
d This describes a single, completed action.

2 Look through the text again and find examples of:
a single completed action.
a repeated action in the past.
an action in progress when another action happened.
a past state (a feeling or situation, not an action).

3 Complete the sentences using the correct form of the verbs in brackets.
1 We _____ (**fly**) by plane to Paris last year on holiday.
2 We _____ (**fly**) over the sea when one engine suddenly stopped.
3 The pilot _____ (**tell**) us that there was nothing to worry about.
4 While he _____ (**tell**) us this, the second engine stopped.
5 I had my eyes closed when somebody _____ (**shout**), 'Look!'
6 I looked out of the window and _____ (**see**) that both engines had started again. Phew!

4 Correct the sentences that have mistakes in them. One sentence has no mistakes. Which one?
1 As we were entering the train station, I was noticing the train was late.
2 I sat in a taxi when the accident happened so I saw the whole thing.
3 Mick was riding his bike almost every day over the summer.
4 People were enjoying the journey when suddenly the ship hit an iceberg.
5 When you called, I watched a programme about the history of transport.

5 Complete the text using the verbs in the box. Put the verbs into the past simple or the past continuous. You will use some verbs more than once.

be • do • fall • get • have • learn • push • ride • say
see • shine • start • take • teach • tell • want

Learning to ride!

I (1) _____ to ride a bike when I (2) _____ eight years old. My dad (3) _____ me. I remember one day in particular. The sun (4) _____ and Dad (5) _____ me to the local park with my new bike. My old bike (6) _____ stabilisers (little wheels at the side, so you can't fall), but this one (7) _____ . When we (8) _____ there, I (9) _____ some children who (10) _____ their bikes, and I (11) _____ to be just like them. I (12) _____ on my bike and Dad (13) _____ to push me. After a moment, I (14) _____ my dad he (15) _____ me too fast, and I couldn't believe his answer!
'I'm not pushing you! You're doing it by yourself!' he (16) _____ .
Of course, I (17) _____ off my bike many times after that, but that (18) _____ a very special day.

6 Do you remember learning to ride a bike? How did you learn? Who taught you? Tell the class.

Vocabulary builder

Public transport

1 Match the words in the box with the correct definitions. There is one word you do not need to use.

cabin • taxi rank • fare • airline
underground • platform • terminal
ferry • coach

1 This is where you stand to wait for a train.
2 This is a company that flies passengers by plane.
3 This is a building for passengers at an airport.
4 This is a system of trains in tunnels in a large city.
5 This is how much you have to pay for a ticket.
6 This is where you sleep on a ship.
7 This is where you find taxis waiting for passengers.
8 This is a bus that runs between towns and cities.

Confusable words

2 Circle the correct word in each sentence.

1 I think that *travel/journey* really teaches you about other people.
2 Mr Carter has gone to Moscow on a business *trip/journey*.
3 Hurry up, or we're going to *miss/lose* the bus!

4 Don't get *on/in* the train unless you know where it's going!

Collocations: transport

3 Complete the table with the means of transport.

bicycle • bus • car • helicopter
horse • hot-air balloon • train
plane • motorbike • ferry • ship
rowing boat • taxi • trolleybus

get on / get off	get in (*or* into) / get out of

4 Match words in list A with words in list B to make compound nouns.

A	B
express	bus
radio	car
double-decker	plane
jet	taxi
sports	train

5 Decide which of the means of transport from exercise 4 each person is talking about.

1 'Wow! This is so cool! It's the latest model too! Let's see if we can do 200!'
2 'Come on! Let's go and sit upstairs so we can see everybody getting off.'
3 'Call one now – and don't forget to tell them we're going to the airport.'
4 'I'm afraid the Inter-city doesn't stop at Porton. You'll have to get a local one.'
5 'It's noisy during take-off, but you can't even hear the engines after that.'

Listening

1 Work in pairs. Make a note of words and phrases you know connected to these means of transport. Try to list as many as you can.

bus: *driver, ticket*, _____

plane: *airport, pilot*, _____

ship: *voyage, captain*, _____

train: *driver, ticket*, _____

2 **1.05** You are going to listen to extracts from three conversations. For each extract, choose the location where the conversation is taking place.

Conversation 1
a at a train station   b on a bus   c in a taxi

Conversation 2
a at a bus station   b on a ship   c at an airport

Conversation 3
a on a plane   b on a train   c in a taxi

3 Listen again and write a word or short phrase in each gap.

Conversation 1

The man wants a(n) (1) _____ return ticket to York. The woman tells him that he needs to catch the (2) _____ from Manchester.

Conversation 2

The man says it takes (3) _____ to get to France. The woman leaves the man to go to her (4) _____.

Conversation 3

The man explains that it's quicker to go (5) _____. The woman agrees, even though the fare will be (6) _____.

Soundbite /æ/ and /e/

 1.06 Circle two words in each line which have the same vowel sound in them. Listen and check.

1	thank	bed	thirty	cat
2	head	had	said	paid
3	apple	ant	ape	arm
4	pet	hut	pat	send

Speaking

1 Make notes of things that trains and buses have in common.

You have to buy a ticket to travel on them.

2 Make notes of things that are different between trains and buses.

A train travels on tracks, but/while/whereas a bus travels on the road.

3 Answer the questions.

Which means of transport do you prefer, the train or the bus? Why?

4 Work in pairs. One of you should read the instructions and the other should talk for one minute. Then swap.

> Compare and contrast these photographs and say which means of transport you prefer.

◉ Look at *Speaking database - Comparing* and *Expressing preferences* on page 165.

Use of English

Would, used to, be used to

Look at *Grammar database* page 170 before you do the exercises.

1 Circle the correct word or phrase in each sentence.
1 Our old car *would/was used to* break down all the time.
2 I *used to/am used to* going to school by bus every day.
3 There *would/used to* be an aircraft factory in this area.
4 I never *used to/wouldn't* like travelling by train.
5 Driving is complicated, but you soon *are/get* used to it.
6 I found flying frightening because I *didn't use to/wasn't used to* it.

2 Rewrite the sentences using the word in bold.
1 When he was a boy, my dad would watch the steam trains go past. **used**
2 Flying a helicopter is difficult at first, but you'll soon find it much easier. **get**
3 When she was four, my sister used to ride her bike around the house. **would**
4 My grandfather took me for rides in his old car when I was small. **used**

Word patterns

3 Complete the sentences using the correct form of the verbs in the box.

work • insist • remind • complain • take

1 John _____ on going by bus as he's afraid of flying.
2 We decided to _____ about the delay to the ticket inspector.
3 We have to _____ into account the traffic at that time of day.
4 To _____ as a bus driver, you need a special licence.
5 This old bus _____ me of the time we travelled around India.

4 For questions 1–10, read the text below and think of the word which best fits each gap. Use only one word in each gap. There is an example at the beginning (0). Write your answers IN CAPITAL LETTERS.

THE SKY'S THE LIMIT!

Not so long (0) __AGO__, almost all pilots were men. Women working for airlines (1) _____ usually be part of the cabin crew, serving drinks and meals to passengers. And while it's still true that the majority of people who work (2) _____ pilots are men, more women are entering the field. Sara Milton is one of them.

'I (3) _____ to be afraid of flying when I was a child,' she says, 'but my parents insisted (4) _____ taking us on holiday abroad. I (5) _____ argue and cry, but it never made any difference, so I eventually (6) _____ used to it. Then, on one trip, we had a female pilot, which I wasn't used (7) _____ seeing, and I suddenly thought that I'd love to do that job! My mum reminded (8) _____ of my fear of flying and how I always complained (9) _____ going on planes, but from that moment on, I was determined to become a pilot. When you (10) _____ into account the long hours and all the training you have to do, it might seem like hard work, but it's worth it!'

Writing

An essay

👁 Look at *Writing database - essays* on page 153 before you do the exercises.

1 Make notes to answer these questions. Then discuss your ideas as a class.

1 'Public transport' includes which forms of transport?
   _____
2 What are two advantages of public transport?
   _____
3 What are two things people don't like about public transport?
   _____

2 Read this writing task.
- Should your answer be formal or informal?
- Do you agree with the statement?

Your class has been studying transport. Your teacher has asked you to write an essay explaining whether you agree or disagree with the following statement:

> People should be encouraged to use public transport more.

Write an **essay** of between **120** and **180** words in an appropriate style.

3 Complete the useful phrases with words from the box.

> addition • argue • begin • convinced
> first • more • of • one • other • to

to introduce your first point

To _____ with, ... In the _____ place, ... The first thing to take into account is ...

to introduce a further point

Secondly, ... What is _____, ... In _____ to this, ... Another point to be made is that ...

to express causes and results

Because _____ this, ... This is due _____ ... , As a result, ...

to express contrast

On the _____ hand, ... On the _____ hand, ... However, ... Despite ...

to introduce a conclusion and express opinion

To conclude, ... In conclusion, ... I am _____ that ... I would _____ that ...

Working model

4 Read the answer to the writing task. Does the writer agree or disagree with the statement?

There is no doubt that traffic adds to pollution. Public transport offers a possible solution to the problem, since many people can be transported in one vehicle. The government has a responsibility to encourage the public to use buses and the underground more. However, there are a number of changes which need to be considered.

In the first place, public transport should be made free. The government should raise taxes to pay for the service. If it was free, most people would decide to leave their cars at home and travel by bus or train.

What is more, the service must be clean and reliable. People need to know that they can get to work on time. They also need to know that their journey will be comfortable.

To sum up, I would argue that a clean, reliable service which was free would encourage many people to use public transport. The government should take action on this to prevent environmental damage.

5 Find words and phrases in the essay which mean:

> because • but • firstly
> in addition • in conclusion

20

6 Read the essay again and circle the correct answer.
1 In the first paragraph, the writer
   a introduces the subject and generally agrees or disagrees with the statement.
   b lists all the reasons why she agrees or disagrees with the statement in detail.
2 In the second paragraph, she
   a explains some points against her point of view.
   b explains some points in favour of her point of view.
3 In the third paragraph, she
   a introduces her conclusion and states her opinion.
   b explains more points in favour of her point of view.
4 In the second and third paragraphs,
   a the first sentence of each paragraph expresses the main idea.
   b the last sentence of each paragraph expresses the main idea.
5 In the final paragraph, she
   a summarises her argument.
   b introduces extra points.

Ready to write!

7 Look at this writing task. Do you agree or disagree with the statement?

Your class has been studying the history of transport. Your teacher has asked you to write an essay explaining whether you agree or disagree with the following statement:

> *The invention of the car changed the world.*

Write an **essay** of between **120** and **180** words in an appropriate style.

8 Make a plan of your answer.
- Do you think the invention of the car changed the world? Why? / Why not?
- What are you going to write in your first paragraph?
- Which point(s) are you going to talk about in your second paragraph?
  Write the first sentence of your second paragraph in your exercise book.
- Which point(s) are you going to talk about in your third paragraph?
  Write the first sentence of your third paragraph in your exercise book.
- Which phrase are you going to use to
  a introduce your concluding paragraph?
  b introduce your opinion?

Now complete *Writing Planner 2* on page 155.

Now write!

9 You are now ready to write your essay.

Check it out!

10 Check your work. Tick (✓) what you have done.

I have used formal language. ☐
I have used some good connecting phrases. ☐
I have explained why I agree/disagree with the statement. ☐
I have used paragraphs. ☐
I have summarised my argument in the last paragraph. ☐
I have checked my spelling and my grammar. ☐
My essay is between 120 and 180 words long. ☐

Look Back

Can you answer these questions? If you can't remember, look through the unit for the answers.
1 When did people first invent the wheel?
2 Who were the first people to fly a plane?
3 What tense describes an action in **progress** at a moment in the past?
4 What's the difference between *would* and *used to*?
5 What is a good phrase for introducing your opinion?

Revision
Units 1–2

1 Choose the correct option.

1 People say my brother's _____ . He likes giving gifts to his friends.
   A brave   B modest   C generous   D optimistic
2 The cruise was wonderful! And our _____ was really comfortable.
   A cabin   B pedal   C terminal   D fare
3 I've always been quite _____ . I want to make a success of my life.
   A depressing   B amusing   C considerate   D ambitious
4 Emily is really _____ ! She seems to think she's better than everyone else!
   A loving   B arrogant   C sensitive   D caring
5 Many _____ children want to learn something about their real parents.
   A adopted   B divorced   C selfish   D only
6 Did you hear that a train came off the _____ yesterday?
   A vehicles   B carts   C bars   D tracks
7 We waited on the _____ for over an hour! Finally, the train arrived.
   A terminal   B rails   C platform   D airline
8 We should be _____ about the future. Things are getting better all the time.
   A amusing   B optimistic   C shy   D pessimistic
9 Let's take the _____ to an island and spend some time on the beach!
   A ferry   B underground   C fare   D coach
10 My dad's really looking forward to his business _____ to Amsterdam.
   A trip   B journey   C travel   D excursion

2 Complete the sentences using the correct form of the verbs in brackets.

1 My sister _____ (stay) at her friend's house for a few days.
2 I _____ (do) my homework when suddenly I heard a loud explosion.
3 We _____ (eat) together as a family about three times a week.
4 I _____ (get) better at remembering words in English these days.
5 In the winter, many birds _____ (fly) south to warmer countries.
6 'Hello? No, Tom _____ (have) a shower at the moment. Can I take a message?'
7 I _____ (swim) almost every day last summer.
8 My mum wants to learn to use a computer, so she _____ (have) lessons.

3 Complete the sentences using the correct preposition.

1 Roger still keeps _____ touch with all his old school friends.
2 When Jill laughs, she really reminds me _____ her mother.
3 You can't blame me _____ all these problems!
4 Our teacher insists _____ giving us homework every day!
5 The police accused the man _____ stealing the money.
6 I usually have to look _____ my brother when my parents are out.
7 When planning a party, take _____ account the cost of food and drink.

4 Make these words negative.

positive	negative	positive	negative
1 legal	_____	5 kind	_____
2 fair	_____	6 relevant	_____
3 honest	_____	7 capable	_____
4 polite	_____	8 attractive	_____

5 Complete the sentences using an appropriate word.
1 If your parents get _____ , they end their marriage.
2 If you are _____ , you have lots of friends.
3 A(n) _____ is a kind of fast ship that lifts out of the water.
4 On a bicycle, you put your feet on the _____ .
5 Taxis wait for passengers at a taxi _____ .
6 A(n) _____ is a kind of bus that travels between towns and cities.
7 If you only care about yourself and your own problems, you are _____ .

6 Complete the sentences using the correct form of the phrasal verbs in the box.

think up • bring up • turn up • come up • make up

1 I hate it when people _____ at my parties without an invitation.
2 A number of problems _____ in the meeting yesterday.
3 When we see Mary, don't _____ her divorce.
4 I wonder who _____ the idea of playing games on computers.
5 Tony is always _____ stories about other people that just aren't true.

7 Circle the correct word or phrase in each sentence.
1 Is that Ashton Kutcher in that car, or **do I see/am I seeing** things?
2 I **don't believe/am not believing** what Caroline told me about what happened.
3 Anybody who **doesn't understand/isn't understanding** can ask me for help after the lesson.
4 What's in this soup? It **tastes/is tasting** delicious!
5 Why are you smiling? What **do you think/are you thinking** about?

8 Complete the following passage using one word in each gap.

Hi, Wendy! Just a quick email to let you know that I'm back from my business (1) _____ to Paris. I had a great time, but I (2) _____ think that Paris was a bit dirty! Everybody was complaining (3) _____ the traffic and the pollution. I'm not used (4) _____ such big cities, so it was a bit difficult to find my way around. I kept getting (5) _____ the wrong bus and going to the wrong place! And the weather was awful! One day, I was waiting at a taxi (6) _____ for an hour in the pouring rain! In the end, I had to call a(n) (7) _____ taxi to come and get me. When it finally turned (8) _____ , I looked like a drowned rat!
Anyway, I hope you dealt (9) _____ everything at work while I was away. We'll have a meeting on Monday and you can (10) _____ up any problems you had.
Take care,
Jackie

Score _____ /60

51–60 Well done! You really know your stuff! 41–50 That's great! Keep it up!
21–40 Maybe it's time for another look! 0–20 What?! Are you sure?

3

Killing Time

Start thinking!

Do you have any hobbies? Do you collect anything? What sort of things do people collect?

Reading

1 🎧 **1.07** Read this article about hobbies. Underline all the hobbies which are mentioned.

Hobbies Past and Present

During the twentieth century, more and more people found that they had leisure time – time when they didn't have to work or study. This raised an interesting question. What do you do when you are free to do anything you like? Many people took up a hobby, and it's interesting to compare the hobbies people, particularly young people, choose today with the hobbies people chose, say, fifty or sixty years ago.

Stamp collecting is one of the first things that come to many people's minds when they think about hobbies. Organising your collection seems like the perfect way to relax for a few hours. It seems that people have been collecting valuable things since ancient times. **1**_____ When stamps appeared in the nineteenth century, they were cheap and colourful and children started to keep them. By the middle of the twentieth century, collecting stamps was a popular pastime for both children and adults, with some stamps worth a large amount of money – far more than most children could afford.

There are still many people today who collect stamps, but technology has had an impact. Emails can be sent instantly and freely around the world, which means that people aren't buying stamps like they used to. **2**_____ Rare stamps are still in demand, and probably always will be, but fifty years ago the number of collectors was higher. It seems that stamp collecting as a hobby of millions of young people has had its day.

Another hobby that has changed because of technology is building models. In the 1950s and 60s, generations of young boys and girls built plastic models of planes, boats and cars. **3**_____ Young people are still making and showing off these models, but the nature of them has changed. In the past, they were simply made of wood or plastic, with few moving parts. Modern models have all kinds of electronic and computerised parts, in some cases making them more like robots than traditional models!

Of course, we can't ignore computers when it comes to free time. Computers have had a huge impact on leisure since they were invented in the middle of the twentieth century. **4**_____ Gradually, however, the computer has become a part of almost every home, where it provides entertainment and a whole set of new hobbies that people fifty years ago would have thought were very weird. Today's teenagers use their computers for playing computer games,

24

2 Match the words and phrases with the explanations.

1 to talk about what happened in the beginning ____
2 to introduce a result ____
3 to introduce a contrast ____
4 to introduce an example ____

a For instance, …
b which means …
c However, …
d At first, …

3 Read the article again. Six sentences have been removed from the article. Choose from the sentences A–G the one which fits each gap (1–6). There is one extra sentence which you do not need to use.

A Hobbies seem to have become less important as time has passed.
B Young people in the past had to rely on people they knew, or perhaps the local library, to learn about their hobby.
C They proudly put these on display in their bedrooms, or wherever else their parents would let them.
D However, most people in the past were too busy and too poor to buy expensive works of art or coins.
E At first, they were seen as strange machines used by big businesses.
F That in turn means that fewer children are becoming interested in the hobby.
G For instance, people still go dancing, even if the rhythm of the music has changed.

running websites, communicating with friends around the world – all hobbies that were impossible until quite recently.

Computers have changed hobbies in other ways too. These days, no matter what hobby you're interested in, you will almost certainly find a huge amount of information on it on the internet. **5** ____ Today's teenagers are instantly in touch with online clubs and social networking sites that tell them all they need to know. People have produced websites on almost every hobby you can think of. You can get advice from experts and easily buy equipment to take your hobby to the next level. Taking up a new hobby, or developing one you already have, has never been easier or more fun.

Some hobbies, though, haven't changed much. Many young people fill their free time with activities that their parents and grandparents enjoyed. **6** ____ Fishing is as popular as it ever was. Young people with good balance do gymnastics. Teenagers play sports and games like they always have done. A teenager from the past might be confused by a video arcade or a CD player, but many things haven't changed, and perhaps never will. Ask your parents what they did with their leisure time and you might be surprised at some of the differences, but also at some of the similarities.

WORD BOX

4 Use words or phrases from the article to complete the sentences. You've been given the first letter to help you.

1 One day, my collection of butterflies might be quite v_____.
2 I don't know if I can a_____ to buy any new stamps for my collection.
3 I prefer t_____ songs to modern pop songs.
4 It might sound a bit w_____, but in my free time I like to study grammar.
5 I like music that has a strong r_____.
6 I'd like to try gymnastics, but I know I would keep losing my b_____!
7 Let's go down to the v_____ a_____ and play *Alien Invasion*.

Have your say!

- Which of the hobbies and activities mentioned in the article do you think are the most/least interesting? Why?
- Would you consider taking any of them up? Why? / Why not?

Grammar clinic

Present perfect tense review

👁 Look at *Grammar database* pages 171–172 before you do the exercises.

1 Read the sentences and phrases from the article on pages 24 and 25. Match each one to an explanation.

1 Computers have had a huge impact on leisure …
2 … people have been collecting valuable things since ancient times.
3 People have produced websites on …

a This is a series of actions continuing up to now.
b This is a situation which continues up to now.
c This is a completed action at a time in the past which is not mentioned.

2 Decide if the statements are true (T) or false (F).

1 I've been studying English for about six years.
   This person is still studying English now.

2 Peter Johnson has written five books about fishing.
   We know that Peter Johnson is still alive.

3 'I've been sorting out my stamp collection,' said Candy.
   Candy finished this action a long time ago.

4 Jan has read *Snowboarding for Beginners*. Ask her about it.
   Jan's present knowledge is the important thing.

3 Correct the sentences that have mistakes in them. One sentence has no mistakes. Which one?

1 I've seen Matt last week, when we were at the karate club.
2 I have a long time to play Monopoly.
3 Sarah hasn't played football since she broke her leg.
4 This is the first time I built a model plane.

4 Complete the sentences using the verbs in brackets in the present perfect simple or continuous.

1 I _____ (**play**) tennis, so I'm quite tired.
2 Luke says he _____ (**never/meet**) anybody who plays the xylophone.
3 _____ (**you/follow**) the new series that's on TV at the moment?
4 My fingers are sore because I _____ (**practise**) the guitar all morning.
5 We _____ (**wait**) for an hour and our dance teacher still isn't here!
6 My dad _____ (**take up**) a new hobby – cooking!

5 Use the verbs in the box to complete the gaps. Use the present perfect simple or continuous.

join • make • plan • read • think • write

For the last few weeks, my friends and I (1) _____ the creation of a free local library, and now it's ready. The idea is that we have a blog that anyone can join for free. The blog's now online, and about 20 people (2) _____ already, so it seems it's popular. When we read a new book, we upload a review of the book. My friends and I (3) _____ and uploaded 16 reviews already! When someone (4) _____ a review, if the book sounds interesting, they can borrow it from the person who owns it. We all live locally so that's not a problem.

Over the past couple of days, we (5) _____ about how we can expand the library so it's for people all round the country. One idea is that we could post books to each other, but that might be expensive, so we (6) _____ a final decision yet. We'll see what happens!

Vocabulary builder

Free time activities

1 Match the free time activities with the verbs *go, do* or *play*.

ballet • basketball • video games • camping • horse-riding • karate • swimming
judo • skiing • gymnastics • fishing • volleyball • the piano • canoeing

'I go/do/play _____ in my free time.'

2 If a word in bold is correct, put a tick (✔). If it's incorrect, rewrite it correctly on the line.

1. How long have you been **playing** karate? _____
2. Let's **go** horse-riding tomorrow. _____
3. Have you ever **been** skiing? _____
4. How much time do you spend **going** video games? _____
5. I **go** ballet twice a week after school. _____
6. We **do** swimming in the sea every weekend in the summer. _____

Idioms: time

3 Match to make sentences using idioms about *time*. What do the idioms mean?

1	Since my mum retired,	a	you have to *take your time* and do it slowly.
2	I don't really like TV so much,	b	*on time* because I've set the video to record it.
3	I know you're very busy with your hobbies these days,	c	she's got a lot of *time on her hands*.
4	When you're working with valuable stamps,	d	*in time* to see Robert win the race.
5	I hope the programme starts	e	but I watch it when I want to *kill time*.
6	We got to the pool just	f	but you have to *make time* for me!

Phrasal verbs with *down*

4 Phrasal verbs with *down* often have negative meanings. Match the phrasal verbs in the box with the correct definitions.

get down • look down on • turn down
come down with • put down

1. If you _____ an offer, you refuse it, or don't accept it.
2. If you _____ someone, you think you are better than they are.
3. If you _____ a minor illness, you start suffering from it.
4. If a vet _____ an animal _____, they kill it because it is old or ill.
5. If something _____ you _____, it depresses you.

Magic metaphors

5 When we talk about *time*, we sometimes use words or phrases that have a connection with *money*. Complete the sentences with the words from the box.

valuable • save • spend • waste

1. To _____ time, we decided to get everything ready first.
2. Stop _____ time watching TV and get your homework done.
3. I _____ most of my free time playing volleyball.
4. As a senior manager, Mr Harrison's time is very _____.

Listening

1 🎧 **1.08** You are going to listen to two people talking about their hobbies. What do they say?

1 In the beginning, Speaker 1 felt that this hobby was
   a enjoyable **b** difficult **c** boring

2 Speaker 2 feels that this hobby is
   a uninteresting **b** embarrassing **c** entertaining

2 🎧 **1.09** Listen to the same two people and two other people talking about their hobbies. For questions 1–4, choose from the list (A–E) what each person says about their hobby. Use the letters only once. There is one extra letter which you do not need to use.

A It teaches you about other cultures.   Speaker 1: ___
B You learn to work with others.   Speaker 2: ___
C It demands a lot of free time.   Speaker 3: ___
D It can be stressful at times.   Speaker 4: ___
E It helps you to stop worrying.

Soundbite /ʌ/

🎧 **1.10** Circle the two words in each line that contain the same vowel sound. Listen and check.

1	come	though	luck	put
2	ran	run	won	rule
3	fun	far	full	fuss
4	truck	trust	track	true

Speaking

Useful Phrases

1 Circle the correct word or phrase to complete the suggestions.

1 I suggest *to get/getting* a games console – we'd have great fun!
2 Why don't we *buy/buying* a video camera? Then we could make films!
3 *Let's get/Getting* a pool table would be a good idea, wouldn't it?
4 A good idea *might/can* be to get a table-tennis table. It's cheaper than a pool table.
5 I'd like to suggest *to buy/buying* a tablet computer so we can check our email.
6 What do you think about *to get/getting* some board games, like chess and backgammon?

2 Work in pairs. Use the phrases from exercise 1 to help you make suggestions.

Imagine you're planning to start a youth club for teenagers in your neighbourhood. Here are some of the things you're thinking of getting for the club. You have about €200 to spend. Discuss how much you think members would enjoy these activities and decide which things you are going to buy for the club.

👁 Look at *Speaking database - Giving/Asking for opinion* on page 165.

Use of English

Articles

👁 Look at *Grammar database* pages 172–173 before you do the exercises.

1 Circle the extra word in each sentence.
1 In my free time, I listen to the music, go to the cinema and play the guitar.
2 The Head gave the Class 7 permission to organise an after-school club.
3 I go to the chess club at the weekend by the bus.
4 Jenny loves the swimming and she'd like to swim the English Channel.
5 We went to the USA and saw the Grand Canyon and the Mount Rushmore.
6 You need a hobby, like playing the flute or collecting the stamps.

2 Correct the sentences. Add articles where necessary.
1 Oscar had lot of time to start new hobbies when he was in prison.
2 I like comedies, whether they are on television or on radio.
3 James has taken up new hobby and spends whole evening making models.
4 Hang-gliding is great fun, but you need hills or even mountain nearby.
5 My hobby is drawing, so when I grow up I'd like to be artist.

Synonyms

3 Match the expressions which mean the same.
1 regret   a feel like doing
2 want to do   b not approve of
3 look forward to doing c wish you hadn't
4 object to   d can't wait to do

4 For questions 1–6, complete the second sentence so that it has a similar meaning to the first sentence, using the word given. Do not change the word given. You must use between two and five words, including the word given. Write the missing words IN CAPITAL LETTERS.

1 My parents asked me if I wanted to have ballet lessons.   **felt**
   My parents asked me if I _____ ballet lessons.

2 The teachers object to our playing football in the corridor.   **of**
   The teachers _____ our playing football in the corridor.

3 I regret giving up the trumpet at the age of 12.   **wish**
   I _____ up the trumpet at the age of 12.

4 I am really looking forward to joining my local basketball team.   **wait**
   I really _____ my local basketball team.

5 Dave can't wait to take part in the karaoke competition!   **looking**
   Dave _____ part in the karaoke competition!

6 Why don't you approve of Sarah playing rugby?   **object**
   Why _____ Sarah playing rugby?

Writing

An informal letter/email

👁 Look at *Writing database - informal letters/emails* on page 154 before you do the exercises.

1 Read this writing task. Why should your email be informal?

> Craig, a friend of yours, is thinking of visiting you and he wants to be able to go to a concert while staying with you. The local tourist office has given you this leaflet and you have made these notes. Write an email giving him the choice of two possible concerts.

Write an **email** of between **120** and **150** words. You must use grammatically correct sentences with accurate spelling and punctuation in a style appropriate for the situation.

Craig arriving June 19th (I think)

I've seen Royal Orchestra – very good!

I haven't got a lot of money.

Washington Hall

We've got some great concerts lined up for you this season at Washington Hall. There's something for everybody. Tickets are available at the box office.

June 12th-18th
The Robbers This rock group will get you dancing and screaming! They're loud, they're fast, and they're coming to Washington Hall.
Tickets: €15-30

June 20th-21st
Royal Orchestra For classical music lovers, the Royal Orchestra is back, bringing you some old classics, and a few new pieces.
Tickets: €20

June 22nd-29th
The Wilson Brothers Country music's most famous brothers are here with their guitars! If you like your music with a good melody and great singing, then let the Wilson Brothers entertain you.
Tickets: €25-40

2 Decide if the statements are true (T) or false (F).

1. You should always use formal language in an email. ☐
2. We normally ask each other about our news in informal letters/emails. ☐
3. You have to include all the information from your notes. ☐
4. You can add extra relevant information not in the notes. ☐

Working model

3 Read the answer to the writing task.

From: Kelly <kelly@dmail.com>
To: Craig <CriagSmith@friend.com>
Subject: Your visit!

Dear Craig,

Hi! Have your exams finished? I can't wait for you to arrive!

You said you want to go to a concert while you're here. You're arriving on the 19th, aren't you? 'The Robbers' are playing up to the 18th, so we'll miss them. It's a shame because they're great!

So really you've got a choice of two concerts. The first is the Royal Orchestra on the 20th or 21st. I've seen them and they were very good. Tickets are €20 each.

The Wilson Brothers are playing after that. Have you heard of them? I don't know what they're like. Still, might be interesting. I don't have much money so we'd have to get the cheapest tickets. They're €25. Decide which one you want to see and let me know. I'll get the tickets before you come.

Got to go! Mum's calling me.

See you soon,

Kelly

4 Underline where Kelly does these things in her email on page 30.

1 asks a friendly question about her friend's life
2 checks a piece of information
3 tells Craig what the first choice is
4 tells Craig what the second choice is
5 tells Craig what she wants him to do next
6 gives a reason for closing the email

Ready to write!

5 Look at this writing task. You are going to write a similar email.

> Imagine your friend, Tom, is coming to stay with you. While he is staying with you, he wants to go to a concert. Use the leaflet on page 30 and the notes you have made to write an email to Tom, offering him the choice of two concerts.

Write an **email** of between **120** and **150** words. You must use grammatically correct sentences with accurate spelling and punctuation in a style appropriate for the situation.

> Tom arriving on June 15th, leaving on June 21st (?)
>
> Cost not a problem – birthday money!
>
> Have to book tickets before 6th

6 Make a plan of your answer. Use your imagination.

- How are you going to start your email?
- What question are you going to ask Tom about his own life?
- What piece of information do you want to check?
- What's the first choice you're going to offer him? What's your opinion of this choice?
- What's the second choice you're going to offer him?
  What's your opinion of this choice?
- Why is money not a problem?
- What do you want him to do next?
- When does he have to do it before?
- How are you going to end your email?

Now complete *Writing Planner 3* on page 156.

Now write!

7 You are now ready to write your email. Use informal language. Include all the information you have to.

Check it out!

8 Check your work. Tick (✓) what you have done.

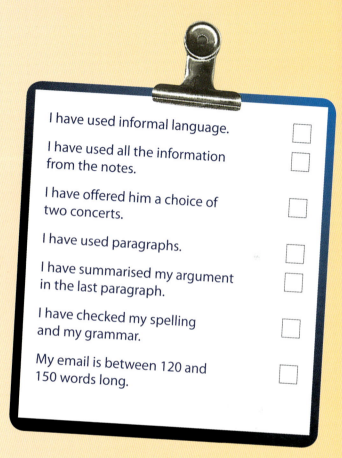

- I have used informal language. ☐
- I have used all the information from the notes. ☐
- I have offered him a choice of two concerts. ☐
- I have used paragraphs. ☐
- I have summarised my argument in the last paragraph. ☐
- I have checked my spelling and my grammar. ☐
- My email is between 120 and 150 words long. ☐

◀ Look Back

Can you answer these questions? If you can't remember, look through the unit for the answers.

1 When did people first start collecting stamps?
2 What's the difference between 'He's been to India.' and 'He's gone to India.'?
3 Which phrase using the word 'time' means 'do something slowly'?
4 If something 'gets you down', what does it do?
5 Can you think of the name of a country we use 'the' before?

4

Work Wonders

Start thinking!

What job would you like to do in the future? Why?
Which is more important, money or job satisfaction?
Would you like to do the same job as your parents? Why? / Why not?

Reading

1 Look at the paragraph headings in the article below. Which of these types of work would you rather do? Why?

MAKING A LIVING by *Ivy Saunders*

'What do you want to be when you grow up?' By the time I was fifteen, I'd answered that question a hundred different ways. A doctor! An actor! An astronaut! (OK, even I knew that wasn't going to happen!) By the time I was twenty-five, I'd had lots of jobs, but none of them had been on my list of careers. I'd flipped burgers in a fast-food place. I'd worked in a shoe shop and a pet shop. Then, gradually, I realised I had been doing things I didn't like. I decided that I liked writing, so I took a course and became a journalist. The point is, it's okay to answer 'I don't know what I want to be!'. Finding a career takes time. If you've got no idea what career you want to do, here are a few ideas to get you started.

A Work in an office

Whatever we say we want to be, a huge number of us will join the staff of large companies and work in an office. And that's not a bad thing. Office work can be secure, well-paid, and many people like working in teams. You could become a manager and go on trips abroad with your expenses paid by the company. On the other hand, some people find it hard to be at the same desk working on the same computer day after day. If you're the outdoors type, then office work might not be ideal for you!

B Work with your hands

For some of us, applying for a job in writing is all the writing we want to do! The usual applicant for jobs such as these is someone who is independent and who prefers to use their physical skills, which could involve being anything from a builder to a chef. This type of work might also suit people who perhaps don't expect to stay in education for a long time. It's work that can involve long hours and you might never make a fortune, but at the same time you feel the satisfaction of making something, which office work often doesn't provide.

C Do voluntary work

It's difficult to make an entire career out of voluntary work because there's no money in it, but it can be a very useful step to something else. You can get lots of experience and you can try out different jobs while you make up your mind. From helping older people to working with animals, voluntary work teaches you skills that you can then use in a paid job. It can even take you to other countries, since many charities do international work.

2 🎧 **1.11 Read the article and decide if the statements are true (T) or false (F).**

1 The writer always wanted to be a journalist. T/F
2 She thinks young people have to decide now what career they want. T/F
3 She thinks young people should stay in education as long as possible. T/F
4 She thinks voluntary work can teach you something useful. T/F
5 She thinks people who work from home can't get another job. T/F
6 This article is aimed at young people considering their future. T/F

3 **Read the article again. For questions 1–6, choose from the types of work (A–E). The types of work may be chosen more than once.**

According to the writer, which type(s) of work:

would be good, if you like working on your own? 1 ___ 2 ___

do you not get paid to do? 3 ___

can you earn a lot of money from? 4 ___ 5 ___

would be good, if you haven't chosen a career? 6 ___

could allow you to travel? 7 ___ 8 ___

would be good, if you like working with other people? 9 ___ 10 ___

D WORK WITH THE PUBLIC

Working in a shop or in another service where you deal with members of the public isn't for everyone. It's ideal for those of you who like meeting people, both people you work with and customers. You might sometimes need a lot of patience, and it's not always easy to keep calm when the customer is wrong. On the plus side, there are lots of opportunities to earn a lot and move up to the level of manager, and maybe even higher!

E SET UP YOUR OWN BUSINESS

There's one advantage of working for yourself. You never have to fill in an application form to get the job! Seriously, though, for someone who likes working alone, running your own business can be very rewarding, even if it can also be very hard work. You could take something that you love, such as a hobby, and start making a salary from it. These days, you can even start your business online and work from home alone, if you wish. You need to have a lot of confidence, but there's nothing like being your own boss.

WORD BOX

4 **Use words or phrases from the article to complete the definitions. You've been given the first letter to help you.**

1 The amount of money you get paid every year to do a job is called your s_____ .
2 An a_____ f_____ is something you fill in when you apply for a job.
3 If a company pays your e_____ , they pay for taxis, meals, travel, etc.
4 When you write a letter to apply for a job, you apply i_____ w_____ .
5 A person applying for a job is called an a_____ .
6 Work which you do for a charity and which you don't get paid for is called v_____ w_____ .
7 The s_____ are all the people who work for a company.

❓ Have your say!

- How important is it to earn a high salary?
- Explain what other aspects of work you think are important.

Grammar clinic

Past perfect tense review

👁 Look at *Grammar database* pages 174–175 before you do the exercises.

1 Read the sentences and decide if the statements are true (T) or false (F).

> 1 By the time I was twenty-five, I*'d had* lots of jobs, …
> This describes an action before the main time in the past. ☐
> The action was completed before the main time in the past. ☐
>
> 2 Then, gradually, I realised I *had been doing* things I didn't like.
> This describes a continuous action before the main time in the past. ☐
> The action was completed before the main time in the past. ☐

2 Circle the correct tense in each sentence.
1 By the time Claire retired, she **worked/had been working** there for 20 years.
2 Before I filled in the application form, I **had called/had been calling** them to ask for more information.
3 It was the first time John **was working/had worked** on a computer.
4 The boss phoned before I **had finished/hadn't finished** the letter he asked me to write.
5 Mr Turner worked as a chef for a while and then **decided/had decided** to apply for a job as a fireman.

3 Correct the sentences that have mistakes in them. One sentence has no mistakes. Which one?
1 The staff were quite tired because customers had been coming in all morning.
2 Because he had never been working from home, my brother didn't know what to expect.
3 Somebody else got the job before I hadn't had a chance to send in my application form.
4 Dad had been driven all day so he was really tired when he got home from work.

4 Complete the sentences using the verbs in brackets in the past perfect simple or continuous.

> 1 When I started working here, it was the first time I _____ (**work**) in an office.
> 2 Luckily, we _____ (**already write**) the report when the boss arrived.
> 3 I _____ (**wait**) for the bus to work for half an hour when it finally turned up.
> 4 Helen decided to speak to her manager because she _____ (**have**) problems with the others in the office.
> 5 Alex _____ (**work**) in a supermarket before, so he knew exactly what to do.
> 6 My uncle _____ (**try**) to find a job for months when he finally found what he was looking for.

V Vocabulary builder

Occupations

1 Match the jobs in the box with the definitions.

accountant • journalist • electrician • plumber
sales rep • civil servant • civil engineer
labourer • architect • miner

This person …
1 does hard physical work, such as repairing roads.
2 designs houses and other buildings.
3 deals with the income and the expenses of a business.
4 writes articles and reports for a newspaper.
5 works in a government office, for example in a tax office.
6 digs coal or gold, etc from underground.
7 deals with the water system in buildings.
8 designs and builds roads and bridges, etc.
9 deals with the electrical system in buildings.
10 sells products to businesses.

2 Complete the explanations of the words and phrases in bold with one word.

1 When you are **on strike**, you don't _____ in order to try to force your employer to change something.
2 When you **get the sack**, you _____ your job, often because you did something wrong.
3 When you work **overtime**, you work _____ hours than usual.
4 When your employer **promotes** you, you are given a(n) _____ job than before.
5 When you **retire**, you _____ working permanently because you are old enough to do that or because your health is bad.

Word formation: suffixes

3 Make the words into nouns using one of the suffixes in the box. Be careful with spelling.

-ness	-ment	-tion	-ity

1 active   6 employ
2 enjoy   7 attract
3 kind   8 pay
4 major   9 promote
5 polite   10 lazy

4 Complete each sentence with one of the nouns you made in exercise 3. You may need to make the word plural.

1 I do so many after-school _____ that I never have time just to relax!
2 I'm hoping to find _____ in advertising when I leave college.
3 The _____ of people don't decide on their career until their late 20s.
4 I work in a shop, and _____ towards customers is very important.
5 I get a lot of _____ out of my job, even though the salary is quite low.
6 Jack lost his job because of his own _____ and lack of interest.
7 I was touched by the boss's _____ when he said I looked ill and should go home.
8 I've applied for a(n) _____ at work, and I hope I get it!
9 One of the _____ of working in the media is meeting famous people.
10 Our manager gave us all an extra _____ for working so hard!

4 Work Wonders

Listening

1 **1.12** You are going to listen to an extract from an interview with two careers officers. As you listen, complete the sentences with a number.

1 Craig has been working as a careers officer for _____ years.
2 He visits approximately _____ schools every year.
3 Susan talks to about _____ pupils about careers each year.
4 Each careers interview lasts about _____ minutes.

2 **1.13** Listen to the whole interview. For questions 1–5, choose the best answer (A, B or C).

1 What does Craig say about the work of a careers officer?
   A It has changed completely over the years.
   B It is similar to what it used to be.
   C It's better than the other jobs he's done.

2 Only one in ten of the people who want to become doctors
   A succeed in their ambition.
   B become lawyers.
   C are successful in other professions.

3 Craig suggested the air force to the young man because he
   A wanted to change his mind about being an astronaut.
   B thought it was probably the best way to achieve his aim.
   C was sure that astronauts started in the air force.

4 Craig's advice is that you should
   A be ready to choose a completely different career.
   B only talk about your ambition if you really mean it.
   C become a doctor if you can't become an architect.

5 Susan's advice is that you should
   A become a lawyer if you like helping people.
   B get legal advice before choosing your career.
   C find out more about the job you want to do.

Soundbite silent letters (1)

 1.14 Read the words and underline any silent letters. Listen and check.

listen	climber	pneumonia
plumber	comb	knight
lamb	tomb	

Speaking  Useful Phrases

1 Complete the words and phrases to express uncertainty.

1 *I don't know …*
   I'm not s_____ …
   I'm not c_____ …

2 *… but I think …*
   … but I s_____ …
   … but I i_____ …

3 *… may …*
   … m_____ …
   … c_____ …

2 In pairs, choose four or more of the questions to talk about. Use the phrases from exercise 1 to help you.

- What do you think is important when choosing a career?
- Do you think people work too hard nowadays?
- How do you think the world of work is changing?
- What do you think it would be like to work from home?
- What problems do people face when they are unemployed?

I haven't really thought about that. I suppose …

The salary is important, and so is …

I imagine the biggest problem is …

Look at *Speaking database - Giving/Asking for opinion* on page 165.

Use of English

Comparatives and superlatives

👁 Look at *Grammar database* pages 175–176 before you do the exercises.

1 Complete the sentences using either the comparative or the superlative form of the adjective in brackets.

1 This job is much _____ (**easy**) than my last one!
2 I imagine the life of a lawyer is _____ (**challenging**) than that of a shop assistant.
3 Chris should make a good actor because he's _____ (**confident**) child I know.
4 Doctors are generally _____ (**well**) paid than nurses.

2 Complete each sentence so that it means the same as the first sentence. Use the words given without changing them. Use no more than five words.

1 I've never read such a boring book about being an actor.   **interesting**
   This is _____ about being an actor I have ever read.
2 I had expected the job to be more difficult than it was.   **as**
   The job _____ I had expected.
3 Everyone in the office took much longer to finish their work than Kim.   **quickly**
   Kim finished her work _____ everyone else in the office.
4 I got more satisfaction from my old job.   **less**
   I am _____ I was in my old job.

3 For questions 1–10, read the text below. Use the word given in capitals at the end of some of the lines to form a word that fits in the gap in the same line. There is an example at the beginning (0). Write your answers IN CAPITAL LETTERS.

AN UNUSUAL JOB

Most people end up in fairly ordinary (**0**) _OCCUPATIONS_. If you're a (**1**) _____, a sales rep or a doctor, when you tell people what you do, they understand what it is. For some, though, their (**2**) _____ produces a surprised stare from the (**3**) _____ of people. For example, Emma Carter is a hand model. A what? Well, let Emma explain. 'It's (**4**) _____ paid than a lot of jobs, and in some ways I suppose it's (**5**) _____. Most people don't understand what I do, even though they've probably seen me do it! My hands appear on TV and in magazine ads all the time. I don't think I've got the (**6**) _____ hands in the world, but I know how to do different (**7**) _____ in different ways, to communicate ideas such as strength or love. The main (**8**) _____ of this job are that I have a lot of freedom to choose when I work, and I get to go on trips abroad with all my (**9**) _____ paid. I get a lot of (**10**) _____ out of it, and my hands are famous, even if I'm not!'

OCCUPY
LABOUR

EMPLOY
MAJOR

WELL
EASY

PRETTY
ACTIVE

ATTRACT

EXPENSE
ENJOY

Writing

A report

👁 Look at *Writing database - reports* on page 151 before you do the exercises.

1 Read this writing task. Who is the report to and what is the subject?

Everyone in your class has spent a day at work with a member of their family. Your teacher has now asked you to write a report for her/him about the job you learned about. She/He wants you to describe the main features of the work, and to explain why it would or wouldn't be suitable for you as a career.

Write a **report** of between **120** and **180** words in an appropriate style.

2 Decide if the statements are true (T) or false (F).

1. The aim of a report is to present information in a clear way.
2. You should never give your own opinion in a report.
3. Reports are usually quite informal.
4. It's usually a good idea to give each paragraph a heading.
5. The last paragraph might be a summary or might contain suggestions.
6. You put your name at the end of a report, like in a letter.

Working model

3 Put these parts of a report into the correct order (A–D).

1 ___ 2 ___ 3 ___ 4 ___

A
CONCLUSION
Being an accountant would not be an appropriate career choice for me. Firstly, I am not interested in working in an office, and I would rather work outdoors. Secondly, I have always wanted to be a vet and work with animals. My experience of a day with an accountant has not changed my plans.

B
INTRODUCTION
To learn about careers, we were each asked to spend a day at work with a member of our family. I chose my aunt, Rachel, who works as an accountant.

C
To: Mrs Edwards
From: Hannah Davies
Subject: My day with an accountant

D
DAILY ROUTINE
On most days, my aunt arrives at the office at nine o'clock and works on her computer until lunchtime. In the afternoon, she visits businesses and has meetings with people. This was her routine on the day I spent with her.

SALARY AND JOB SATISFACTIONS
My aunt receives a good salary, and she often earns more by doing overtime. As well as a good salary, my aunt gets a large amount of job satisfaction from her work. I observed her solving people's financial problems and helping them manage their money. She enjoys this part of her job.

4 Read the model again and complete the sentences with a word or short phrase.

1 Mrs Edwards asked the pupils to spend a day at work to _____ careers.
2 Hannah spent the day with a(n) _____ called Rachel, who is a member of her family.
3 On the day Hannah spent with Rachel, they spent the morning in _____ .
4 They spent the afternoon having _____ with people at their businesses.
5 Rachel likes helping people with their _____ .
6 Hannah would rather be a(n) _____ than an accountant.

Ready to write!

5 Look at this writing task. Who is the report to and what is the subject?

> Everyone in your class has been asked to find out about a different career, either by speaking to people you know or by searching online. Your teacher has now asked you to write a report for her/him about the career you learned about. She/He wants you to describe the main features of the work and to explain why it would or wouldn't be suitable for you as a career.

Write a **report** of between **120** and **180** words in an appropriate style.

6 Write short answers to these questions. Find information online, speak to someone you know, or use your imagination where necessary.

1 What job have you found out about?
   _____
2 Where did you get information about that job from? _____
3 What is the usual salary for that job?
   _____
4 What are the main things that person does each day? _____
5 Apart from money, what might a person doing that job enjoy? _____

7 Make a plan of your answer. Use your notes.

- How are you going to start your report?
  To: ....
  From: ....
  Subject: ....
- What's the title of your first paragraph?
- How are you going to start it?
- What are the titles of your other paragraphs?
- How are you going to start your final paragraph?
- Do you think this career would be suitable for you?
- What are the main two reasons? Why? / Why not?
- Is there a career that would suit you better? Which?

Now complete *Writing Planner 4* on page 156.

Now write!

8 You are now ready to write your report. Use formal language and present your information clearly. Make a clear recommendation.

Check it out!

9 Check your work. Tick (✓) what you have done.

- I have started the report in the correct way. ☐
- I have used formal language. ☐
- I have given my paragraphs clear headings. ☐
- I have made a good recommendation. ☐
- I have checked my spelling and my grammar. ☐
- My report is between 120 and 180 words long. ☐

◀ Look Back

Can you answer these questions? If you can't remember, look through the unit for the answers.

1 What do you fill in to apply for a job?
2 Who does a civil servant work for?
3 What's the noun from 'lazy'?
4 What do we call the person who gives us advice on choosing a job?
5 Which of these words has a silent letter?
   mumble   climber   grumble

Revision
Units 3-4

1 Choose the correct option.

1 All the _____ for the job seem to have a lot of experience.
 A expenses   B applicants   C staff   D applications

2 My aunt's really worried that she's going to get the _____ and be unemployed.
 A sack   B strike   C post   D vacancy

3 Why don't you send in an application _____ for the job? You might get it!
 A paper   B form   C report   D list

4 Diane's really successful! She's just been _____ to Senior Manager.
 A employed   B placed   C promoted   D applied

5 Greg's a waiter, and his _____ isn't really very high.
 A expenses   B payment   C salary   D wage

6 Imagine how exciting it must be to be a(n) _____ and to interview famous people!
 A sales rep   B journalist   C miner   D accountant

7 This might sound a bit _____, but I love doing exams!
 A weird   B valuable   C traditional   D balanced

8 Have you ever thought of doing _____ work, maybe for a charity?
 A expensive   B worthless   C voluntary   D priceless

9 My grandfather used to be a teacher, but he _____ years ago.
 A afforded   B promoted   C balanced   D retired

10 I'd like to be a _____ because you have a lot of security working for the government.
 A sales rep   B civil servant   C plumber   D labourer

2 Complete the sentences using the correct form of the verbs in brackets.

1 I suppose I _____ (**know**) Tony for six years now.

2 By the time Ian got to the station, the train _____ (**leave**).

3 Diane _____ (**cook**) since five o'clock and she still hasn't finished dinner!

4 We _____ (**see**) this programme before.

5 I _____ (**learn**) English for about five years now.

6 I was tired when you saw me yesterday because I _____ (**work**) all day.

7 My dad _____ (**visit**) China twice and India once.

8 Let's go to the cinema when you _____ (**finish**) your homework.

3 Circle the correct verb in each sentence.

1. Last summer, I **went/did/played** fishing almost every day.
2. My sister **goes/does/plays** gymnastics three times a week.
3. **Going/Doing/Playing** swimming is probably my only hobby.
4. Some people spend too much time **going/doing/playing** video games.
5. I'm really looking forward to **going/doing/playing** camping next month.
6. I think more boys should think about **going/doing/playing** ballet.
7. Have you ever **been/done/played** skiing? It looks really difficult.

4 Complete the sentences using an appropriate word.

1. Don't rush! _____ your time and you'll do a much better job.
2. People who are unemployed often have more time on their _____ .
3. I got to school just _____ time for the start of the lesson.
4. I'm quite busy, but I try to _____ time to do my hobbies.

5 Choose the correct option.

1. Many teachers leave the profession _____ the long hours.
   A because   B because of
2. Many people _____ that working overtime is a good way of making more money.
   A think   B think so
3. Let's all hide and surprise Janette when she _____ back from the shop!
   A gets   B will get
4. You need to _____ a degree in architecture to become an architect.
   A get   B get to

6 Circle the correct article in each sentence. If no article is necessary, circle the hyphen (-).

1. During **a/the/-** 1980s, many people used computers at work for the first time.
2. In **a/the/-** United States, professional people work very long hours.
3. I hope to go to **a/the/-** university to study engineering.
4. Emma was off work last Monday with **a/the/-** cold.
5. 'Hello? No, Mr Green is at **a/the/-** work. Can I take a message?'
6. I hate this job. I work all week, and then I have to work on **a/the/-** Sunday morning too!
7. My car broke down so I went home on **a/the/-** foot.

7 Read this text. For questions 1–10, use the word given at the end of each line to form a word that fills the gap. There is an example at the beginning (0). You will get two marks for each correct answer.

Many people, perhaps even the (0) ___*majority*___ , are not particularly	MAJOR
happy in their job. They go to work, get paid, and (1) _____ for	EMPLOY
them is just a way of paying the bills. This leads to (2) _____ at	LAZY
work and unhappy workers often don't show enough (3) _____	POLITE
to customers or (4) _____ to their fellow workers. Many people	KIND
feel that they have no chance of (5) _____ and they are unhappy	PROMOTE
with the (6) _____ conditions.	WORK
If you want to get (7) _____ from your work, make sure that it	ENJOY
involves doing an (8) _____ that you like. Ask yourself whether	ACTIVE
the job will have the same (9) _____ after five years. A careful	ATTRACT
choice now can save you a lot of (10) _____ in the future.	HAPPY

Score _____ /60

5

The Global Village

Start thinking!

What does the word 'media' mean to you?
How much TV do you watch?
What kinds of TV programme do you like?

Reading

1 1.15 Read the magazine article. What is surprising about what it says?

How it all began

Without even thinking about it, we click the remote to turn our TVs on. Then we turn over to find a channel we want to watch and sit back to enjoy full colour entertainment, news and sport. Television is a global success story. How did it all begin? Amazingly, it first took its modern form in the mind of a thirteen-year-old American boy called Philo T. Farnsworth.

The basis for modern telecommunications was created in the nineteenth century. The telegraph, which was invented in 1837, meant that messages could be sent round the world. The telephone followed in 1876. For the first time, people's voices could be sent over long distances. **1**____ It was only with the invention of the radio in 1901 that suddenly people were capable of sending messages through the air over long distances. The first radio shows were almost twenty years away.

The idea of sending images along with sound seemed to be an impossibility. Although cinema had been invented in 1895, there seemed no way to get these moving pictures to fly through the air. At first, inventors such as John Logie Baird in Britain worked on mechanical systems. This used spinning discs inside the television which allowed light through small holes. **2**____ In order to develop, television needed to be electronic, and the story of electronic television goes back to the small town of Rigby, Idaho, in 1922.

Philo T. Farnsworth was a very clever student. He was fascinated by electricity and built electrical machines to make the work on his parents' farm easier. He read an article in a magazine that described mechanical television and realised that it could never be fast enough to produce good pictures. **3**____ Gradually, an idea formed in his mind. Magnets could be used to control electrons to make a picture.

He went to the only other person in Rigby who he felt might understand the ideas – his chemistry teacher, Justin Tolman. He drew diagrams on the blackboard explaining how it would work. **4**____ There was no way they could build a working model, though, and soon Philo's family was forced to move to find work.

Eventually, Farnsworth went to Brigham Young University, where he continued to develop

2 Match these dates to what happened.

1 1837 _____
2 1876 _____
3 1895 _____
4 1901 _____
5 1922 _____
6 1927 _____

a Electric TV was first explained.
b The telephone was invented.
c The radio was invented.
d The telegraph was invented.
e The first pictures were seen on electric TV.
f The cinema was invented.

3 Read the article again. Six sentences have been removed from the article. Choose from the sentences A–G the one which fits each gap (1–6). There is one extra sentence which you do not need to use.

A Television became a part of everyday life, as it still is.
B It finally came when he got a job with two rich investors, George Everson and Leslie Gorrell.
C However, wires were needed to connect people who wanted to communicate.
D Nobody understood how it worked, but it was very impressive.
E Over the next few weeks, they developed the ideas together until they were convinced it could succeed.
F Although images were sent, they were very basic.
G As he worked in the fields, his brain played with the idea of television.

his ideas for electronic television. After university, he set up his own business repairing radios. All the time he was doing this, he was looking out for the chance to raise money to develop his world-changing invention. **5** _____ After work one day, Farnsworth explained his idea and the men agreed to provide some of the money and raise the rest.

Farnsworth finally registered the patents for his idea in 1927. Later that year, he managed to see the first images on his system. It was still many years before television became the force it is today, but it was on its way. Shortly after the end of the Second World War, TV pictures were being broadcast into homes across America and, soon, across Europe and the rest of the world. **6** _____ Billions of us every day around the world stay up to date with the news headlines, follow our favourite sports team or laugh at a comedy show. And it's all because of an idea in the mind of a young boy nearly a hundred years ago.

WORD BOX

4 Find words or phrases in the article that mean the following. You've been given the first letter to help you.

1 change channels on a TV
   t_____ o_____
2 worldwide
   g_____
3 electronic means of communication
   t_____
4 pictures
   i_____
5 send (a programme) through the air
   b_____
6 informed about the latest news
   u_____ t_____
   d_____
7 titles of news stories
   h_____

Have your say!

- How do you think television has changed the world?
- Do you think it will still be important in the future? Why? / Why not?

Grammar clinic

The passive

👁 Look at *Grammar database* pages 176–177 before you do the exercises.

1 Read the sentences and phrase from the magazine article on pages 42 and 43. Tick (✓) the reasons why we might use the passive.

The basis for modern telecommunications was created in the nineteenth century.

For the first time, people's voices could be sent over long distances.

Although cinema had been invented in 1895, …

We might use the passive when

a We don't know who did something. ☐
b It's not important who did something. ☐
c We want to emphasise something. ☐
d We think our reader doesn't understand. ☐

Now underline all the examples of the passive you can find in the article.

2 Rewrite the sentences in the passive.

1 Someone first suggested the idea of the internet in the 1960s in America.
2 They deliver our newspaper to the house every morning.
3 Someone told me that the BBC is planning a new channel.
4 People say that the internet is a great way to receive international news.
5 Jill gave me a great book about working in the media.

3 Choose the correct passive version of each sentence.

1 They broadcast the news report by satellite.
 a The news report broadcasts them by satellite.
 b The news report was broadcast by satellite.
2 Satellite television is bringing people closer to each other.
 a People are being brought closer to each other by satellite television.
 b People are bringing satellite television closer to each other.
3 They showed that new Spielberg film on cable last night.
 a Cable has shown that new Spielberg film last night.
 b That new Spielberg film was shown on cable last night.
4 Somebody has stolen our television, so I missed the big match.
 a Our television was being stolen by someone so I missed the big match.
 b Our television has been stolen so I missed the big match.

4 Read this short article about communication. Then rewrite it in the passive.

Someone sent the first modern email in 1971. Someone sent the first text message in 1992. Both of these forms of communication have changed the world. They have brought people together and they have made the world smaller. Today, we send over 300 billion email messages per day! And people send over 1 billion text messages per week – in just the UK!

_____
_____
_____
_____
_____

Vocabulary builder

Television programmes

1 Complete the sentences with a word or phrase from the box.

documentary • sitcom • game show
reality show • soap opera • chat show

1 A _____ is funny and each programme usually lasts for half an hour. Every show has the same characters.
2 A _____ is a factual programme and it might be about the environment or politics.
3 On a _____ , famous people are interviewed about their careers and their recent work.
4 A _____ is a show about different characters who live in the same area or who work together. They usually have very dramatic problems and the story continues for a long time.
5 On a _____ , members of the public play games or answer questions to try to win prizes.
6 On a _____ , we watch members of the public living together. We follow their relationships and one of them leaves each week.

Can you name one of each type of programme? Which types of programme do you prefer to watch?

2 Match the people with the descriptions of what they do.

1 presenter   a tries to win prizes on a game show
2 contestant   b tells people watching about important events
3 viewer   c films the show so that people at home can see it
4 producer   d watches a TV programme
5 cameraman   e decides which TV programmes should be made
6 newsreader   f introduces the show and the people on it

Phrasal verbs with *on*

3 Phrasal verbs with *on* often have meanings connected to starting something or continuing something. Circle the correct phrasal verb in each sentence.

1 Do you think you could **open on/turn on** the TV for me, please?
2 Sorry, but I can't hear the radio if you **carry on/put on** making so much noise.
3 I hated this programme at first, but now it's **coming on/growing on** me.
4 I'm going to **bring on/log on** and see if I've got any email.
5 There are two people on *Life in the House* who just don't **take on/get on** with each other at all!
6 I don't think they should **put on/come on** violent programmes in the early evening.

Now match each phrasal verb with a definition. Put the phrasal verbs into the infinitive.

have a good relationship   _____
broadcast on TV   _____
start something working   _____
connect to the internet   _____
continue   _____
become more attractive
to you after some time   _____

Which other phrasal verb means 'continue'? _____ on

Idioms: the media

4 In pairs, talk about what you think these idiomatic phrases might mean.

be front-page news   hit the headlines
a couch potato   be on the air
be on the spot

Listening

1 🎧 **1.16** You are going to listen to extracts from five different programmes. As you listen, match each extract to a programme type.

Extract 1	**a** documentary
Extract 2	**b** sitcom
Extract 3	**c** game show
Extract 4	**d** chat show
Extract 5	**e** soap opera

2 🎧 **1.17** You will now hear the extracts again in a different order. For questions 1–5, choose the best answer (A, B or C).

1 You hear this woman speaking on the TV. What is she saying?
   A She is planning to get divorced.
   B Brad isn't who people thought he was.
   C Brad's cousin isn't really her son.

2 You hear this man speaking on the TV. What does the government say?
   A The number of unemployed people has gone down.
   B The number of businesses closing has gone down.
   C The number of people missing has gone down.

3 You hear this conversation on the TV. What does Chris want?
   A to take the dog with him
   B to get something he left behind
   C to prove that the woman is wrong

4 You hear this man speaking on the TV. What does the man say about his guest?
   A The show she is in has made her famous.
   B She was a failure in films.
   C She is enjoying success at the moment.

5 You hear this man speaking on the TV. What does the man tell Amy?
   A If she is nervous, she won't win the prize.
   B If she loses, she will still get some money.
   C If she wins the car, she'll also win some money.

Soundbite /ɜː/

🎧 **1.18** Circle the words that have the same vowel sound in them. Listen and check.

1	word	sorry	fear	bird
2	hard	heard	murder	bread
3	fair	fur	first	far
4	mean	meant	learn	burn
5	sir	occur	part	sour

Speaking

1 Make notes to answer the questions.
Have you ever been on television?
When? What was it like?
Would you like to be? Why? / Why not?

2 In pairs, ask and answer the questions. Try to say as much as you can. Use the phrases below to help you.
- Have you ever watched TV programmes in English?
- Have you ever been on television? Would you like to be?
- Has anybody you know ever been in the news?
- Do you like phone-in programmes? Have you ever called one on TV or on the radio?

Useful Phrases

Actually, no, I haven't, but I would like to because …

In fact, yes, I have. It was …

Yes, and it was a great experience. I …

No, luckily, and I think that …

👁 Look at *Speaking database - Expressing preferences* on page 165.

Use of English

Countable and uncountable nouns

👁 Look at *Grammar database* pages 177–178 before you do the exercises.

1 Are these nouns countable, uncountable or both?

advice • sheep • equipment • furniture • wood • chicken • paper • hair • news • luggage • chocolate clothes • information • fact • interest • jeans • money • journey • trousers • bone • rice

2 Correct the sentences that have mistakes in them and tick (✓) the correct ones.
1. Any television studio has a lot of valuable equipments in it. ☐
2. The programme was interrupted to bring the viewers an important news. ☐
3. Most people who read the news on TV wear a suit, rather than a jean. ☐
4. I used to write for a paper and give advices to readers with problems. ☐
5. Most of us get a great deal of information through the media. ☐

Homonyms

3 Write a verb from the box to match each definition. You will use each verb twice.

argue • feel • order • realise • run • suggest

1. quarrel, row _____
2. move quickly _____
3. remind you of _____
4. touch with your hands _____
5. suddenly understand _____
6. manage (a business) _____
7. propose _____
8. make a point _____
9. command _____
10. experience an emotion _____
11. ask for _____
12. make (a dream) come true _____

4 For questions 1–10, read the text below. Use the word given in capitals at the end of some of the lines to form a word that fits in the gap in the same line. There is an example at the beginning (0). Write your answers IN CAPITAL LETTERS.

THE HISTORY OF TV SHOWS

Whether you like (0) <u>DOCUMENTARIES</u> or whether you prefer to watch a (1) _____ interview people on a chat show, we are all used to seeing a (2) _____ of programmes on our screens. We often forget, though, that someone had to invent each type of show. For example, the first (3) _____ appeared on the first game show, called *Spelling Bee*, in America in 1938, although the (4) _____ of game shows really began to grow in the late 1950s. The first (5) _____ of a sports event took place in 1936 and showed the Berlin Olympics®. The first situation (6) _____ (or 'sitcom') was called *Pinwright's Progress* and was made in 1946 by the BBC. The first soap operas were on radio, and the (7) _____ were often companies that made soap powder – that's where the name comes from! They started to appear on TV in the 50s, and (8) _____ soon fell in love with these shows. And what about (9) _____ shows? They grew out of (10) _____ shows about ordinary people and really took off with the first series of *Big Brother* in the Netherlands in 1999.

DOCUMENT
PRESENT
VARY

CONTEST
POPULAR

BROAD
COMIC

PRODUCE

VIEW
REAL
EARLY

 Writing

A story

👁 Look at *Writing database - stories* on page 152 before you do the exercises.

1 When you write a story, descriptive language is important. Put the adjectives into the correct column. Some of them may go in more than one column.

terrible • excited • wonderful • depressed • terrific • nervous
dreadful • awful • great • cool • horrible • perfect • amazing

'very good'	'very bad'	feelings

Add more adjectives to the boxes and compare your ideas.

2 Underline any adjectives from your lists that can be made into adverbs by adding *-ly*.

Working model

3 Read this writing task. Who do you think is going to read the story?

> A local radio station is holding a competition for stories written by listeners. The winning stories will be read on the radio. The competition rules state that all stories must begin with these words:
> *I had never imagined I would see myself on the news.*

Write a **story** of between **120** and **180** words in an appropriate style.

4 Read the answer to the writing task. Underline all the descriptive adjectives and adverbs the writer has used.

IT WASN'T ME!

I had never imagined I would see myself on the news. It was awful! The newsreader was talking about a robbery and there, on the screen, was a picture of me. 'Mum! I'm on television!' I shouted, and she ran into the living room.

'That's great!' she said and then suddenly stopped. She looked at me, and then back at the screen. 'I didn't do it. I'm innocent!' I said quickly. 'What should I do?'

My mum suggested that we go to the police station. I wasn't sure. I didn't want to go to prison for a crime I hadn't committed! Mum said that I had to convince them that they wanted the wrong person.

We got to the police station and I went inside nervously. I explained who I was and they asked me lots of questions. I answered them honestly. Eventually, they believed I was innocent. It was a wonderful feeling when I finally walked out of the police station!

The next night, they said on the news that the police had caught the person who committed the robbery. He looked a little like me. My nightmare was finally over.

5 Decide if the statements are true (T) or false (F).

1. The writer starts with the right words.
2. The writer sometimes uses short sentences for dramatic effect.
3. The writer uses direct speech to tell us what people said.
4. The writer uses exclamation marks to add drama and excitement.
5. The story doesn't have a beginning, a middle or an end.

Ready to write!

6 You are going to write your own story to enter the competition. Make a plan of your answer. Use your imagination.

- Where do you have to put the sentence you have been given?
- How did you feel when you saw yourself on the news?
- Why were you on the news?
- Who else was involved?
- How did they feel? Did they say anything?
- What happened after you saw the news?
- Then what happened?
- What happened in the end?
- How did you feel in the end?

Now complete *Writing Planner 5* on page 157.

Now write!

7 You are now ready to write your story. Make sure you use good descriptive language. Try to create drama by using direct speech. Write between 120 and 180 words

Check it out!

8 Check your work. Tick (✓) what you have done.

- I have started with the sentence given and I haven't changed it.
- I have used some good descriptive adjectives.
- I have used direct speech at least once.
- My story has a beginning, a middle and an end.
- I have used paragraphs.
- I have checked my spelling and my grammar.
- My story is between 120 and 180 words long.

◀ Look Back

Can you answer these questions? If you can't remember, look through the unit for the answers.

1. How old was Philo T. Farnsworth when he had the idea for electronic TV?
2. What do we call the title of a news story?
3. We make the passive using which auxiliary verb?
4. What is a 'couch potato'?
5. Which noun is countable?
   jeans   news   facts
6. What two meanings of 'argue' do you know?

The Global Village

6

Come Rain or Shine

🗨 Start thinking!

What's the weather usually like in each season in your area?
Think about:
- spring
- summer
- autumn
- winter

📖 Reading

1 🎧 1.19 Read this extract from a book. Would you like to do what the writer suggests?

2 Read the sentences. Do you think the writer of the book agrees or disagrees with them?
1. Traditional wisdom isn't very reliable.
2. The professionals rely on the amateurs.
3. You should know the usual weather patterns.
4. You can benefit from your forecasts.

Do-It-Yourself Forecasts

*When the wind is in the west,
the weather is always best.
When the wind's in the south,
the rain's in its mouth.*

Have you heard sayings like these before? Or have you heard that when cows lie down it's going to rain? Maybe you've heard that a sunny Christmas Day means we're going to have a warm Easter. Many cultures have traditional ideas about how to forecast the weather and they all have one thing in common: they are not very
7 accurate. Most of **them** are about as accurate as saying that the weather tomorrow will be more or less the same as today. The weather is too complicated to be forecast easily and simply.

How do meteorologists go about trying to forecast the weather? The first thing they need is information, and lots of it. Data is constantly collected from weather stations around the world. Weather balloons tell us what is happening at high altitude. Satellites give us images of cloud cover and wind direction. All this information is processed by computer and combined with information about the normal climate of a region to produce the forecast. Even so, we can only accurately forecast the weather for the next couple of days.

Can't we amateurs forecast the weather at all, then? Yes, we can, but to be a great amateur meteorologist you need to do some of the things the experts do. First of all, collect your information. You need to know about the climate in the area where you live. What's a typical summer like? How much rain normally falls in October? If your area never gets fog in the summer, then a forecast of fog in July is unlikely to be accurate.

The next thing you need to take into account is local geography. Are there any mountains nearby? They could affect the wind. Are you by the coast? That could affect rainfall. All these factors need to be considered when you are trying to understand what the weather is going to do next. You'll also need some basic equipment: a good thermometer, a barometer to measure pressure in the atmosphere and, if possible, a wind meter. Start to keep records of the temperature, pressure and wind speed and direction each day.

Then it's a question of using your eyes, and even your ears. Listen to the radio. Is there a lot of static? Together with falling atmospheric pressure, that probably means that the weather is going to get worse. Go outside and listen. Do sounds seem clearer than usual? Is there a kind of ring around the Sun or Moon? It could mean that it's

3 Read the text again. For questions 1–6, choose the answer (A, B, C or D) which you think fits best according to the text.

1 What does 'them' in line 7 refer to?
 A different cultures
 B traditional ideas about the weather
 C most weather forecasts
 D the weather on different days

2 The writer does not mention that forecasters collect information about
 A the weather very high in the atmosphere.
 B the accuracy of forecasts in the past.
 C the amount of cloud over an area.
 D the way the wind is blowing.

3 What does the writer say you need to know about your area?
 A the forecasts of the experts
 B the general patterns of weather
 C how rain affects local people
 D how summer fog is caused

4 The writer suggests that the amateur forecaster should
 A buy a lot of accurate equipment.
 B get a good map of the area.
 C make notes about changes in the weather.
 D live in a flat area away from the sea.

5 You might be able to forecast good weather when
 A the reading on your barometer is falling.
 B you can hear sounds very clearly.
 C low clouds start to disappear.
 D the Moon is very bright in the sky.

6 To make accurate forecasts, you need to have
 A experience of forecasting.
 B good planning.
 C time to watch the weather change.
 D a good memory.

going to rain. Is your barometer rising and do the clouds seem to be getting higher? It probably means that the weather is clearing up.

With a little practice, your forecasts will become more accurate. Soon, you'll be able to plan your day better. Are you playing football tomorrow? Well, a quick look at your equipment and a few minutes spent outside will tell you whether it's going to rain or not. Are you going skiing next week? Maybe you should forget it if there's no chance of snow.

Making your own forecasts can be a lot of fun, and who knows? You might even beat the experts!

WORD BOX

4 Match the words with the definitions.

1 forecast (paragraph 1) — a unwanted electrical noise (on a radio)
2 meteorologist (paragraph 2) — b the general weather pattern of a place
3 data (paragraph 2) — c (of the weather) become better, less cloudy, etc
4 climate (paragraph 2) — d person who studies the weather
5 amateur (paragraph 3) — e predict
6 barometer (paragraph 4) — f information, especially in the form of numbers
7 static (paragraph 5) — g device for measuring atmospheric pressure
8 clear up (paragraph 5) — h person who does something for pleasure, without being paid

❓ Have your say!

- Are you interested in making your own amateur weather forecasts?
- Would you like to be a professional meteorologist when you're older?

G Grammar clinic

The future (1)

👁 Look at *Grammar database* pages 178–179 before you do the exercises.

1 Look at the book extract on pages 50 and 51. Find as many examples as you can of these ways of referring to the future and underline them.
- be going to
- will
- could/might
- present continuous

2 Choose the correct option in each sentence.
1. A hurricane is going to hit Florida in the next few days.
   a This is an arrangement. **b** This is a prediction.
2. Shall we check the weather forecast before we plan the picnic?
   a This is a suggestion. **b** This is an offer.
3. I'm sorry, but I'm not carrying your umbrella for you.
   a This is an arrangement. **b** This is a refusal.
4. If the weather's okay, we're visiting your grandma this weekend.
   a This is an arrangement. **b** This is a suggestion.

3 Circle the correct word or phrase to complete the email.

To: Jackie
Date: 4th November
Subject: Hi!

Hi Zoe,

Thanks for your email!

This is just a quick message because (1) **I'm meeting/I'll meet** Alison at the gym in a few minutes.

Anyway, here's what I need to know. (2) **Do you still go/Are you still going** to Dave's barbecue on Saturday afternoon? I hope so, because I think (3) **we'll have/we're having** a great time! What do you think the weather (4) **will be/is being** like? If it's warm, (5) **I/I'll** wear my new shorts. (6) **I'm going to/I** call Dave this evening to ask him what we should bring with us. (7) **Are/Will** you seeing him tomorrow?

Got to go now. (8) **I'm texting/I'll text** you later when (9) **I/I'll** get back from the gym.

Bye for now!
Jackie

4 Correct the sentences that have mistakes in them. One sentence has no mistakes. Which one?
1. We should take coats with us. The forecast says it's raining later today.
2. I hope it stops snowing! I meet Ben at the café at six.
3. It's getting very windy! We will have a storm!
4. Shall I turn the central heating on? It's getting a bit cold, isn't it?
5. That was lightning! It starts raining in a minute, I bet!
6. I think that in 100 years' time we are able to control the weather.

Vocabulary builder

The weather

1 Match the words in the box with the correct definitions.

hurricane • heatwave • blizzard
shower • hail • frost • mist

1 This is frozen rain.
2 This is a short period when it rains.
3 This is a heavy snowstorm.
4 This is white ice, like a powder on the ground.
5 This is light fog.
6 This is a very strong storm with powerful winds.
7 This is a period of very hot weather.

We can make adjectives by adding -y to three of the words in exercise 1. Which ones?

What other adjectives ending in -y do you know for describing the weather? Make a list.

2 Complete the words and phrases using the words in the box.

stone • gust • flake • puddle • flash • drop

snow_____   rain_____

hail_____   a _____ of lightning

a _____ of wind   a _____ of water

Collocations

3 Choose the correct option in each sentence.

1 We didn't go to the concert in the end because it was _____ with rain.
  a dripping   b showering   c pouring
2 I heard that there were really _____ winds in France last night.
  a strong   b heavy   c wet
3 In our area, we usually have warm summers and _____ winters.
  a light   b mild   c easy
4 It looks like a _____ shower, so we'll just wait for it to stop raining.
  a moving   b travelling   c passing
5 Don't go out without your coat. It's raining _____ .
  a hard   b greatly   c powerfully

Confusable words

4 Complete the sentences using the correct form of the words in the boxes.

look • see • watch

1 We were _____ the match when suddenly it started to snow!
2 I love _____ at all the trees when it's been snowing.
3 It was the first time Lee had ever _____ snow.

nervous • upset

4 Daisy will be really _____ if we cancel the trip because of the weather.
5 I get a bit _____ when I have to speak in public.

have • spend • pass

6 We always _____ our holidays in hot countries.
7 Did you _____ a good time playing in the snow?
8 If we can't play out because of the rain, let's play cards to _____ the time.

Listening

1 **1.20** You are going to listen to an extract from an interview about rainbows. Answer the questions.

1 What's the programme called?
2 What does Nicola want to know?
3 Where does Kate work?

2 **1.21** Listen to the whole interview. For questions 1–7, complete the sentences.

The sun's energy is composed of **1** _____, microwaves and light.
Light reaching the Earth is bent by **2** _____ in the air.
Kate suggests looking closely at a(n) **3** _____.
We don't see rainbows in winter because the raindrops are **4** _____.
You can create a rainbow by **5** _____ into the air.
To do Kate's experiment, you need a mirror, the sun, a bowl of water and a(n) **6** _____.
The next question is about the causes of **7** _____.

Soundbite — weak forms (1)

1.22 Some words are pronounced differently when they aren't stressed. Listen to how we say the underlined words in these sentences.

and — I get a bit scared when there's lots of thunder <u>and</u> lightning.
an — Don't forget to take <u>an</u> umbrella.
as — It's not <u>as</u> cold <u>as</u> yesterday, is it?
at — It started snowing <u>at</u> 10 o'clock and didn't stop.
can — If it's warm, we <u>can</u> go to the beach.
for — It seems like it's been raining <u>for</u> days.

Now try saying the sentences in the same way. If necessary, listen again.

Speaking

1 Here are some pictures of unusual things. Talk about what you think they might be. Use the phrases given. **Useful Phrases**

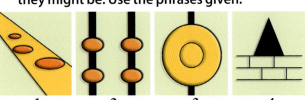

1 2 3 4

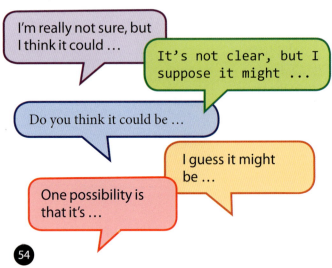

- I'm really not sure, but I think it could …
- It's not clear, but I suppose it might …
- Do you think it could be …
- I guess it might be …
- One possibility is that it's …

2 In pairs, discuss the questions about the picture. Use the phrases from exercise 1 to help you.

- Where do you think the photograph was taken?
- Where do you think the people are going?
- How do you think they feel?

👁 Look at *Speaking database - Giving/Asking for opinion* on page 165.

Use of English

Question tags

👁 Look at *Grammar database* page 180 before you do the exercises.

1 Complete the questions.

1. Lightning usually means there's going to be a storm, _____ ?
2. There's been a lot of unusual weather this year, _____ ?
3. Nobody said we were going to have a storm, _____ ?
4. They should put the weather on before the news, _____ ?
5. You haven't heard what they're forecasting for tomorrow, _____ ?

Connectors

2 Complete the sentences using the connectors in the box.

although • however • despite
since • so • in spite

1. The weather affects us all, _____ we can protect ourselves from some of its effects.
2. We can never protect ourselves from extreme weather completely, _____ nature is too powerful.
3. Hurricanes will always be a threat, _____ all our efforts.
4. Scientists have made progress in controlling the weather, _____ of the difficulties.
5. We can't make rain fall in desert areas, _____ drought is still a problem.
6. Control over the weather could save many lives. _____ , we don't have the technology yet.

3 For questions 1–10, read the text below and decide which answer (A, B, C or D) best fits each gap. There is an example at the beginning (0).

SEASONAL AFFECTIVE DISORDER

Have you (0) ___*ever*___ thought, 'Oh, no! Not another grey rainy day!'? Bad weather can really affect your mood, (1) _____ it? Most of us get depressed at some point (2) _____ the winter, and we can't wait for spring to come. For some people, (3) _____ , those dark, cold winter days can cause real medical problems.

Doctors have (4) _____ a condition which is (5) _____ as SAD (Seasonal Affective Disorder) and it can be a big problem in countries in northern Europe where the winters are long and dark. SAD sufferers find it difficult to (6) _____ , often feel depressed or anxious and their behaviour affects the people (7) _____ them.

The whole problem is caused by a lack of sunlight. Bright light affects the chemistry of the brain, although scientists don't understand (8) _____ how. There are two main cures. The first is to travel to a country that has a warm (9) _____ , with bright, sunny winters. The second is to use (10) _____ light. So, if it's raining and you're depressed, perhaps it's time you had a holiday in the sun!

0	A hardly	B ever	C soon	D every
1	A doesn't	B wouldn't	C can't	D isn't
2	A during	B while	C into	D of
3	A despite	B although	C yet	D however
4	A invented	B developed	C discovered	D produced
5	A called	B known	C regarded	D named
6	A imagine	B consider	C wonder	D concentrate
7	A around	B among	C nearby	D by
8	A accurately	B mainly	C closely	D exactly
9	A weather	B sunshine	C climate	D season
10	A false	B artificial	C fake	D pretend

Writing

An article

👁 Look at *Writing database - articles* on page 153 before you do the exercises.

1 Read this writing task. Who is going to read this article?

> You have been asked by an international students' magazine to write an article about your local climate and how it affects people's way of life.

Write an **article** of between **120** and **180** words in an appropriate style.

2 Choose the correct option in each sentence.

1 Your readers are _____ you.
   a about the same age as   **b** much older than

2 This kind of article _____ be very formal.
   a should   **b** shouldn't

3 Your main purpose is to _____ your readers.
   a persuade   **b** entertain

4 Your style of writing should be quite _____.
   a conversational   **b** formal

5 This kind of writing _____ have a title.
   a should   **b** shouldn't

Working model

3 Read the answer to the writing task.

Is your idea of fun lying on the beach, or is skiing more your style? In my area we are doing both! I live on the east coast of Greece and we have a Mediterranean climate. We do have cold days, but the sun is never far away. The summers are warm and dry. Temperatures can reach at 40° Celsius, although it's not usually so hot. The days are sunny and bright and most people spend their time swimming or sitting in cafés.

Autumn can be wet and windy. We have great storms, with lots of thunder and lightnings, and people usually visit friends or stay at home.

The winters are mild and sunny. It might snow in February or March, but it doesn't last long. Everybody loves to go for the lunch in villages in the mountains and play in the snow.

Spring finally arrives and the days get warmer again. Some people like going for picnics in a countryside.

My area has a wonderful climate, which is why we get such many tourists. Everybody enjoys themselves, whatever season it is.

4 The writer has forgotten to give the article on page 56 a title. Which of these would be a good title? Why?
1 Meteorological Phenomena and Humans
2 How I Spend My Holidays
3 Fun All Year Round

5 The writer has made a few mistakes. Read the article again and find one mistake in each paragraph. Correct it.

Ready to write!

6 Look at this writing task. Who is going to read your article?

> You have been asked by an international students' magazine to write an article about problems caused by the weather in your country.

Write an **article** of between **120** and **180** words in an appropriate style.

7 Make a plan of your answer.
- What might be a good title for your article?
- It's often good to start an article with a question to get your readers' attention. What question could you start with?
- What's the first kind of weather you're going to talk about? What problems does it cause?
- What's the second kind of weather you're going to talk about? What problems does it cause?
- What's the third kind of weather you're going to talk about? What problems does it cause?
- What style are you going to use, formal or informal?

Now complete *Writing Planner 6* on page 157.

Now write!

8 You are now ready to write your article for the magazine. Use an appropriate style. Answer the question!

Check it out!

9 Check your work. Tick (✓) what you have done.

- I have given my article an appropriate title.
- I have used an informal style of writing.
- I have described problems caused by different kinds of weather.
- I have used paragraphs.
- I have checked my spelling and my grammar.
- My article is between 120 and 180 words long.

◀ Look Back

Can you answer these questions? If you can't remember, look through the unit for the answers.
1 What are the signs that it might rain soon?
2 What does a barometer measure?
3 What tense do we generally use to talk about future arrangements?
4 What is a blizzard?
5 We use question tags to invite someone to agree with us and _____ .

Revision
Units 5-6

1 Choose the correct option.

1. This area has a very comfortable _____ all year round.
   A weather   B climate   C barometer   D data

2. About a hundred trees were destroyed in the _____ .
   A static   B shower   C hurricane   D mist

3. Watch you don't step in that great big _____ of water!
   A flake   B gust   C flash   D puddle

4. On *Win A Million*, the game show, four _____ answer questions to win money.
   A producers   B presenters   C contestants   D cameramen

5. We might have to cancel the trip because it's starting to rain _____ .
   A tough   B hard   C badly   D wetly

6. Put the news on. I just want to see the _____ .
   A headlines   B titles   C headings   D labels

7. Let's hope the weather _____ up before the wedding.
   A clears   B cleans   C comes   D goes

8. Last year it snowed, but this winter has been quite _____ .
   A mild   B soft   C gentle   D smooth

9. I don't like _____ at all. The stories are too dramatic and the characters aren't real.
   A cartoons   B game shows   C sitcoms   D soap operas

10. Can I borrow your umbrella? It's _____ with rain outside.
    A dropping   B pouring   C running   D flowing

2 Write nouns derived from these words.

1. real (adj)   _____
2. argue (v)   _____
3. inform (v)   _____
4. entertain (v)   _____
5. know (v)   _____
6. decide (v)   _____
7. relation (n)   _____
8. advise (v)   _____

3 Complete the questions with an appropriate question tag.

1. Joanne's very kind, _____ ?
2. Tom's party was a lot of fun, _____ ?
3. There's some butter in the fridge, _____ ?
4. Ron's been to Washington, _____ ?
5. You won't tell Sam what I said, _____ ?
6. Let's get a pizza tonight, _____ ?
7. Lisa seems to know a lot about football, _____ ?

4 Circle the correct word in each sentence.
1. My mum was quite *upset/nervous* when she heard I'd broken her new vase.
2. Let's have a game of chess to *spend/pass* the time.
3. Have you *seen/watched* the new exhibition at the museum yet?
4. I always get a bit *upset/nervous* before I have to speak in front of people.
5. Polly *spends/passes* a lot of time watching her favourite programmes on TV.

5 Complete each sentence so that it means the same as the first sentence. Use the words given without changing them. Use no more than five words. You will get two marks for each correct answer.
1. A storm damaged the church near our house. **by**
   The church near our house _____ a storm.
2. It was very noisy here while they were building the new road. **being**
   While the new road _____, it was very noisy here.
3. People think that TV news is very shocking. **thought**
   TV news _____ very shocking.
4. Someone has taken my books out of my bag! **have**
   My books _____ out of my bag!
5. I think South Africa will probably win the match. **be**
   The match _____ South Africa.
6. I told everyone about the changes to the timetable. **been**
   Everyone _____ about the changes to the timetable.
7. My mum gave each of us €100 to spend at the fair. **given**
   We _____ €100 to spend at the fair.

6 Complete the sentences using phrasal verbs with *on*.
1. I never used to _____ with my brother so well, but now we have a great relationship.
2. The channels _____ a lot of violent programmes late at night, don't they?
3. You know, I didn't like this song at first, but it _____ you after a while.
4. It's so hot! Could we _____ the air-conditioning?
5. The soldier was too tired to _____ so he started to look for a place to spend the night.
6. Why don't you find someone your own size to _____, instead of bullying small kids?

7 Write a word or phrase to match the definitions. You've been given the first letter to help.
1. worldwide — g_____
2. frozen rain — h_____
3. a programme where famous people are interviewed — c_____ s_____
4. predict — f_____
5. someone who introduces a TV show — p_____
6. person who studies the weather — m_____
7. person who does something for pleasure, without being paid — a_____
8. a period of very hot weather — h_____
9. make (a dream) come true — r_____
10. a heavy snowstorm — b_____

Score _____ /60

51–60 Well done! You really know your stuff! 41–50 That's great! Keep it up! 21–40 Maybe it's time for another look! 0–20 What? Are you sure?

7

A Matter of Taste

Start thinking!

Where do you think potatoes came from?
Who do you think invented chips?
When do you think crisps were invented?

Reading

1  **1.23** Read this magazine article to check your answers.

Imagine a tasty plate of chips, fried in hot oil until golden-brown, topped with a little salt and served with ketchup. Think of a hot jacket potato, filled with butter and cheese. Imagine a packet of delicious crisps that leave the flavour on your fingers to be licked off when you've finished.

Wherever you go, you can't get away from them. They are everywhere, eaten by everyone with practically every meal. **1** ____ But have you ever asked yourself where they came from? (And I don't mean the supermarket!)

It all started in Peru. There, they grew potatoes over 2,000 years ago. They weren't like **the ones** we know today. **2** ____ The first Europeans to try the potato were the Spanish. In 1537, Spanish explorers discovered people eating what they called papas. They brought this strange vegetable back to Spain in the 1550s.

People generally didn't like the potato. Lots of other vegetables were introduced into Europe at the same time, like tomatoes and sweet potatoes, and people preferred **those** to the unattractive potatoes. **3** ____ Very slowly, they spread through Europe, although many people still thought potatoes were poisonous for quite a long time.

There is a story that King Louis XVI (that's 'the sixteenth' to me and you) of France liked the potato and wanted to encourage people to eat them. He planted them in the royal gardens, since he knew this would make them seem valuable and desirable. **4** ____ Once they got used to this strange plant, it became a popular part of the French diet.

So, what about chips? Well, the Belgians claim that they invented fried potatoes, although nobody really knows for sure. The first mention of 'chips' in England is by the writer Charles Dickens in 1859. **5** ____ The Americans call them 'French fries' because soldiers from

2 What do the words and phrases refer to? Circle the correct option.

1. the ones (paragraph 3)
   people in Peru/potatoes
2. those (paragraph 4)
   attractive potatoes/other vegetables
3. he (paragraph 7)
   the customer/George Crum
4. them (paragraph 8)
   your friends/the chips

3 Read the article again. Six sentences have been removed from the article. Choose from the sentences A–G the one which fits each gap (1–6). There is one extra sentence which you do not need to use.

A He mentions 'chips of potato' fried in oil in one of his books.
B He kept sending them back to be sliced again.
C Ordinary people stole them and planted them in their own gardens.
D The original potatoes were smaller and tasted bitter.
E They are a good source of vitamins, surprisingly.
F They were given to slaves and prisoners because they were so cheap.
G We seem to love potatoes however they are cooked.

America went to France during the First World War and loved the dish. Now, the Americans eat over 20 million tons of chips a year. (That's altogether, not each!)

Crisps are an American invention, although they call them 'chips' (don't get confused!). Everybody agrees that a Native-American chef, George Crum, made the first crisps in 1853. One day, a difficult customer wanted fried potatoes, sliced thinly. When they arrived, **he** said they weren't thin enough. **6** _____ In the end, Crum got annoyed and sliced the potato as thinly as he could and fried it, then added lots of salt. The dish was an immediate success.

So now you know. Next time you're in your favourite fast-food place with your friends eating chips, amaze **them** with your potato knowledge! Who knows? They might even share their chips with you.

WORD BOX

4 Use words or phrases from the text to complete the sentences. You've been given the first letter to help you.

1. Doctors say that eating too much food f_____ in oil isn't very healthy.
2. They sell lots of different ice cream and my favourite f_____ is banana!
3. In fast-food places in Britain, they ask for c_____ , but in America they ask for F_____ f_____ .
4. When I went to New York, I asked for a packet of c_____ as a snack, but they said they were called c_____ .
5. Try to s_____ the bread more thinly next time, so it fits in the toaster!
6. A j_____ p_____ is one that has been baked in the oven with its skin on.
7. I don't like b_____ tastes like coffee and dark chocolate. I prefer something sweet.

Have your say!

- Which of the facts in the article do you think is most surprising? Why?

7 Grammar clinic

Reported speech

👁 Look at *Grammar database* pages 181–182 before you do the exercises.

1 Read this sentence from the magazine article on pages 60 and 61.

When they arrived, he said they weren't thin enough.

What did he actually say?
a 'They weren't thin enough.'
b 'They aren't thin enough.'

2 Choose the correct reported version of each sentence.

1 'I'm making chips for lunch,' said Linda.
 a Linda said she will make chips for lunch.
 b Linda said she was making chips for lunch.

2 'What have you been doing all day?' my father asked me.
 a My father asked me what had I been doing all day.
 b My father asked me what I had been doing all day.

3 'You must be more careful in the kitchen,' Mum said.
 a Mum said I had to be more careful in the kitchen.
 b Mum said me to be more careful in the kitchen.

4 'We'll be happy to keep a table for you,' the waiter said.
 a The waiter said we should be happy if they kept a table for us.
 b The waiter said they would be happy to keep a table for us.

3 Rewrite the statements using reported speech.

1 'We ate in a great restaurant last night,' George said.
2 'I'll have chicken and another glass of this wine,' Mr Brown said.
3 'Don't put your knife in your mouth, Tom,' his father said.
4 'Are you having chips?' asked my friend.
5 'What have you cooked for dinner?' she asked her husband.

4 Match the reporting verbs with the correct meanings.

1 refuse   a say that something is true without proof
2 deny   b say that you won't do something
3 suggest   c say that you did something wrong
4 admit   d say that you didn't do something you are accused of
5 claim   e offer a plan or idea to be considered

5 Complete the sentences using the verbs in the box.

refused • suggested • denied
admitted • claimed

1 'We serve the best food in town,' the owner said.

 The owner _____ the best food in town.

2 'Yes, I ate the cake in the fridge,' she said.

 She _____ the cake in the fridge.

3 'No, I won't cook your dinner while you watch TV,' Sally said to her husband.

 Sally _____ her husband's dinner while he watched TV.

4 'Don't look at me! I didn't drink all of the orange juice!' shouted Oliver.

 Oliver _____ all of the orange juice.

5 'How about all of us meeting outside *BurgerBar* at nine?' said Ron.

 Ron _____ outside *BurgerBar* at nine.

Vocabulary builder

Food and cooking

1 Match the ways of cooking with the definitions.
1 fry   a cook in the oven with oil (meat, etc)
2 boil   b cook in hot water
3 bake   c cook under direct heat
4 grill   d cook in hot oil
5 roast   e cook in the oven (bread, a cake, etc)

2 Complete the paragraph using the words in the box.

snack • recipes • meal • ingredients • cooker
chefs • saucepans • raw • dishes • dairy

Cookery books are usually written by famous (1) _____ . These books are full of (2) _____ , telling you how to cook different (3) _____ . They usually tell you what (4) _____ you need first. These might be (5) _____ meat, vegetables or (6) _____ products like milk and butter. Then, they tell you what equipment you need, such as (7) _____ or bowls. When you've got everything, and you've turned the (8) _____ on, you just follow the instructions in the book. Anybody can cook! Whether it's a complete (9) _____ or just a(n) (10) _____ , all you have to do is follow the advice of an expert. It's easy with the right book.

3 Circle the correct word to describe each taste.
1 strong coffee, dark chocolate   **spicy/bitter**
2 a lemon   **sour/salty**
3 crisps, peanuts, sea water   **sweet/salty**
4 sugar, strawberries, cake   **sweet/spicy**
5 chilli, Mexican food, curry   **spicy/salty**

Phrasal verbs with *out*

4 Phrasal verbs with *out* often have meanings connected to something stopping or disappearing. Read the sentences and match the correct phrasal verb to each definition.
1 Firemen have finally *put out* the fire.
2 It was so hot that I *passed out*!
3 You can't *back out* of helping me now!
4 We've *run out of* eggs so we can't bake a cake.
5 My brother *dropped out* of his course at college.
6 Let's not *fall out* over who is cooking dinner!
7 Just *cut out* the sugar and it'll be fine.
   a not have any left
   b faint, lose consciousness
   c argue
   d not include, remove
   e leave a course before the end
   f extinguish, stop something burning
   g decide not to do something you had agreed to do

Collocations: cooking

5 Match to make phrases.
1 frying   a tray
2 mixing   b spoon
3 serving   c bowl
4 carving   d pan
5 baking   e knife

6 Write a phrase from exercise 5 under each picture.

1 _____

2 _____

3 _____

4 _____   5 _____

7 Listening

1 🎧 **1.24** You are going to listen to four short conversations. Decide who the man is in each conversation.

In Conversation 1, the man is _____ .
A a waiter
B a customer
C a restaurant manager

In Conversation 2, the man is _____ .
A a chef
B a student
C a waiter

In Conversation 3, the man is _____ .
A a customer
B a waiter
C a student

In Conversation 4, the man is _____ .
A a chef
B a waiter
C a restaurant manager

2 Listen again. For questions 1–4, choose the best answer (A, B or C).
1 Why are they having this conversation?
  A to plan for the coming month
  B to decide what to have for dinner
  C to appoint a new chef
2 Why does the woman want the man to try the food?
  A to show him that she's a good cook
  B to help him carry out his job better
  C to show him what he's doing wrong
3 What does the man think of the woman's suggestions?
  A He follows them.
  B He ignores them.
  C He questions them.
4 What does the man suggest to go with the lamb?
  A a spicy dish
  B something cheesy
  C some simple food

Soundbite /k/, /g/ and /ŋ/

🎧 **1.25** Listen to these words. Pay attention to the ends of the words.

bag • bang • back • bank

Now listen to these sets of words. Decide in what order you hear the words by writing the letters a to c next to the words.

1 thing _____   think _____   thick _____
2 sang _____   sank _____   sag _____
3 sick _____   sink _____   sing _____
4 bring _____   brick _____   brink _____

Speaking

Useful Phrases

1 Match to make useful phrases for agreeing and disagreeing.

1 Yes, I totally   a a good point.
2 You're absolutely   b disagree.
3 Yes, I think that's   c I agree with you.
4 I'm not sure   d agree with you.
5 I'm afraid I have to   e right.

2 Work in pairs. Use the phrases from exercise 1 to help you agree and disagree.

- Plan a special meal out for both your families.
- Talk about how much you think they would like to eat these meals.
- Decide which two choices you would like to suggest to your families.

👁 Look at *Speaking database - Agreeing/Disagreeing* on page 165.

Use of English

Indirect questions

👁 Look at *Grammar database* pages 182–183 before you do the exercises.

1 Read the questions. Decide if the statements are true (T) or false (F).

direct questions	indirect questions
What is a fortune cookie?	Could you tell me what a fortune cookie is?
What do they have inside?	I wonder if you could tell me what they have inside.
Where was the fortune cookie invented?	Do you know where the fortune cookie was invented?

a The word order in indirect questions is the same as in direct questions. ☐
b All indirect questions need a question mark at the end. ☐

2 Rewrite the questions as indirect questions starting with the words given.

1 Do you like Chinese food?   I wonder _____
2 Have you ever been to China?   Could _____
3 What is the capital of China?   Do you know _____
4 How much does a fortune cookie cost?   I would like _____
5 Where is the nearest Chinese restaurant?   Could _____

Prepositions

3 Complete the sentences using the prepositions in the box. Use some prepositions more than once.

> about • on • during • back • to • at • in

1 Some traditions, like eating lamb at Easter, go quite a long way _____ .
2 I'd like to welcome you here _____ this very special occasion.
3 _____ the end of the recipe, the chef says that it should be served cold.
4 I wrote the number of the restaurant _____ a bit of paper, but I've lost it.
5 How much do you know _____ the history of your country's food?
6 I've always been interested _____ food from different countries.
7 We often eat special food _____ traditional celebrations.
8 My parents went _____ an expensive restaurant for their wedding anniversary.

4 Read this passage about fortune cookies and answer the questions in exercise 1.

The Fortune Cookie

Are you interested (0) __IN__ world cuisine? Do you know anything (1) _____ Chinese food? I wonder (2) _____ you have ever heard of fortune cookies. Fortune cookies are small biscuits that are traditionally served (3) _____ the end of a meal in a Chinese restaurant. They are sweet and have a piece of paper inside them. Written (4) _____ the piece of paper is your fortune. They often say things like 'You will write a book one day' or 'You will be lucky (5) _____ love'. Do you know how far (6) _____ the tradition goes? The Chinese have always given each other sweet Moon Cakes (7) _____ special occasions. When the Mongols occupied China in the 13th century, the Chinese needed a way to send secret messages to each other. They put the messages inside Moon Cakes. When gold was discovered in California in 1849, many Chinese people went (8) _____ America to work (9) _____ the railway. Life was hard, but (10) _____ celebrations they put messages of hope inside biscuits. When they settled in California and opened restaurants, they continued the tradition.

5 Read the passage again. For questions 1–10, think of the word which best fits each gap. Use only one word in each gap. There is an example at the beginning (0). Write your answers IN CAPITAL LETTERS.

Writing

A formal letter/email

👁 Look at *Writing database – formal letters/emails* on page 150 before you do the exercises.

1 Read this writing task. Why should your email be formal?

> You work for your school magazine. A local chef has agreed to do an interview but wants more information. The editor of the school magazine has sent you this article from the local newspaper and asked you to write an email to the chef. Using the information in the article and the notes you have made, write your email.

Write an **email** of between **120** and **150** words. You must use grammatically correct sentences with accurate spelling and punctuation in a style appropriate for the situation.

Local Chef Gets TV Series

Denise Jordan, chef at the Grand Hotel, has finally made it to the top. Next week, her new series, *Full of Flavour*, begins on Channel 6. Denise believes that it's never too early to start cooking and her new series is aimed at children. She hopes to give them good advice to get them started in the kitchen. From sandwiches to pies, she'll be showing us how good food doesn't have to be hard work.

- tell her what we'd like to ask her about
- suggest either 12th or 13th March, in the morning
- can she bring some examples of easy food?
- can we take some photographs?

Working model

2 Read the answer to the writing task.

From: Maria
To: Denise Jordan
Subject: Your interview

Dear Mrs Jordan,

I work for my school magazine, 'Talking in Class'. Our editor has asked me to give you more information about the interview you have agreed to do.

We are very interested in your new series. Would you mind if we asked you a few questions about it? We would also like to ask you about your experiences working in a hotel.

I wonder if you would be available on either the 12th or the 13th of March. The interview would take place at about 10 o'clock in the morning, because of the school timetable.

Your new series is about learning to cook easy dishes. I wonder if you could bring some examples to show us what you mean. Would you mind if we took photographs during the interview?

Please contact me if you need more information.

Yours sincerely,
Maria Zerva

3 Underline sentences in the email where Maria:
1 tells Denise what she'd like to ask her about.
2 suggests possible days for the interview.
3 asks her to bring examples of easy food.
4 asks if they can take photographs.

Which of these are indirect questions?

Ready to write!

4 Look at the extract from an article about another local chef.

Cooking in the Classroom

Should we all learn how to cook at school? Yes, says Peter Murphy, a local chef, whose new book, *Fit for a King*, is published this week. He believes that schools should provide lessons in healthy cooking and healthy eating for all pupils. Peter thinks that fast food is great, but young people can also make other delicious dishes. Customers at his restaurant in the centre of town certainly agree that he knows what he's doing! Peter Murphy has agreed to do an interview with your school magazine and you have been asked to give him more information. Here are the notes you have made:

- tell him what we'd like to interview him about
- suggest we interview him at his restaurant
- ask him to prepare one or two easy recipes for students
- can we take photographs?

5 Make a plan of your answer. Use your imagination.
- How are you going to start your email?
  a Dear Peter,
  b Dear Peter Murphy,
  c Dear Mr Murphy,
- What's your school magazine called?
- What would you like to interview him about? (at least TWO things)
- Write a formal sentence to suggest an interview at his restaurant.
- Write an indirect question to ask him to prepare recipes for students.
- Write an indirect question to ask if you can take photographs.
- How are you going to end your email?
  a Best wishes,
  b Yours sincerely,
  c All the best,
- What will be the last thing you write?
  a Thank you
  b your first name
  c your first and last names

Now complete *Writing Planner 7* on page 158.

Now write!

6 You are now ready to write your email to Peter Murphy. Include all the information in the notes. Ask him all the questions you have to. Write between 120 and 150 words.

Check it out!

7 Check your work. Tick (✓) what you have done.

- I have started and finished the email in the correct way.
- I have included all the information in the notes.
- I have asked him all the questions I had to ask him.
- I have used indirect questions to be polite.
- I have used paragraphs.
- I have checked my spelling, grammar and punctuation.
- My email is between 120 and 150 words long.

Look Back

Can you answer these questions? If you can't remember, look through the unit for the answers.

1. In what year were crisps invented?
2. What's the American word for crisps?
3. How would you describe the taste of a lemon?
4. Do all indirect questions need a question mark?
5. When was gold discovered in California?

Out and About

Start thinking!

What is your dream holiday like?
Where do you want to go?
What do you want to do?

Reading

1 **1.26** Read this magazine article. Which holiday sounds most interesting to you?

2 Choose the correct option.
1. Where would you find a text like this?
   a a magazine
   b a business report
   c a textbook
2. Who would read a text like this?
   a hotel owners
   b teenagers
   c business travellers
3. Why would they read it?
   a to learn about tourism
   b to plan their holiday
   c to meet new friends

3 Read the article again. For questions 1–6, choose from the reports (A–E). The reports may be chosen more than once.
Which writer(s) …

was uncertain about the holiday at first?	1 _____	
found the journey tiring?	2 _____	
mentions eating out?	3 _____	
were bored by the end of the holiday?	4 _____	5 _____
made friends while on holiday?	6 _____	7 _____
usually go abroad on holiday?	8 _____	9 _____

68

Wish you were

Is it the beach as usual for you this year, or are you planning to do something a little more adventurous? To give you some ideas, we sent five daring teenagers off on holiday and we got them to report back. Read on to find out more …

A Name: Amy Barker, 14
Holiday destination: Sydney, Australia

We were exhausted when we arrived because the flight takes about 24 hours, with a stopover in Singapore. We all had jet lag and the first thing we did was go to bed! We were there for ten days, so we didn't have time to travel around too much – Australia is huge and it takes days to get anywhere. We stayed in Sydney, but there was plenty to do there. I was a bit unsure when Dad suggested going to the Sydney Opera House (dance music is more my style!), but we saw a fantastic rock concert. The Harbour Bridge is really impressive, and I bought some great souvenirs as presents for my friends.

Recommended? Definitely.

B Name: Ryan Fletcher, 13
Holiday destination: Skopelos, Greece

We go abroad every year, and I'd been to Greece twice before so I knew what to expect, but it was the first time I'd been to Skopelos. We normally stay in hotels, but this time we decided to try self-catering rooms. Mum and Dad soon realised that they didn't want to do much cooking so we went out every night, which was great. I love Greek food, especially seafood. We spent most of our time on the beach, and Skopelos has some great beaches. The resort of Skopelos itself was a bit quiet, but I met a couple of local people my age so it wasn't too bad. I'd had enough of the beach, really, after two weeks.

Recommended? Yes, although I prefer staying at a hotel.

Name: Rebecca Key, 13

Holiday destination: Summer Camp, France

It was the first time I'd been on holiday without my parents and sister, so I was really looking forward to it. At the same time, I was a bit nervous about meeting so many new people. It was a real adventure holiday. The camp was in the countryside and they'd organised things like rock climbing, horse-riding and canoeing. I soon made friends and we had a lot of fun. You can keep the rock climbing (I was never very good at heights!), but the canoeing was brilliant! I keep in touch with some of the people by email and we're planning to go again next year.

Recommended? Great for action-lovers. Didn't meet any French people, though!

Name: Simon Watson, 12

Holiday destination: Maldon Farm, Kent

We hadn't had a holiday in Britain for a very long time. Usually, it's Italy or Spain. Maldon Farm looked nice in the brochure, and it's only an hour from where we live, so we got there very quickly. You stay in rooms on the farm and you're expected to help out with the animals every day. My mum and dad thought it would be good for me and my brother to learn about that sort of thing. Well, it just seemed to me more like hard work than a holiday! I enjoyed swimming in the pool, but we couldn't use it for three days because of the rain! There wasn't much to do and I was glad to get home. Mum and Dad seemed to enjoy it, anyway.

Recommended? OK for people who like looking after animals.

Name: Hanna Bridgeman, 14

Holiday destination: Disneyland®, Florida, USA

When my mum and dad said we were going to Disneyland®, I thought, 'That's great for my sister (she's nine), but what about me? I'm too old for people in Mickey Mouse costumes.' I was looking forward to going to America, though. When we finally got there, I couldn't believe it. The whole theme park is like a separate world. I ignored Mickey Mouse (and Donald Duck!) and headed straight for the rides. Space Cruiser was really cool, and so was the roller coaster. In the end, we all had a great time. I'd say there's something there for everyone.

Recommended? Yes, especially for families with young children.

WORD BOX

4 Use words or phrases from the box to complete the definitions.

destination • stopover • jet lag • souvenir
abroad • self-catering • resort
adventure holiday • brochure

1 If you stay in _____ rooms, you have to cook your own food.

2 A(n) _____ is a kind of small magazine that often advertises holidays.

3 A(n) _____ is a town where lots of people go on holiday.

4 You suffer from _____ when you arrive in a country where the time is very different from the country you left.

5 Your _____ is the place you are going to.

6 A(n) _____ is a break in the middle of a very long flight.

7 _____ s are fun for people who enjoy physical exercise and trying new activities.

8 When you go _____ , make sure you take your passport with you.

9 I got a model of the Acropolis as a(n) _____ of my trip to Athens.

Have your say!

- Which of the places that you've just read about would you most like to visit? Why?
- Are there any that you wouldn't be interested in visiting? Why?

G Grammar clinic

Full infinitives (with *to*) and *-ing* forms after verbs

👁 Look at *Grammar database* pages 183–184 before you do the exercises.

1 Read these sentences from the article on pages 68 and 69.

… or are you planning **to do** something a little more adventurous?

… I prefer stay**ing** at a hotel.

Find other verbs in the article which are followed by the full infinitive or the *-ing* form.

2 Complete the sentences using the correct form of the verbs in brackets.
1. I don't think we can really afford _____ (**go**) abroad this year.
2. My dad is planning _____ (**find**) some cheap flights on the internet.
3. I'd quite like _____ (**visit**) an Asian country, like India.
4. If you enjoy _____ (**swim**), why not try an adventure holiday?
5. My friends and I have arranged _____ (**meet**) at summer camp again next year.
6. China seems _____ (**be**) a very popular tourist destination at the moment.
7. I would suggest _____ (**book**) a room in a hotel before we leave.

3 Use the notes to make complete sentences.
1. Imagine/see/the sun/as it/go down/behind the Pyramids!
2. A trip around the world/involve/make/a lot of arrangements.
3. When I/be/there last year,/local people/seem/be/very friendly and/offer/help us.
4. We decide/avoid/stay/in places where lots of tourists go.
5. Tina/promise/bring/me back a souvenir from South Africa.
6. My grandmother/refuse/consider/go/on foreign holidays.

4 Read the situations. Circle the correct word or phrase in each sentence.
1. You went to Paris last year. In your mind, you can see the Eiffel Tower.
   'I remember *to see/seeing* the Eiffel Tower in Paris last year. It was fantastic!'
2. You are in the car going to the beach. You want to buy something to drink.
   'I'm thirsty. Shall we stop *to get/getting* something to drink?'
3. You and a friend are in a strange city and you can't find your hotel.
   'I think we're lost. Why don't we try *to ask/asking* someone for directions?'
4. You get to the airport and you suddenly realise that you haven't got your passport.
   'Oh, no! I must have forgotten *to pick/picking* up my passport when we left!'
5. You are staying in a hotel and you have accidentally broken the key.
   'I'm sorry. I was trying *to open/opening* the door and the key broke.'

5 Find eight mistakes in this text message and correct them.

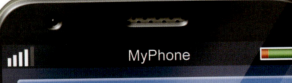

Hi from New York! Got here last night and planning staying for about two days. The shops are fantastic! I've managed finding some great clothes! We hope going up the Statue of Liberty tomorrow. Sharon's refused coming, but I've agreed going with Mum and Dad. Not sure if I'll enjoy to climb all those stairs or not! I promise getting you an I♥NY T-shirt – if I can afford buying it!

Vocabulary builder

Travel and tourism

1 Rearrange the letters to complete the definitions.

1 _____ put the things you are taking with you into your suitcase
kacp

2 _____ a person who arranges holidays and sells tickets, etc
rtvale / tagne

3 _____ the area of an airport where passengers wait to board their planes
rapudrete / elogun

4 _____ have your ticket checked and hand over your luggage when you are travelling by plane
cchke / ni

5 _____ a kind of holiday where the accommodation, travel, etc are all organised for you
kegpaca / dailyoh

6 _____ a person in a resort who looks after people on a package holiday
liyhoda / pre

7 _____ the way you go when you are travelling
ruoet

8 _____ the people who check what you are bringing into the country
stomucs

9 _____ visiting the interesting places, buildings, etc in an area while on holiday
iehgtsensgi

2 Complete the story using the correct form of some of the words and phrases in exercise 1.

It all started to go wrong when we arrived at the airport. We (1) _____ and decided to go through passport control to the (2) _____ .

I suddenly realised that I'd forgotten (3) _____ my guidebook, with all the information about the holiday. The (4) _____ had given me a map when I booked the holiday and I'd forgotten that too. I just hoped the (5) _____ would be there to meet us when we got off the plane. We arrived in Jamaica seven hours later and it took us ages to get through (6) _____ . They opened and checked every single bag we had! By the time we got out, there was nobody else there! I couldn't remember which (7) _____ we were supposed to take to the hotel and there weren't any taxis around. Finally, we got to the hotel, and it wasn't even finished! That's the last time I go on a (8) _____ !

Word formation: irregular forms

3 Complete the sentences with the correct form of the word in bold.

1 The holiday rep explained the history of the local area to us in _____ . **deep**

2 I demanded an _____ from the hotel manager as to why our room hadn't been cleaned. **explain**

3 There was such a wide _____ of interesting local dishes that I really didn't know what to choose. **vary**

4 I wasn't sure we'd made the right _____ when the rep told us that we were visiting a volcano the next day. **choose**

5 I don't think I'd be very good on an adventure holiday because I'm quite scared of _____ . **high**

6 It was very interesting to be in a country that has such different religious _____ . **believe**

Magic metaphors

4 When we talk about *life*, we sometimes use words or phrases that have a connection with *travel* and *journeys*. Complete the sentences with the correct form of the words from the box.

direction • arrive • step • go through
progress • pace

1 The fast _____ of modern life causes a lot of stress for some people.

2 I feel like I've _____ at an important point in my life.

3 You can never predict exactly which _____ your life is going to take.

4 Many teenagers find themselves _____ a difficult period, emotionally.

5 I've got quite a good career, and I think the next _____ is to get married.

6 My life has got a bit boring recently and I seem to have stopped making _____ .

8 Out and About

Listening

1 🎧 **1.27** You are going to listen to a woman being asked questions about a recent holiday. Which four of the problems does she mention?

- problems with the food
- problems with money
- problems with the journey
- problems with other tourists
- problems with pollution
- problems with the weather
- problems with the sights
- problems with the hotel

2 Listen to the interview again. For questions 1–6, complete the sentences.

> They spent a total of **1** _____ in a hotel in Glasgow.
>
> The hotel staff recommended **2** _____ which were inside.
>
> They especially enjoyed the **3** _____ in Glasgow.
>
> The woman says they should develop the **4** _____ system.
>
> Seeing **5** _____ reminded the woman of another trip.
>
> They didn't have enough information when their plane **6** _____ .

Soundbite /s/ and /z/

🎧 **1.28** Sometimes the letter 's' sounds like 's' in 'see' and sometimes it sounds like 'z' in 'zebra'. How is 's' pronounced in these words? Listen and check.

1 says 4 interested 7 increase
2 advise 5 doesn't
3 stress 6 peas

Speaking   Useful Phrases

1 Write a word from the box in each gap.

another • for • instance • like • one • such

> There are lots of problems you could have when you go on holiday. (1) _____ problem might be with communicating when you're abroad. (2) _____ example, maybe you want to ask someone for directions but you don't speak the same language. (3) _____ problem might be with your accommodation. For (4) _____ , maybe your hotel isn't as nice as you expected. You may have big problems if you lose things, (5) _____ as your wallet or passport. You might also have problems if you don't know about the local culture – how much to tip waiters, what you're not allowed to wear on the beach, things (6) _____ that.

2 In pairs, discuss the following question. Remember to give examples. Use the words and phrases in exercise 1 and the ideas below to help you.

> What problems can people have when they go on holiday?

communication • accommodation
losing things • travel delays • local culture
health • money • food • weather
disagreements • accidents

👁 Look at *Speaking database - Giving/Asking for opinion* on page 165.

Use of English

Prefer, would rather, had better

👁 Look at *Grammar database* page 184 before you do the exercises.

1 Correct the sentences.
1. I'd prefer travelling by ferry to France when we go on holiday this summer.
2. We would better call the hotel to see if they still have any rooms.
3. I prefer seeing the sights than lying on the beach all day.
4. Vietnam was great, but I didn't prefer to eat some of the local dishes.
5. I had rather not to stay in a hotel where there are lots of other tourists.

2 Complete each sentence so that it means the same as the first sentence. Use the words given without changing them. Use no more than five words.

1. I think I'd prefer to go to Spain this year and not France. **than**
   This year, I would _____ go to France.
2. Mum says she prefers visiting countries she hasn't been to before. **would**
   Mum says she _____ she has been to before.
3. My doctor suggested taking some time off work to relax. **better**
   'You _____ some time off work to relax,' my doctor said.
4. I like travelling, but sometimes I'd rather just stay at home. **to**
   Sometimes, I _____ travelling.

Parts of speech

3 Complete the table. Note: the brackets show negative forms.

verb	noun	adjective	verb	noun	adjective
(___)agree	___agree___	---	---	difficult___	difficult
(___)appear	___appear___	---	discuss	discuss___	---
apply	appl___ appl___	---	interest	inter___	(___)interest___ (___)interest___
damage	damag___	---	---	(___) responsib___	(___)respons___
describe	descri___	---	visit	visit visit___	---

4 For questions 1–6, complete the second sentence so that it has a similar meaning to the first sentence, using the word given. Do not change the word given. You must use between two and five words, including the word given. Write the missing words IN CAPITAL LETTERS.

1. My parents discussed where we were going to go on holiday. **about**
   My parents _____ where we were going to go on holiday.
2. It might be cold in Poland, so take some warm clothes. **better**
   You _____ some warm clothes in case it's cold in Poland.
3. Organising social events is usually the holiday rep's responsibility. **responsible**
   The holiday rep _____ organising social events.
4. They didn't have many applicants for the job at the travel agent's. **receive**
   They didn't _____ for the job at the travel agent's.
5. I'd much rather stay in hotels than go camping when I'm on holiday. **prefer**
   I much _____ than going camping when I'm on holiday.
6. We found it difficult on holiday to understand the local people. **difficulty**
   We had _____ the local people.

Writing

A review

 Look at *Writing database - reviews* on page 152 before you do the exercises.

1 Read this writing task. In pairs or as a group, discuss these questions.
- Which tourist attractions in your area could you write about?
- What can people do there?
- Would you recommend them? Why? / Why not?

You recently saw this message on a website for teenagers.

---

www.teenworld.com

Reviews needed!

Have you recently visited a tourist attraction in your area? If so, could you write us a review of the place? Include information on what kind of place it is, what activities you can do there, and whether you would recommend the place to other people.

Write a **review** of between **120** and **180** words in an appropriate style.

2 Write a word from the box in each gap to complete these sentences expressing opinion.

> as • in x2 • personally • to

1 _____ my mind, most teenagers will enjoy a tour of the castle.

2 _____ my view, people of all ages will love a day out at Bodmin Park.

3 _____ my opinion, there aren't many activities for teenagers to do there, so they will probably find a trip there a little boring.

4 I _____ believe that this is one of the best attractions in the whole country.

5 _____ far as I'm concerned, this is one of the most expensive and least interesting places in the area to visit.

Working model

3 Read the answer to the writing task and decide if the statements are true (T) or false (F).

1 The review has a title. ☐
2 The first paragraph is an introduction. ☐
3 The second paragraph describes in detail the activities in the park. ☐
4 The final paragraph summarises the writer's opinion. ☐
5 Each paragraph has its own heading. ☐
6 The writer uses contractions such as *don't*, *there's*, *I'd*, etc. ☐

Bodmin Park

Bodmin Park is one of the most popular tourist attractions in the Chudford area. The park is open all summer, and there are a large number of activities for people of all ages to enjoy.

The park's just a short 15-minute drive from the town of Chudford. There is free parking for visitors, and the entrance fee is not expensive: €10 for adults, €5 for children between 5 and 15. Children under the age of five don't have to pay. There's also a family ticket which costs €25.

Inside the park, there's a gift shop, a café and a lovely picnic area. The main attraction, though, is the adventure park. This has a large number of fun activities, such as death slides, rope bridges and climbing walls. Safety equipment is provided and there are always members of staff available to help you. For people who want a quieter time, there are beautiful walks through the forest.

I'd definitely recommend a trip to Bodmin Park, particularly if the weather's nice. In my view, people of all ages will really enjoy a day out there.

4 Read the answer to the writing task again and write YES or NO to answer each question.

1. Is the park open all year round? _____
2. Is the park near the town of Chudford? _____
3. Do you have to pay to park your car there? _____
4. Can a three-year-old child enter free? _____
5. Do families get a discount? _____
6. Are there places to eat in the park? _____
7. Do they provide safety equipment in the adventure park? _____
8. Is playing at the adventure park the only activity you can do there? _____
9. Is it better to go there when it's not raining? _____
10. Does the writer recommend the park only for young people? _____

Ready to write!

5 You are going to write a review in answer to the same writing task. Choose an attraction in your area and complete the chart.

Name of attraction:
Location:
How to get there:
Entrance fee(s):
Main facilities (café, shop, etc):
Main activities you can do there:

6 Make a plan of your answer.

- What's the title of your review?

- Paragraph 1: What key information will you give to introduce the place?

- Paragraphs 2 and 3: You'll go into detail here about how to get there, how much it costs and the facilities and activities on offer. What points will you make in each paragraph?

- Paragraph 4: Are you going to recommend the place? If so, who to? If not, why not?

Now complete *Writing Planner 8* on page 158.

Now write!

7 You are now ready to write your review. Use your plan from exercise 6 to help you. Write between 120 and 180 words.

Check it out!

8 Check your work. Tick (✓) what you have done.

- I have given my review a title. ☐
- I have written four main paragraphs. ☐
- I have said where the attraction is. ☐
- I have described the main facilities. ☐
- I have described the main activities. ☐
- I have said whether I recommend the place or not. ☐
- I have checked my grammar and spelling. ☐
- My review is between 120 and 180 words long. ☐

◀ Look Back

Can you answer these questions? If you can't remember, look through the unit for the answers.

1. Which Australian city has a famous Opera House?
2. What kind of magazine tells you about holidays?
3. Which of these verbs is followed by the *-ing* form?
   plan   suggest   hope
4. Write one noun from the verb *vary*.
5. Which of these do we not say?
   would prefer   would rather   would better

Out and About 8

Revision
Units 7-8

1 Choose the correct option.

1 On our way to Australia, we had a _____ in Singapore.
   A destination   B jet lag   C stopover   D resort

2 You _____ the bread and I'll butter it and we'll make some sandwiches.
   A slice   B boil   C fry   D carve

3 Let's look through some _____ and decide where we're going this summer.
   A souvenirs   B brochures   C customs   D departures

4 I asked Eric if he'd broken the window, but he _____ it.
   A denied   B admitted   C accused   D refused

5 Could you pass me the _____ pan, please?
   A mixing   B serving   C carving   D frying

6 Don't forget your swimming costume when you _____ your suitcase.
   A put   B pack   C fill   D place

7 Would you like _____ fries with your burger?
   A American   B German   C Belgian   D French

8 Then, you have to _____ your meat in the oven for about an hour.
   A fry   B roast   C boil   D bake

9 I saw a flight to Germany in the _____ window for only €10!
   A holiday rep's   B holiday brochure's   C travel agent's   D travel guide's

10 When we get to the airport, the first thing we should do is check _____ .
   A in   B out   C up   D off

2 Complete each sentence so that it means the same as the first sentence. Use the words given without changing them. Use no more than five words. You will get two marks for each correct answer.

1 'I'm meeting Mark outside the cinema,' said Philip.   **he**
   Philip said _____ outside the cinema.

2 'I've been here before,' Marianna said as we entered the old house.   **there**
   As we entered the old house, Marianna said _____ before.

3 'Why don't we see what's on at the cinema?' said Alex.   **suggested**
   Alex _____ on at the cinema.

4 'Put your dirty clothes in the washing basket,' my mum said.   **told**
   My mum _____ dirty clothes in the washing basket.

5 'I've been working all day so I'm tired,' Mrs Lewis said.   **because**
   Mrs Lewis said she _____ been working all day.

6 'No, I'm not going to lend you any money,' Nancy said to me.   **refused**
   Nancy _____ any money.

7 'I think Grandma will be here at the weekend,' my dad said.   **there**
   My dad said he _____ at the weekend.

3 Circle the correct word or phrase in each sentence.

1 Do you remember *to go/going* to see that fantastic film last year?
2 I suggest *to visit/visiting* the Science Museum while you're in town.
3 The old man appeared *to be/being* quite ill when I saw him.
4 My sister avoids *to eat/eating* fast food because it's unhealthy.
5 I'm going to learn *to play/playing* the drums this summer.
6 Do you think we can afford *to go/going* on holiday this year?

4 Complete the sentences using the correct preposition.

1 I was surprised when the hero got killed right _____ the end of the film.
2 Could you please put your name _____ this piece of paper and give it back to me?
3 Tell me more. I'm very interested _____ local history.
4 What are you working _____? Can I have a look?
5 I'm afraid I don't know much _____ the Second World War.

5 Write a phrasal verb with *out* to match the definitions.

1 see with difficulty   _____ out
2 not have any left   _____ out of
3 not include, remove   _____ out
4 be in the end   _____ out
5 argue   _____ out

6 Read this letter. For questions 1–10, use the word given at the end of each line to form a word that fills the gap. There is an example at the beginning (0). You will get two marks for each correct answer.

Dear Mr Coco,
Thank you for your (0) *application* for the position of manager. I am afraid that after a long (1) _____ we have decided to appoint someone else. We would like to explain our (2) _____ . All of us were a little surprised by your (3) _____ when you came for the interview. 'Dressed like a clown' was the (4) _____ used by one of us. A great (5) _____ of different people work for us, but we thought the red nose showed a lack of (6) _____ . We were all in (7) _____ that many of our customers would have great (8) _____ in taking seriously a manager in size 76 shoes. We hope this (9) _____ helps. I would like to finish by expressing my (10) _____ that you will go far in business … show.
Yours faithfully,

Justine Carter
Personnel Manager

APPLY
DISCUSS
CHOOSE
APPEAR
DESCRIBE
VARY
RESPONSIBLE
AGREE
DIFFICULT
EXPLAIN
BELIEVE

Score _____ /60

9

Lab Report

Start thinking!

How often do you do these things?
use computers
send and get emails
send and get text messages
buy something online

Do you or does anyone in your family have:
a netbook
a tablet computer
a smartphone

What new technology do you expect to see in the next two or three years?

Reading

1 🎧 **2.01** Quickly read the magazine article. Write the number of a paragraph 1–6 next to each heading. There is one heading you do not need to use.

a Better batteries _____
b A huge number of uses _____
c Reasons to be concerned _____
d More functions, better functions _____
e In the past _____
f Tomorrow's world _____
g Money matters _____

AN APPETITE FOR APPS!

'How did apps become such an important part of our lives, and where do we go from here?' asks Jemima Deacon.

1 A few short years ago, phones were firmly stuck on a piece of furniture, and were used mainly for calling people. Then we all got mobile phones and got into sending and receiving text messages on the go. Early mobiles did have a few handy little features such as a calculator and a calendar, but were still mainly used for communicating with people we knew. And taking a few poor quality photos that you didn't quite know what to do with. And then – all of a sudden, it seemed – this useful little device morphed into an enormously powerful computer with the potential to do … well, to do everything your PC did at home, and sometimes more. What led to this development, and where does it go from here?

2 Several key aspects had to come together to create the modern smartphone as we know it. Firstly, battery life had to improve. If you use a mobile phone for more than just a few phone calls, you need a powerful long-lasting battery. Batteries have become increasingly powerful over the past ten years or so, and will undoubtedly continue to do so.

3 Secondly, the cost of downloading large amounts of data onto a phone had to decrease. There's no point having the ability to check your email on your phone if you can't afford to use the service. Using the mobile phone network for data is still too expensive for many people, but they're able to make use of Wifi, which has become extremely widespread and is essentially free. If we didn't have wireless networks, we almost certainly wouldn't have smartphones.

4 Thirdly, the actual functionality of phones has improved enormously. They have much better cameras than they did just a few years ago, they can hold more data, their sound quality is much clearer and louder, they have touch screens, and they know when they're being rotated or held or touched in a certain way.

5 If you combine all these elements, and have reasonably-priced smartphones being used by millions of people, you create an environment where the uses of a smartphone become almost infinite. All it takes is a little imagination to think of a new way to use it, and you've created something people want. And that's what happened with apps. At the time of writing this article, there are hundreds of thousands of apps that can be used for millions of different purposes. If you want an app to tell you where the nearest chemist to where you're standing is, it's available. If you need an app to send free

2 Read the article again. Underline a phrase in the article that has a similar meaning to the phrase given.
1 weren't mobile (paragraph 1)
2 while doing things out of the house (paragraph 1)
3 it was important for different things to combine (paragraph 2)
4 to become more powerful in the future (paragraph 2)
5 it's a waste of time (paragraph 3)
6 very common (paragraph 3)
7 have a situation (paragraph 5)
8 the chances are (paragraph 6)

3 Write a word or short phrase from the article to complete each sentence.
1 People started _____ while doing things out of the house.
2 The _____ of cameras on early mobile phones was not good.
3 It's important that a mobile phone battery is powerful and _____ .
4 With smartphones today, _____ are downloaded onto the phone.
5 To access information, smartphones can use the mobile phone network, or _____ .
6 A smartphone knows when it's _____ to the left or right.
7 Many people use _____ to pay bills through their phone, computer or tablet.
8 A(n) _____ in a future phone will be able to detect pollution and pollen.

messages to someone else with the same app, it exists. If you want an app to do your online banking, or play funny noises to your cat, or point out the names of all the stars and planets right above you, you can find it. And by the time you read this, there will be thousands more apps available.

But what about the future? It's always dangerous to predict what technology's going to be like in a few years' time and we often get it wrong, but it seems likely that the future apps will rely on sensors and functions that current smartphones don't have. For example, if future smartphones have some kind of air sensor, there will be a whole new range of apps which can tell you if the air you're breathing is too polluted, or, for people with allergies, how much pollen is in the air. As image-recognition and video-streaming become more effective, another range of apps might combine the real and the digital. For example, in the future there might be games we play on our smartphones where the background and setting is the actual room we're sitting in, or the street we're standing in.

WORD BOX

4 Find words in the article to match the definitions. You've been given the first letter to help you.
1 h_____ (adj) useful
2 d_____ (n) a machine or piece of equipment that does a particular thing
3 d_____ (n) progress, improvement
4 i_____ (v) get better
5 u_____ (adv) definitely, certainly
6 d_____ (v) go down, become smaller/lower
7 q_____ (n) how good something is
8 r_____ (adj) not too expensive
9 f_____ (n) the ability to do different things
10 d_____ (adj) electronic, not physical

Have your say!

- What are the most useful apps? Why are they so useful? Can you think of any other apps that someone might invent in the future?

G Grammar clinic

Conditionals (1): zero, first, second

👁 Look at *Grammar database* page 185 before you do the exercises.

1 Read the sentences from the article on pages 78 and 79. Match each one to an explanation.

1 If you use a mobile phone for more than just a few phone calls, you need a powerful long-lasting battery. ____
2 If future smartphones have some kind of air sensor, there will be a whole new range of apps … ____
3 If we didn't have wireless networks, we almost certainly wouldn't have smartphones. ____

a This expresses a present or future possibility.
b This expresses a general truth.
c This expresses an unlikely or hypothetical situation.

2 Choose the correct option in each sentence.

1 If I were a scientist, _____ a new kind of computer.
  a I would invent   b I invent   c I will invent
2 Smartphones _____ a possibility if we didn't have long-lasting batteries.
  a won't be   b isn't   c wouldn't be
3 If you _____ nonsense into a computer, you get nonsense out.
  a would put   b put   c were putting
4 You should think carefully about what you need if you _____ to get a computer.
  a are planning   b were planning   c would plan
5 An air sensor in a smartphone will be useful if it _____ people with allergies.
  a would help   b helped   c helps

3 Put the verbs into the correct form to complete the sentences. Use contractions (*I'll, I'd*, etc) where possible.

1 If I _____ (be) you, _____ (I/get) a smartphone.
2 The browser opens a new tab if _____ (you/click) on any of these links.
3 If the internet _____ (not/exist), we _____ (not/be) able to send emails round the world.
4 If you buy a new tablet, _____ (make) sure you get one with a good-quality camera.
5 If _____ (you/lower) the screen of a netbook, it goes into 'sleep' mode automatically.
6 If _____ (you/use) a smartphone before, _____ (you/find) using a tablet very easy.

4 Use this information about a student to make six conditional sentences as in the examples.

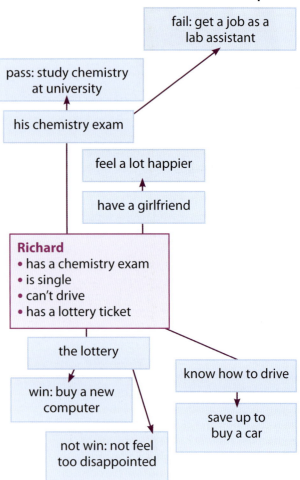

If Richard had a girlfriend, he would feel a lot happier.
Richard would feel a lot happier if he had a girlfriend.

Vocabulary builder

Science and technology

1 Write the correct letter to label the picture using the words and phrases from the box.

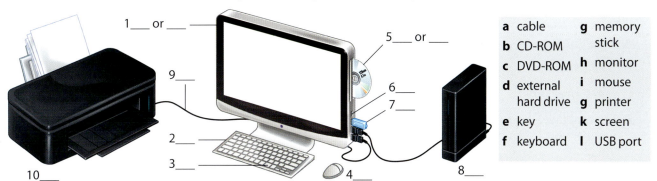

a	cable	g	memory stick
b	CD-ROM		
c	DVD-ROM	h	monitor
d	external hard drive	i	mouse
		g	printer
e	key	k	screen
f	keyboard	l	USB port

2 Complete the sentences using the nouns in the box. Some of them may need to be in the plural.

invention • discovery • theory • laboratory
experiment • research

1 The computer is one of the most important _____ of the late 20th century.
2 Dr Hawking has an interesting _____ about how the universe developed.
3 Today's _____ have a lot of complicated scientific equipment in them.
4 According to recent _____ , most people don't understand modern science.
5 This _____ with white mice is designed to test their intelligence.
6 Astronomers have announced the _____ of a new planet.

Collocations

3 Write each word or phrase from the box next to all the verbs it can go with. Be careful! You will write the words and phrases more than once.

a memory stick • a theory • an experiment
research • software

1 do _____
2 carry out _____
3 have _____
4 come up with _____
5 download _____
6 install _____
7 connect _____
8 plug in _____

Phrasal verbs with *off*

4 Phrasal verbs with *off* often have meanings connected to removing, stopping or cancelling something. Match the phrasal verbs in the box with the correct definitions.

go off • make off • take off • put off
turn off • call off

1 _____ stop liking something you used to like
2 _____ remove an item of clothing, etc
3 _____ delay something until a later time
4 _____ cancel a planned event
5 _____ escape, often after a crime
6 _____ stop a machine

5 Complete the sentences using the correct form of the phrasal verbs from exercise 4.

1 The burglars stole a flat screen TV and _____ in a white car.
2 We've decided to _____ the experiment _____ until the weather improves.
3 Before you go into the lab, please _____ your shoes.
4 I've really _____ violent video games.
5 My cousin was planning to marry a woman over the internet, but at the last minute they _____ it _____ .
6 Don't you think you should _____ your computer _____ and go and play football outside with your friends?

Listening

1 🎧 **2.02** You are going to listen to five people talking about new computer games. Decide which computer game each person enjoyed the most.

A *Night Thief*   Speaker 1: ___
B *Cave Warrior*   Speaker 2: ___
C *Mad Driver City*   Speaker 3: ___
D *Tower of Evil*   Speaker 4: ___
E *Cup Final*   Speaker 5: ___

2 You will now hear the five speakers again. For questions 1–5, choose the best answer (A, B or C).

1 You hear a boy talking. What did he not like about *Cave Warrior*?
  A He couldn't find the lost treasure.
  B He knew what was going to happen next.
  C He thought there was too much action.

2 You hear a woman talking. What was the problem she had with some of the games?
  A She doesn't like playing sports.
  B She couldn't react quickly enough.
  C She can't drive a car.

3 You hear a girl being interviewed in the street. Why doesn't she like *Night Thief*?
  A It seems like hard work.
  B It involves criminal activities.
  C She isn't very good at maths.

4 You hear a boy talking. What does he dislike about *Mad Driver City*?
  A He doesn't have enough time to play it.
  B His friend is much better at it.
  C They want to play at the same time.

5 You hear a girl talking. What does she say about computer games?
  A Buying sports games is a waste of money.
  B You can waste money if you make the wrong decision.
  C Driving games are the best value for money.

Soundbite /s/ and /ʃ/

🎧 **2.03** Listen and circle the words you hear.
1 Only half of the people were *saved/shaved*.
2 Could you get me a *seat/sheet* from the office, please?
3 Did you *sew/show* all of them?
4 They have lots of different *sorts/shorts*.

Speaking

1 What do you want to do in the future?

I'd like to go to university, if I get good exam results.

I want to get married if _____ .

I hope to have a family if _____ .

It'd be nice to work as a(n) _____ if _____ .

I'd love to visit _____ one day if _____ .

I'd like to live _____ if _____ .

2 In pairs, ask and answer the questions. Try to say as much as you can. Use the phrases below to help you.
- What would you like to do when you leave school?
- What job would you like to do in the future?
- Do you have any ambitions?
- What are your hopes for the future?
- Is there anything you'd really like to do one day?

 Useful Phrases

That seems like a long way in the future. I'd say that …

I'm quite an ambitious person. One thing I'd like to do is …

Well, if I had the chance, I think I'd love to …

👁 Look at *Speaking database - Expressing preferences* on page 165.

Use of English

Unless, in case, as long as

👁 Look at *Grammar database* page 186 before you do the exercises.

1 Rewrite the sentences using *unless, in case* or *as/so long as*.
1. Promise to give it back tomorrow and you can borrow my new computer game.
   You can _____ .
2. I have to finish my homework before I can play on my computer.
   I can't _____ .
3. Save your documents on an external hard drive or memory stick – your computer might get a virus.
   Save your documents _____
   _____ .

Word patterns

2 Choose the correct option in each sentence.
1. I think I'm a little scared of computers _____ I don't know much about them.
   a because of   **b** because
2. Some people have complained about this game _____ the violence.
   a because of   **b** because
3. I didn't _____ Jason when he said he'd got a new mobile phone.
   a believe   **b** believe in
4. Some people don't _____ UFOs.
   a believe   **b** believe in
5. When you buy the new K256 mobile, a hands-free set is _____ .
   a provided with **b** provided

3 For questions 1–12, read the text below and think of the word which best fits each gap. Use only one word in each gap. There is an example at the beginning (0). Write your answers IN CAPITAL LETTERS.

Time Travel

Scientists still aren't sure whether the laws of physics allow us (0) __TO__ build a time machine. Some scientists argue that it's (1) _____ possible, using this logic: if we built a time machine and travelled back into the past, we (2) _____ be able to stop our parents meeting. Then we'd never be born! (3) _____ , however, argue that that isn't a real problem. We just wouldn't be born in this universe, but we'd still be born in a parallel universe. Strange, isn't it?
(4) _____ you want to travel into the past, it's actually very easy. Just look (5) _____ at the night sky. When you see a star in the sky, (6) _____ you see it as it is right now? No, you see it as it was millions of years ago. This is (7) _____ the light from the star has taken millions of years to travel across the universe to reach your eyes.
Travelling into the future is more difficult, but Einstein proved (8) _____ is theoretically possible. You can achieve this so (9) _____ as you have a spaceship that goes really fast – nearly at the speed of light, (10) _____ is very fast indeed. If you go off in your spaceship and fly around for, let's say, six months, when you come back (11) _____ Earth you'll be in the future. How much in the future? If your spaceship goes at 99.99% of light speed, all your friends you left behind (12) _____ be almost 50 years older than you. It's incredible, but it's true!

Lab Report 9

Writing

An informal letter/email

👁 Look at *Writing database - informal letters/emails* on page 154 before you do the exercises.

1 Read this writing task. Why should your email be informal?

You have a friend who lives in another country. She/He is writing a report for school on technology and has asked you for some information about how you and your family use technology in your daily life. Write an email to your friend, telling her/him what she/he needs to know.

Write an **email** of between **120** and **180** words in an appropriate style.

2 Decide if the statements are true (T) or false (F). In informal letters/emails …

1 we usually ask our friend about their health/news/etc first. ☐
2 we never use contractions (*I've, don't, can't*, etc). ☐
3 it's sometimes okay to write incomplete sentences. ☐
4 you should never use exclamation marks (!). ☐
5 you don't need to write in paragraphs. ☐
6 you don't need to worry about answering the question. ☐

Working model

3 Read the answer to the writing task. The writer has not used paragraphs. Decide where new paragraphs should begin.

To: Ashley
Sent: 18th February
Subject: Technology!

Dear Miss Ashley Williams,

How are you? How did your French test go? I bet you passed! You asked me about tecnology. Well, the first thing I should tell you is that I've got a new computer! So far, I've used it for playing games and for serfing the internet. It's not as complicated as I thought. I'm even teaching my dad how to use it! What else? Of course, we've got things like a TV and a DVD player. We watch a few hours of TV every day, and we watch a DVD once a weak. My brother watches more than I do. Lazy boy! My dad says he's thinking of getting satelite TV, so maybe I'll start watching a bit more. The only other thing I can think of is my mobile phone. It's a smartphone and it's really cool! I never go anywhere without it. I use it all the time and send about 20 text mesages every day! (Luckily, Mum and Dad pay the bill.) Got to go. Love to your sister.

Take care,
Jessica Saunders

4 There are mistakes with the names and five spelling mistakes in the email. Correct them.

Lab Report 9

84

Ready to write!

5 You are going to answer the same question. First, look at this extract from your pen friend's last email.

> ... and then there's this football match on Saturday. If we win that, we're in the final. Who knows? Oh, yeah. I wanted to ask you something. We have to write a report on technology for school. Could you tell me a few things about how you use technology in your life? You know, computers, mobiles, TV, that sort of thing. Oh, and tell me something about the other members of your family too, and how they use technology.
> Anyway, I was talking to Sam the other day and he says that ...

Which of these things does your friend want to know about?
- your opinion on violent video games
- what kind of computer you want to get
- how much television you watch
- whether you have a computer at home
- how good you are at football
- whether your parents have mobile phones
- what the best model of mobile phone is

6 Make a plan of your answer. Use your imagination.
- How are you going to start your email?
- What news are you going to ask your friend about first?
- What's the first kind of technology you want to talk about?
  How do you use it?
- What's the second kind of technology you want to talk about?
  How do you use it?
- What's the third kind of technology you want to talk about?
  How do you use it?
- Which phrases are you going to use in your email?
- What name are you going to write at the end?

Now complete *Writing Planner 9* on page 159.

Now write!

7 You are now ready to write your email to your friend. Use informal language. Write between 120 and 180 words.

Check it out!

8 Check your work. Tick (✓) what you have done.

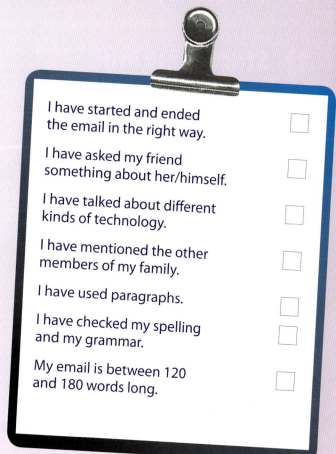

- I have started and ended the email in the right way.
- I have asked my friend something about her/himself.
- I have talked about different kinds of technology.
- I have mentioned the other members of my family.
- I have used paragraphs.
- I have checked my spelling and my grammar.
- My email is between 120 and 180 words long.

 Look Back

Can you answer these questions? If you can't remember, look through the unit for the answers.
1. What's another way of saying 'a wireless network'?
2. Do you *carry out* or *come up with* a new theory?
3. How many parts of a computer can you name?
4. What's the difference between *put off* and *call off*?
5. Which phrase means 'only if'?

10

Let Me Entertain You

Start thinking!

What different forms of entertainment can you think of?
Do you ever go to the theatre?
Do you ever read TV, film or theatre reviews?

Reading

1 🎧 2.04 Read this newspaper column. Which programme would you most like to watch?

2 Read the statements from the column and decide if they are facts or express the writer's opinion.
1. SuperTV has been broadcasting for five years.
2. The presenters of *VJ-TV* aren't very intelligent.
3. *Staff Room* is replacing *Train Driver*.
4. *Life in Aylesford Street* is very popular.
5. *Joke-a-Cola* will be funny.
6. There is a lot of choice of entertainment.

TV REVIEW

Lucy Chang tells you what's new (and not so new!) on your screens this summer.

I always look forward to this time of year, and I'm always disappointed! It's the time of year when the TV channels tell us their plans for the summer and every year I tell myself that it might be different. It never is. Take SuperTV, for example. This channel, on our screens for five years now, broadcasts a depressing mix of game shows and music videos. So what do we find in the new schedule? *I'm The One*, a game show with holidays as prizes, and *VJ-TV*, yet another music video programme with brainless presenters.

13 **They**'re also planning to repeat the dreadful chat show *Star Quality*, which is about as entertaining as watching grass grow. Why can't they come up with new ideas?

Channel 9 does a little better. Now that *Train Driver* has finished, they've decided to replace it with *Staff Room*, a reality show that follows teachers around all day. It should be the hit of the summer, giving us an idea of what really goes on when the lesson is over. Who doesn't want to see and hear what teachers say about their students at the end of the schoolday? Great stuff! Together with *Life in Aylesford Street*, the soap opera that everyone's talking about, it looks like Channel 9 could be the channel to watch this summer.

Over on BTV1, Max Read is back with *Joke-a-Cola*, the comedy show. The first series was slightly amusing, the second hilarious. Let's wait and see what the third series is like. Comedy is difficult to get right, but it ought to be great. I wish I could say the same about the sitcom, *Oh! Those Kids!* It's enough to look at the expressions on the faces of the cast! It's obvious they know it's rubbish and the script is just so badly written! Oh! Those writers!

3 Read the text again. For questions 1–6, choose the answer (A, B, C or D) which you think fits best according to the text.

1. At this time of year
   A the TV channels change all their programmes.
   B the writer disappoints the TV channels with her reviews.
   C the writer hopes for something that never happens.
   D the writer's favourite programmes often disappear.

2. What does 'They' in line 13 refer to?
   A SuperTV
   B the TV channels
   C the presenters of *VJ-TV*
   D TV viewers

3. The writer says that *Staff Room* will probably
   A be successful.
   B shock students.
   C be worse than *Train Driver*.
   D be on instead of *Life in Aylesford Street*.

4. The writer thinks that *Joke-a-Cola* is now
   A more difficult to understand.
   B more popular with viewers.
   C funnier than before.
   D more like a sitcom.

5. Because of the choice of entertainment
   A people watch more television.
   B people move to areas with more facilities.
   C programme makers have to tell lies.
   D programmes have to be more exciting.

6. The writer thinks that television
   A will never be as popular as the theatre is.
   B should show more programmes about hobbies.
   C could lose its popularity in the future.
   D ought to provide more than just entertainment.

WORD BOX

4 Use words or phrases from the text to complete the definitions. You've been given the first letter to help you.

1. M_____ v_____ are short films showing musicians singing their songs.
2. If something is e_____ , it is enjoyable and interesting.
3. A h_____ is a great success.
4. If something is a_____ , it's a little funny, but not very.
5. If something is h_____ , it's very funny.
6. The group of people who act in a programme, film or play is called the c_____ .
7. The s_____ contains all the words the actors have to learn.
8. Another phrase meaning 'free time' or 'spare time' is l_____ t_____ .

The programme makers must think we'll watch anything. That's just not true. People might have hundreds of channels on their TV or might live near a cinema with a dozen screens. There is so much choice of entertainment these days – TV, the cinema, the theatre, even the internet – that they have to work hard to keep their audience. What they should be doing is making new, exciting programmes. Where are the programmes that make people think they must stay in to watch them?

We have to ask ourselves what entertainment is. We have to think about what people do with their leisure time. Television has been popular for about 50–60 years, but it might not be popular forever. More people are going to the cinema and theatre than ever before. More people are surfing the internet or playing computer games than ever before. If *Oh! Those Kids!* is all that the TV can offer, why should we watch it? With one or two exceptions, this summer's programmes will make more people turn off than turn on.

Have your say!

- Which of the programmes mentioned in the TV review would you like to watch?
- Do you watch any programmes similar to the ones mentioned in the review?

G Grammar clinic

Modals (1)

👁 Look at *Grammar database* pages 187–188 before you do the exercises.

1 Read the sentences and phrases from the article on pages 86 and 87. Match each one to an explanation.

1 … every year I tell myself that it *might* be different.
2 Why *can't* they come up with new ideas?
3 It *should* be the hit of the summer, …
4 The programme makers *must* think we'll watch anything.
5 What they *should* be doing is …
6 We *have to* ask ourselves what entertainment is.

This expresses …
a something which is probable.
b an ability/inability.
c something which is possible.
d a way of giving advice.
e a certain opinion.
f an obligation.

2 Choose the correct option to show the meaning of the verb in italics.

1 They *should* close down the theatre in this town because nobody ever goes.
   a giving advice   b giving permission
2 I think I *might* stay in and watch the film on Channel 4 this evening.
   a expressing obligation   b expressing possibility
3 My mum says I *can* be in the school play.
   a expressing ability   b giving permission
4 Do you *have to* go to university to become an actor?
   a asking about obligation
   b asking about probability

3 Choose the correct verb in each sentence.

1 You really _____ go and see Spielberg's latest. It's brilliant!
   a could   b should   c might
2 Oh, Dad! Do we _____ watch that opera programme again?
   a must   b should   c have to
3 I read somewhere that Isla Fisher _____ be on TV tonight.
   a might   b can   c has to
4 Ask your parents if you _____ come to the concert with me.
   a can   b ought to   c will
5 I really _____ get some new clothes to go to the theatre.
   a might   b must   c could

4 Rewrite the sentences using the verbs in brackets.

1 Justin Bieber's new song will probably win an award. (**should**)
   Justin _____.

2 There's a possibility that Madonna is recording a new album. (**might**)
   Madonna _____.

3 People's ears are often damaged by listening to very loud music. (**can**)
   Listening _____.

4 You can get me a CD if you like, but it's not necessary. (**have to**)
   You _____.

5 We should probably check to see if there are any tickets left. (**ought to**)
   We _____.

6 I'm thinking of going to the theatre while I'm in London. (**might**)
   I _____.

V Vocabulary builder

Entertainment

1 Use the words in the box to answer the questions.

rehearsal • audition • play • critic
review • stage • act

1 Where do the actors perform in a theatre?
2 What do we call a dramatic performance in a theatre?
3 What do actors do?
4 What do we call the test actors do before they get the part?
5 Who judges theatre performances for a newspaper or magazine?
6 Where do we read a judgement of a theatre performance?
7 What do we call a practice of a performance?

2 Complete the sentences with the correct form of the words in exercise 1.

1 The _____ were terrible! I'm surprised the play didn't close sooner.
2 We saw a great _____ the other day. *Blue Murder*, it was called.
3 I can't meet you on Friday because I'm in the school play and we've got a(n) _____ .
4 The _____ absolutely loved the performance, but the public just didn't seem to be interested.
5 The curtain went up and two actors came out onto the _____ .
6 I'm really nervous about the _____ . Hope I get the part.
7 I know she's beautiful, but she can't _____ and I'm not having her in my show.

Confusable words

3 Circle the correct word or phrase in each sentence.

1 I was always very *popular/famous* at school.
2 Nobody seems to like my favourite group, but they're very *popular/famous*.
3 In my free time, I like to *hear/listen to* music, especially rap music.
4 Sh! I think I can *hear/listen to* music coming from upstairs.
5 I'm going to call Sarah to *tell/say/speak* to her about the tickets.
6 What did Mark *tell/say/speak* you about the film he saw?
7 Some people *tell/say/speak* that pop music is a kind of art.
8 I love *reading/studying* romantic books and books for teenagers.
9 I love *reading/studying* English grammar, believe it or not!

Collocations: entertainment

4 Match to make common phrases about entertainment.

1 get   a a joke funny
2 find   b the joke
3 tell   c fun
4 have   d fun of somebody
5 make   e a joke

I don't get it!

5 Write a word in each gap. Use the phrases from exercise 4 to help you.

My friends and I often sit around and (1) _____ jokes. We (2) _____ a lot of fun, but no-one ever (3) _____ my jokes funny! I don't know why. Maybe I just haven't got a good sense of humour. And I hate it when someone tells a joke and I don't (4) _____ it. I always feel stupid! I also don't like it when someone makes (5) _____ of somebody else in the group – probably because it's usually me they're making fun (6) _____ !

10 Let Me Entertain You

Listening

1 You are going to listen to an interview on an online radio station. Before you listen, look at the sentences in exercise 2. In pairs talk about:
- what type of word or phrase (noun, verb, etc) might fill each gap.
- what actual words or phrases might fill each gap.

2 🎧 **2.05** Listen to the interview. For questions 1–8, complete the sentences.

> In a previous show, they asked for ideas of enjoyable things teenagers can do 1_____.
> Liz says making a short film is lots of fun and very 2_____.
> It's not a good idea to film yourselves without 3_____.
> Liz says that 4_____ is not necessary.
> There may sometimes be difficulties with outdoor 5_____ quality.
> You can choose whether to write a (n) 6_____ or just a rough outline.
> The person holding the camera should also be 7_____.
> Choose the characters, time and place carefully so that the actors can 8_____.

Soundbite /ə/

🎧 **2.06** Listen and pay attention to the vowel sound in the syllables underlined.

There's <u>a</u> new theat<u>re</u> <u>a</u>cross <u>the</u> road <u>from</u> me.

One syllable in each word contains the sound /ə/. Underline the syllable. Listen and check your answers.

| letter | about | entertain | teacher |
| leisure | exercise | occur | |

3 Were any of your guesses in exercise 1 right or nearly right?

Speaking

1 Decide what you like and dislike about the activities. Write something in each box. Use your imagination.

	… reading books because …	… going to pop concerts because …
I like …		
I dislike …		

2 Work in pairs. One of you should read the instructions and the other should talk for one minute. Then swap.

What do you like and dislike about each form of entertainment?

I'd like you to compare and contrast the two photos and say what you like and dislike about each form of entertainment.

👁 Look at *Speaking database - Comparing* and *Expressing preferences* on page 165.

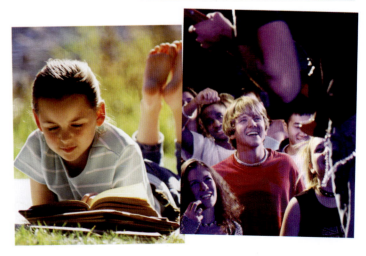

Use of English

Parts of speech

1 Choose the kind of word that is needed to complete the sentences.

1 The audience clapped _____ and the actors came back onto the stage.
   a adverb   **b** adjective

2 The stadium is great for concerts because of its _____ .
   a adjective   **b** noun

3 I love reading _____ books with characters my age in them.
   a adjective   **b** adverb

4 Do you think we could _____ what we're doing this evening?
   a noun   **b** verb

5 I really get a lot of _____ out of watching and reading about sports.
   a noun   **b** adjective

2 Now decide what parts of speech the words in the box are. Use five of them to complete the sentences in exercise 1.

> loud • loudness • sizeable • decide
> enjoyable • exciting • excited • decision
> decisive • size • loudly • enjoyment
> indecisive • enjoy

3 Choose two words from the box you didn't know before. Write sentences using those words. In groups, compare your sentences.

Word formation: prefixes

4 Use the prefixes to form the negative of the adjectives and nouns. One of them has two answers.

un-	dis-	in-
able	believable	expected
ability	clear	lucky
advantage	comfort	organised
approve	comfortable	suitable
belief	employed	

5 For questions 1–10, read the text below. Use the word given in capitals at the end of some of the lines to form a word that fits in the gap in the same line. There is an example at the beginning (0). Write your answers IN CAPITAL LETTERS.

BUSKING

Street (0) __PERFORMERS__ , or 'buskers', help make any city centre a place   PERFORM
of (1) _____ . In every major European city you can find   ENTERTAIN
young, (2) _____ people juggling, playing the guitar or even   EMPLOY
doing magic tricks for money. All they need is a(n) (3) _____   SUIT
place to perform and a good crowd.
Some people might (4) _____ of busking and find it   APPROVE
annoying, but most people in the city centre agree that it's a(n)
(5) _____ break from shopping and having to rush around   ENJOY
when there's a(n) (6) _____ show in the street. Some young   EXPECT
people, (7) _____ to afford a luxury trip around the world,   ABLE
busk in order to travel. It can be (8) _____ , but it   COMFORT
is a very cheap way to see the world. A few hours playing, unless you are
(9) _____ , will pay for a bed or a bus ticket. The   LUCK
(10) _____ is that you need to have some talent or you   ADVANTAGE
might go hungry!

10 Writing

An essay

👁 Look at *Writing database - essays* on page 153 before you do the exercises.

1 Make notes to answer the questions.
1 What programmes are there on TV for children?
2 Which programmes are popular?
3 Which of these would you like to see more of? Why?
- cartoons
- drama for children
- news for children
- game shows for children
4 Should children's TV educate or entertain? Why?

Talk about your answers with the class. Explain clearly why you agree or disagree with other students.

2 Read this writing task. What kind of style would be appropriate?

> You have had a class discussion on TV programmes for children. Now your English teacher has asked you to write an essay, giving your opinions on this question:
> *Should children's TV educate or entertain?*

Write an **essay** of between **120** and **180** words in an appropriate style.

Working model

3 Read the answer to the writing task.

1 Children today are under more pressure than ever and need to relax. They often do this by watching television. Although parents worry about how it will affect them, I believe television should entertain, rather than educate.

6 First of all, there is no reason why television for children should be different from television for adults. The most popular programmes tend to be game shows and drama series. Adults watch them to relax after a busy day at work and children should also be able to relax after a hard day at
12 school.

Secondly, programmes such as these do teach us things. Game shows improve your general knowledge. Drama series teach us about human relationships and the problems people face. Despite their parents' disapproval, children learn a lot while
18 they are being entertained.

To sum up, children's television should provide quality entertainment. Instead of uninteresting educational programmes, there should be game shows and drama series made for children. It should be a way for them to escape their
24 problems, although watching too much television might cause problems with schoolwork, for instance.

4 Do you agree with the writer? Why? / Why not?

5 The words in red are important! Decide what each word in red refers to.

1 They (line 2)
2 this (line 2)
3 it (line 3)
4 them (line 9)
5 these (line 13)
6 their (line 17)
7 It (line 23)
8 them (line 23)

6 The words and phrases in blue are also important. Decide which words and phrases in blue are used …

1 to refer to an example. _____
2 to introduce the conclusion. _____
3 to refer to a negative point. _____ / _____
4 to introduce the first main point. _____
5 to introduce the next main point. _____

Ready to write!

7 Read this writing task.

> You have had a class discussion about television. Now your English teacher has asked you to write an essay, giving your opinions on this question: *Do children nowadays watch too much TV?*

Write an **essay** of between **120** and **180** words in an appropriate style.

8 Before you write, complete the essay plan.

what I'm going to include
Paragraph 1 _____
Paragraph 2 _____
Paragraph 3 _____
Paragraph 4 _____

Now complete *Writing Planner 10* on page 159.

Now write!

9 You are now ready to write your essay. Use your notes to help you. Use some of the connecting phrases. Use 'it', 'this', 'them', etc to connect your sentences.

Check it out!

10 Check your work. Tick (✓) what you have done.

- I have used an appropriate formal style. ☐
- I have explained the reasons for my opinion. ☐
- I have used some good connecting phrases. ☐
- I have used 'it', 'this', 'them', etc to connect my sentences together. ☐
- I have used paragraphs. ☐
- I have checked my spelling and my grammar. ☐
- My essay is between 120 and 180 words long. ☐

◀ Look Back

Can you answer these questions? If you can't remember, look through the unit for the answers.

1 What is another word for a great success?
2 Which of these modals can be used for giving advice? *could   should   might*
3 What do critics write?
4 If lots of people like you, are you popular or famous?
5 What is a busker?

Revision
Units 9-10

1 Choose the correct option.

1 I thought the new Ben Stiller film was _____ ! It's the funniest film I've ever seen!
   A famous   B entertaining   C hilarious   D amusing

2 I don't have much time to _____ the internet for things I'm interested in.
   A ride   B surf   C travel   D tour

3 My brother wants to be an actor. He's been to a hundred _____ so far, but he never gets the part.
   A auditions   B reviews   C critics   D rehearsals

4 My mum was in a pop group that had a _____ in the 90s and then she got married and had a family.
   A top   B screen   C hit   D win

5 All the members of the _____ were shocked when the leading actress left the show.
   A script   B stage   C play   D cast

6 The _____ of America changed the way Europeans saw the world.
   A discovery   B invention   C theory   D research

7 I'd love to see the new James Bond film. It's had really good _____ .
   A critics   B auditions   C reviews   D rehearsals

8 The action scenes were quite good, but the main actor really couldn't _____ . He was rubbish!
   A act   B play   C star   D appear

9 Our teacher didn't _____ the joke I told so I had to explain it to her.
   A find   B have   C take   D get

10 I don't think it's nice to make fun _____ kids who are younger than you.
   A to   B of   C at   D with

2 Match to make complete sentences.

1 If we had more money,
2 If you open your computer,
3 If we've got enough money,
4 If the shop were closed,
5 If I were you,
6 If you opened your computer,

a we'll go and get you a new computer.
b I'd find out about computer courses in the local area.
c you wouldn't do any damage to it.
d we can see where the hard drive is.
e the lights wouldn't be on, would they?
f we'd be able to get a home cinema.

3 Write the negative form of these words using an appropriate prefix.

1 comfortable _____
2 organised _____
3 ability _____ or _____
4 comfort _____
5 able _____
6 approve _____
7 suitable _____
8 employed _____

4 Complete the sentences using the correct form of the phrasal verbs in the box.

put off • call off • go off
turn off • take off • make off

1 I used to really like Leonardo DiCaprio's films, but I _____ him recently.
2 I think we'll have to _____ our holiday until the end of the summer.
3 Why don't you _____ that hat? You look ridiculous.
4 The thieves _____ with over €1 million.
5 Unless it stops raining, we'll have to _____ the barbecue.
6 Don't forget to _____ your computer before you go to bed.

5 Complete the explanations using the words in the boxes.

famous • popular

If a lot of people like you, you are (1) _____ . If a lot of people know who you are, you are (2) _____ . You can be both, but it isn't always true!

tell • say • speak • hear • listen

If you have some information or an opinion, you can (3) _____ someone about it. To do that, you (4) _____ to them. They (5) _____ to what you (6) _____ and talk to you, unless it's so noisy that they can't (7) _____ you!

study • read

When you (8) _____ something that is written, you look at it to understand what it says. When you (9) _____ something, you try hard to understand it and to learn it, often because your teacher has asked you to.

6 Complete this table.

noun	verb	adjective	adverb
1 _____	✗	loud	loudly
2 _____	decide	decisive	decisively
enjoyment	enjoy	3 _____	4 _____
size	✗	5 _____	✗

7 For questions 1–8, choose the option which best completes the passage. You will get two marks for each answer.

BECOMING A SCIENTIST

If you're interested in becoming a scientist, there are a few things you (1) _____ do. First of all, you (2) _____ decide which area of science you want to work in. Is it biology and animals or physics and space that you think (3) _____ interest you most? Another thing you (4) _____ do is speak to your science teacher about it. He or she will tell you what your options are and (5) _____ have some helpful experience. You (6) _____ almost certainly need to go to university to study your chosen science. This can be the hardest time because you (7) _____ prove that you understand many different areas. After your degree, you need to specialise in an area that really interests you. It can be a long, hard road, but at the end of it, you just (8) _____ make a discovery that changes the world.

1 A should   B shall   C will   D would
2 A can   B may   C have to   D shall
3 A might   B must   C can   D has to
4 A shall   B will   C ought to D would
5 A has to   B may   C must   D can
6 A can   B may   C might   D will
7 A may   B might   C shall   D have to
8 A will   B should   C might   D can

Score _____ /60

11 The Learning Curve

Start thinking!

What do you think makes a good school?
How would you improve your school?
Would you like to be a head teacher?

Reading

1 🎧 2.07 Quickly read the newspaper article. Ignore the gaps for now. How has Abbot Hill School changed since Elaine Atkins became head teacher?

Top Marks!

Elaine Atkins, head teacher of Abbot Hill School in Manchester, has turned one of the worst schools in the country into one of the best. Ollie Dawson finds out how she did it.

Three years ago, Abbot Hill School had a dreadful reputation. Teachers didn't want to work there. Parents didn't want to send their children there. The pupils – as seen by the number of children who regularly played truant from school – clearly didn't want to go there. It was a failing school, and a school failing the community. Then Elaine Atkins was appointed head teacher. **1** _____ So how has **she achieved the impossible**?

'It actually wasn't that difficult,' says Elaine with her usual modesty. 'The school was in such a bad state that no-one – not the parents, not the students, not the teachers – valued anything about it. That made it much easier for **an outsider** to come in and say, " **2** _____ We're going to do it differently." And I did have a lot of help too.'

One of the first things Elaine did was call a meeting of all the students, staff and parents. 'Not all of them came, of course, but it was actually very well attended. That's when I realised I had **a chance**. They hadn't given up completely.' She told them some of the things which she wanted to change and put some key issues to the vote. **3** _____ 'I said: "If I introduce a school uniform, will you support me?" The vast majority said they would.'

Elaine believes in things like school uniforms. 'It's all about creating **an environment** where there's discipline and a sense of pride. When I took over, Abbot Hill was out of control. Children were being bullied, and no-one stopped the bullies. **4** _____
A uniform is a symbol that there are limits and that we're all part of the same community.'
Elaine is convinced that discipline is central to students' learning. 'How can they learn anything if there's chaos in the classroom? **5** _____ We've managed to bring that back to Abbot Hill, and it's clearly working. Students are now leaving the school with the qualifications they need. That never happened before. Of course, some students still get in trouble. Children always will. But they know what the rules are, and they know they'll be enforced. There's much less bullying now.'

2 Some words and phrases in the text are in bold. For each one, choose what you think it's referring to.

1 she achieved the impossible (line 9)
   a Elaine's becoming head teacher
   b Elaine's making the school successful
2 an outsider (line 15)
   a Elaine   b someone else
3 a chance (line 22)
   a the possibility of being able to improve the school
   b the opportunity to talk to the parents, staff and pupils
4 an environment (line 29)
   a the natural world   b a school
5 things (line 51)
   a lessons   b activities
6 the things which she'd done (line 63)
   a the changes Elaine has made to the school
   b Elaine's jobs before coming to the school

3 Read the article again. Seven sentences have been removed from the article. Choose from the sentences A–H the one which fits each gap (1–7). There is one extra sentence which you do not need to use.

A No, we're not going to do it like that anymore.
B The teacher has to be in control.
C There were actually many occasions when I thought I'd never succeed in changing the school.
D I wanted them to feel they were part of what was going to happen.
E I have a great time while I'm here, and I know it's teaching me loads of things I need.
F They can choose from sports, aerobics, photography, pottery, drama, dance classes.
G Today, the main problem she faces is a waiting list of parents who are desperate to get their children into the school.
H The students thought they could get away with anything.

It's not all about punishment and discipline, though. Elaine has also introduced a large number of after-class activities. 'Everyone used to go home after the last lesson. Now, there are a
51 huge number of **things** which the students can choose from. None of them are compulsory, so the students don't feel they're being forced to do them. **6**
You name it – we offer it! We also have regular school trips, which are educational and a lot of fun. Some parents come on them too, and that's a great way for us all to get to know each other better. I've always believed that the better you know someone, the easier it is to work together.'
I wondered what the students thought of
63 their head teacher and **the things which she'd done**. Sharon Tucker, 16, who I met outside the school gates, summed up the mood of all the students: 'I used to hate coming to this school. I dreaded it every single morning. Now, I look forward to coming. **7** Mrs Atkins has changed all our lives. We owe her a lot.'

WORD BOX

4 Use words or phrases from the whole article to complete the definitions. You've been given the first letter to help you.

1 If everyone at school wears a s_____ u_____, they all wear the same clothes.
2 If you are b_____, other children often make fun of you or even hit you.
3 People who have q_____ have passed exams and have received certificates.
4 If you are i_____ t_____, you are going to be punished for doing something wrong.
5 If something is c_____, you have to do it.
6 On s_____ t_____, you go with your classmates to visit places like parks and museums.

Have your say!

- Do you think schools should offer after-class activities?
- Discuss some of the advantages and disadvantages.

G Grammar clinic

Relative clauses

👁 Look at *Grammar database* pages 189–190 before you do the exercises.

1 Read the sentences from the article on pages 96 and 97. Decide if statements a and b are true (T) or false (F).

> 1 I wondered what the students thought of their head teacher and the things *which she'd done*.
>   **a** Without the words in italics, the sentence makes complete sense. ☐
>   **b** We could replace *which* with *that*. ☐
>
> 2 We also have regular school trips, *which are educational and a lot of fun*.
>   **a** Without the words in italics, the sentence makes complete sense. ☐
>   **b** We could replace *which* with *that*. ☐

Read through the article again and underline all the examples of 'which' and 'who'. Decide whether they are like sentence 1 or sentence 2 above.

2 Decide whether the words in bold are defining (D) or non-defining (N) relative clauses.

1 My dad, **who went to the same school as me**, remembers all the teachers.   D/N
2 My favourite subject, **which we have twice a week**, is chemistry.   D/N
3 We had a lesson last week **that we all found interesting**.   D/N
4 Mrs Edwards, **who teaches us German**, is very strict.   D/N
5 The only teacher **that I don't like** is Mr Leech.   D/N
6 The room **where we have science lessons** is on the fifth floor.   D/N

3 Choose the correct option in each sentence.

1 The students _____ had finished were allowed to leave.
  a whose   **b** who   **c** whom

2 Our school, _____ opened in 1975, has about 2,000 pupils.
  a that   **b** which   **c** who

3 I went to school in Germany, _____ I was born.
  a when   **b** where   **c** which

4 The school _____ my parents went to has been knocked down.
  a whose   **b** that   **c** whom

5 My favourite teacher is Mrs Woods, _____ husband is also a teacher.
  a whose   **b** that   **c** which

6 Any student _____ in the school play should contact Mr Butler.
  a which   **b** whose   **c** who's

V Vocabulary builder

Education

1 Match the words and phrases in the box with the correct definitions.

suspend • play truant • lesson • break up
prefect • term • expel • subject

1 _____ a period of time (often 45 minutes) when students learn in a classroom
2 _____ miss school without permission or without a good reason
3 _____ a period of time (often 3 months) when a school is open
4 _____ start a school holiday, such as the Christmas holiday
5 _____ tell a student they can't come to school for a short time because they did something wrong
6 _____ something you study at school, such as maths, French, etc
7 _____ a student who is given extra responsibility for making sure other students obey the rules
8 _____ tell a student they can't come to school ever again because they did something wrong

2 Complete the sentences using the correct form of the words from the box in exercise 1.

1 Nick is having problems in history so he's having extra _____ .
2 My cousin was caught _____ and got into a lot of trouble.
3 They usually choose older students to be _____ .
4 We have exams at the end of every _____ and at the end of the year.
5 My brother was _____ for two days for fighting in the playground.
6 They _____ a student last week for stealing from other students' bags.
7 I can't wait until we _____ next week for the summer holidays!
8 It's difficult to choose a favourite _____ , but I quite like computer science.

Phrasal verbs with *over*

3 Phrasal verbs with *over* often have meanings connected to movement or control. Choose the correct option.

1 A car almost _____ our cat just outside our house. Luckily, she was OK.
  a ran over   b got over   c took over
2 Our teacher was very ill, but she finally _____ it and came back to school.
  a took over   b got over   c looked over
3 Why don't you _____ to our house for dinner tomorrow?
  a bring over   b look over   c come over
4 Mrs Riley had to leave the classroom so she asked another teacher to _____ .
  a go over   b look over   c take over
5 If you _____ the page, you'll see the answers.
  a turn over   b pass over   c put over

Magic metaphors

4 When we talk about the *mind*, we sometimes think of it as a *container*, like a box. Complete the sentences with the phrases from the box.

in your mind • at the back of my mind
filled with • an open mind • out of my mind

1 What picture do you have _____ if I say 'summer holiday'?
2 I've been studying really hard and I feel like my mind is _____ facts and figures.
3 I heard a song on the radio this morning and I can't get it _____ .
4 When you meet people from other countries, it's important to keep _____ .
5 I like our history teacher, but I've got a feeling _____ that she doesn't really like me.

11 The Learning Curve

🎧 Listening

1 You are going to listen to five people talking about a school. Before you listen, talk about what the people might mention.

The head teacher: *exam results? achievements?*
A pupil: *lessons? favourite teachers?*
A teacher: *students? lessons?*
The caretaker: *cleaning? damage?*
A parent: *exam results? their child?*

2 **2.08** Listen to five people talking about a school. For questions 1–5, choose from the list (A–F) what each person says about the school. Use the letters only once. There is one extra letter which you do not need to use.

A This school doesn't have such good sports teams.
B Someone is planning to leave the school.
C Pupils don't have to do too much work at home.
D This school doesn't cover modern subjects much.
E People contact me when they have a problem.
F This school is better than a lot of others.

Speaker 1: ____
Speaker 2: ____
Speaker 3: ____
Speaker 4: ____
Speaker 5: ____

Soundbite stress (1)

 2.09 Read the phrases below and decide which words you think are stressed the most. Underline them. Listen and check.

As far as I'm concerned, …
In my opinion, …   } home
If you ask me, …   education
To my mind, …   is a great
From my point of view, … } idea.

🎤 Speaking

1 Complete the phrases using the words in the box.

out • as • second • least • of • as

- X is not _____ useful _____ Y because …
- The most useful _____ all is Z because …
- _____ of these ideas, X is most useful because …
- After X, Y is the _____ best idea because …
- Z is probably the _____ useful idea because …

2 Work in pairs. Use the phrases from exercise 1 to help you make suggestions.

- Discuss how popular these after-class activities would be at your school.
- Decide which one you would recommend to your teacher.

a school website

a debating group

an arts and crafts group

a drama group

👁 Look at *Speaking database - Comparing* and *Giving/Asking for opinion* on page 165.

Use of English

Relative pronouns and prepositions

Look at *Grammar database* page 190 before you do the exercises.

1 Match to make complete sentences.

1 They had corporal punishment at the school which
2 The day which my dad left school
3 Yesterday, I saw the old head teacher of the school where
4 Our school is throwing a big party, to which
5 The day when my dad met my mum
6 Every year, we have a school play, which

a my mum and dad went.
b was the school Sports Day.
c my parents went to.
d all parents are invited to.
e all parents are invited.
f on was his 16th birthday.

Word patterns

2 Complete these phrases with the correct preposition.

1 fond _____
2 keen _____
3 aware _____
4 concentrate _____
5 refer _____
6 complain _____
7 interested _____

3 For questions 1–10, read the text below and decide which answer (A, B, C or D) best fits each gap. There is an example at the beginning (0).

SUMMERHILL SCHOOL

What would you do if your teacher said you could either stay to have your (0) __*lesson*__ or you could go home? Well, just imagine a school where attendance wasn't (1) _____ at all! In Suffolk, in the United Kingdom, that school (2) _____ . Summerhill School was founded in 1921 by a man called A.S. Neill. Neill was (3) _____ of the kinds of problems many children have at school and he believed that the only solution was to give (4) _____ complete freedom.

Children at Summerhill are under no (5) _____ at all to attend lessons. Most of them do, (6) _____ . Often, they come from schools at (7) _____ they were unhappy and (8) _____ to do any work at all. After a while, though, they settle down and usually decide that attending lessons is more interesting.

The other unusual thing about Summerhill is the weekly meeting. All teachers and students decide the school rules democratically, with one (9) _____ each. If a student wants to (10) _____ about a teacher or a teacher wants to tell everyone about a student's bad behaviour, they can do so in the meeting.

Life at Summerhill is full of all kinds of challenges, but most of the people there agree that it's a very special place.

0	A subject	B work	C lesson	D timetable
1	A necessary	B compulsory	C needed	D forced
2	A is	B runs	C exists	D opens
3	A interested	B concentrated	C expert	D aware
4	A them	B these	C those	D their
5	A stress	B rules	C pressure	D control
6	A although	B however	C yet	D despite
7	A that	B there	C where	D which
8	A refuse	B object	C deny	D oppose
9	A choice	B vote	C count	D decision
10	A refer	B mention	C discuss	D complain

4 What do you think of Summerhill School? Would you like to go to a school like that?

11 Writing

An informal letter/email

👁 Look at *Writing database - informal letters/emails* on page 154 before you do the exercises.

1 Read this writing task. Why should your letter be informal?

> Your pen friend is doing a class project on the educational system in different countries. She has asked you for some information about your country. Read this extract from your pen friend's letter and use the notes you have made to write your letter.

Write a **letter** of between **120** and **150** words. You must use grammatically correct sentences with accurate spelling and punctuation in a style appropriate for the situation. Do not write any addresses.

> nursery, primary, secondary – mention ages
> take exams in school every year
> take important exams at 18 for university

> Anyway, apart from that, I wanted to ask you for a favour. We're doing a project at school on education in different countries. Is there any chance you could give me some information about your country? You know, what kind of schools you have, when you take exams, that sort of thing.
>
> Thanks.
>
> Got to go (yes, more homework!).
>
> Love,
> Andrea

2 Tick (✓) the correct statements about the writing task in exercise 1.

1. You don't need to write in paragraphs. ☐
2. You can use contractions such as *don't*. ☐
3. You can use chat phrases such as *lol*. ☐
4. You don't need to write in sentences. ☐
5. You should write addresses at the top. ☐
6. Correct spelling is important. ☐
7. You should include all the information given. ☐
8. Correct punctuation is important. ☐

Working model

3 Read the answer to the writing task written by a French student.

4 Decide if the statements are true (T) or false (F).

1. The writer has included all the information he had to. ☐
2. He has used an informal tone. ☐
3. He didn't need to use paragraphs in an informal letter. ☐
4. He asks his friend about a piece of news to begin. ☐

> Dear Andrea,
>
> Thanks for your letter! How was your party? You asked about the educational system here. Well, most people go to nursery school between two and six years old. I went when I was four and I loved it! Then, from six onwards, education is compulsory and everyone goes to primary school. The schools are usually quite small and you stay there until you're 10.
>
> From 11 to 14, we go to secondary school. At 15, we move to another school – a bit like senior high in America. We stay there till 18 and then either get a job or go to university.
>
> We take exams at school every year, but the really important ones come at the age of 18. You have to get good grades to get into university.
>
> I have to go shopping with my mum now. I hope that was useful! Write soon!
>
> Best wishes,
> Paul

Ready to write!

5 Complete the passage using the words and phrases in the box.

> secondary • sixth form • senior high • primary
> elementary • junior high • nursery

Education systems in Britain and America

Britain and America have different education systems. In both countries, most children go to (1) _____ school (or kindergarten) between the ages of three and five. Then, in Britain, they start (2) _____ school, where they stay until they are 11. This is followed by (3) _____ school until age 16. If they stay at school, they go into the (4) _____ until they are 18. Sometimes, this means going to a special college.

In America, children go to (5) _____ school from five to 11. Then, they go to middle school (also called (6) _____ school) until age 14. From 15–18, American children attend high school (sometimes called (7) _____ school).

6 You are going to answer the writing task in exercise 1. You are going to write about your country. Make a plan of your answer.

- How are you going to start your letter?
- What news are you going to ask your pen friend about first?
- What are you going to tell her about nursery schools?
- What are you going to tell her about primary schools?
- What are you going to tell her about secondary schools?
- What are you going to say about exams?
- How do you want to close your letter?
- How are you going to write your name at the end?

Now complete *Writing Planner 11* on page 160.

Now write!

7 You are now ready to write your letter to your pen friend. Use informal language. Include all the information you have to. Write between 120 and 150 words.

Check it out!

8 Check your work. Tick (✓) what you have done.

- I have started and finished the letter in the correct way. ☐
- I have used informal language. ☐
- I have told my pen friend about the educational system in my country. ☐
- I have included all the information I had to. ☐
- I have used paragraphs. ☐
- I have checked my spelling, grammar and punctuation. ☐
- My letter is between 120 and 150 words long. ☐

Look Back

Can you answer these questions? If you can't remember, look through the unit for the answers.

1. What do the children at Abbot Hill School wear now?
2. Which of these is correct?
   school journey   school trip   school excursion
3. When a relative clause just gives us extra information, do we use commas or not?
4. What do you not do if you 'play truant'?
5. What is unusual about Summerhill School in the UK?

Fighting Fit

Start thinking!

How important is keeping fit?
What do people do to keep fit?
What do you personally do to keep fit?

Reading

1 **2.10** Read this information about a local fitness centre. How popular are places like this in your country?

Your Chance to Make Waves!

The Waves Fitness Centre is now open for business! It's the biggest and best fitness centre in the local area, and it's got lots to offer the whole community. Whether you want to get in shape or you're just looking to have fun, we've got everything you need at Waves! And many of our activities are available to non-members for a small fee!

A Waves Pool
Our pool is much more than just a place to swim. It's big enough to keep the whole family entertained! Our wave machine, our water slide and our Ducklings area for pre-school children mean that there's something for everyone. And because swimming is low impact and easy on your body, it's a great form of exercise for the over-60s and people with disabilities. It's never too late to start! We offer Water Walking sessions from 10–11am on weekdays for those who are not used to exercise – walking against the water really helps to build those muscles! – and Power Pool sessions at the weekend from 9–10am for those with more experience. Please note that the Waves Pool has a strict admissions policy and children under eight must be accompanied by an adult unless they are able to pass a short swimming test (call for details).

B Waves Gym
Come and work out in style at the Waves Gym. It's such a cool gym that you'll want to come every day! And with opening hours from 7am–7pm you can! Simply sign up, wait a day for your gym membership to be approved, and then away you go! We offer everything from body building to simply getting fit, with an Active Start programme for complete beginners (please book a place in advance) and a personal trainer for those of you who really want to achieve their goals. On Tuesday and Thursday mornings, you can join one of our aerobics classes, a great way to meet people and get fit, while every Friday at 12 there's a chance to join our Expert Group, for those who really want a challenge. Please note that no children under 12 are allowed in the gym.

C Dance classes
Dance classes are such a great way to exercise that you won't want to stop! We have a full schedule of classes, from modern dance (Mon–Fri, 2–3pm) to traditional ballroom dancing (Weds–Sat, 1–2pm). Whether you want to improve your social life or your appearance, dance is a motivating way to a new you, and it's not just for the young and healthy. Our Senior Dance on Tuesday evenings is great for those over 55. It's so easy that anyone can do it! For those who are more adventurous, we also run high-energy World Dance classes with fast music from around the world to keep you on your toes. Please note that all dance classes need to be booked in advance and charge an individual course fee. Children under 12 are welcome at all our sessions except World Dance.

2 Look through the information again to find the answers to these questions. Don't read the passage in detail.

1 When can you do ballroom dancing?
_____
2 When can you do Water Walking?
_____
3 When can you play squash?
_____
4 When can you learn about Pilates?
_____
5 When does the Expert Group meet?
_____

3 Read the information again. For questions 1–6, choose from the activities (A–E). The activities may be chosen more than once.

Which activity/activities would you recommend for someone who:

wants to take part in a competition? 1 ____

doesn't want to spend more than their membership fee? 2 ____ 3 ____ 4 ____

wants to meet new people? 5 ____ 6 ____

wants a healthier body and a healthier mind? 7 ____

wants to take part in an activity immediately? 8 ____

is 10 and wants to do an activity without an adult? 9 ____ 10 ____

Racket Sports
Whether it's indoor tennis, badminton or squash, you can have a full-body workout on the court. Racket sport sessions are available during the centre's opening hours (7am-7pm, seven days a week) and are included in the membership fee (extra charge for equipment hire). Racket sports are so popular that the courts are often fully booked. Please make sure that you book courts at least one day in advance, or two days in the case of non-members. For those of you who are competitive, we run Waves Contests in all racket sports, which are free to members – just ask at Reception for an entry form and details of charges for non-members. Children under 12 must be accompanied at all times on the courts.

Pilates Classes
Pilates is a system of exercise that is designed to improve your physical and mental health. It is popular around the world, and we're pleased to be able to offer five sessions a week with a professional instructor. Choose any two weeknights to suit you and come along to the session from 6 till 7pm. You'll strengthen your central muscles and also train your mind to concentrate, which will help at work or in your studies. Our introductory session, which everyone who is interested must attend before joining a class, is on the first Saturday of each month and it will help you decide if Pilates is for you. Just bring along some comfortable clothes and a desire to learn! Please note that Pilates sessions are adults-only and are not included in the membership fee.

For further information on any of our activities, contact Waves Reception.

WORD BOX

4 Use words or phrases from the article to complete the sentences. You've been given the first letter to help you.

1 I really want to get i_____ s_____ , so I've started going to a gym twice a week.
2 You have to be very careful when you w_____ o_____ because it's easy to injure yourself.
3 Many famous people have their own personal t_____ who advises them on their fitness.
4 My mum's started going to a_____ c_____ to get fit and she likes meeting all the other women there.
5 I'm not used to a lot of exercise, so my m_____ start to hurt when I play too much sport.
6 If you do b_____ b_____ , you have to work very hard to get ready for shows and competitions.

Have your say!

- Do young people you know get enough exercise?
- What could we do to encourage them to exercise more?

12 G Grammar clinic

Result clauses: so, such, too, enough

👁 Look at *Grammar database* pages 191–192 before you do the exercises.

1 Read the extracts from the article on pages 104 and 105 and decide if the statements are true (T) or false (F).

Racket sports are *so* popular *that* the courts are often fully booked.

It's big *enough* to keep the whole family entertained!

Dance classes are *such* a great way to exercise that you won't want to stop!

It's never *too* late to start!

1 *So* can be followed by an adjective and a *that* clause. ☐
2 *Enough* is followed by an adjective or adverb. ☐
3 *Such* is used in exactly the same way as *so*. ☐
4 *Too* is followed by an adjective or an adverb. ☐

2 Complete each sentence with a word from the box. You will use some words more than once.

so • such • too • enough

1 I'm _____ unfit that I have to join a gym.
2 I might be fit _____ to run a marathon soon!
3 The gym was _____ a success that they've opened another one.
4 It's _____ late to go to the gym today.
5 Are you old _____ to join the dance classes?
6 The gym is _____ expensive I can't afford it.

3 Complete each sentence so that it means the same as the first sentence. Use the words given without changing them. Use no more than five words.

1 Fried food is very unhealthy, which means it can lead to a heart attack. **so**
   Fried food _____ it can lead to a heart attack.
2 Some people take so many pills that it must be bad for them. **such**
   Some people take _____ that it must be bad for them.
3 My grandma is too ill to leave the house. **enough**
   My grandma _____ to leave the house.
5 Lots of people don't do enough exercise. **so**
   There _____ people who don't do enough exercise.
6 I'm so clumsy that I couldn't be a surgeon. **too**
   I'm _____ a surgeon.

4 Complete the sentences to make statements about yourself. Use your imagination if you like!

1 I'm so _____ that _____ .
   eg *I'm so fit that I can run a marathon in three hours!*
2 I'm such a(n) _____ that _____ .
   eg *I'm such a lazy person that I never tidy my room!*
3 I'm not _____ enough to _____ .
   eg *I'm not old enough to drive a car.*
4 I'm too _____ to _____ .
   eg *I'm too short to be a basketball player.*

V Vocabulary builder

Medicine and health

1 Match the words in the box with the correct definitions.

prescription • diagnosis • allergy • cure • symptom • surgery • GP • injection

1 _____ a sign such as spots or a cough that shows you are ill
2 _____ a general practitioner, a kind of general doctor you see when you think you are ill
3 _____ a doctor's office
4 _____ a piece of paper a doctor gives you which you take to a chemist to get the right medicine
5 _____ a doctor's opinion of what is wrong with you
6 _____ a remedy or treatment
7 _____ the action of putting medicine into your body using a syringe
8 _____ a medical condition where your body reacts badly to some things you eat, breathe, etc

Collocations: *make* / *do*

2 Complete the phrases using either *make* or *do*.

_____ an appointment
_____ a complaint
_____ some exercise
_____ the housework
_____ a noise
_____ up your mind
_____ your best
_____ a fuss
_____ a mess
_____ a phone call
_____ the washing-up
_____ a suggestion

_____ your homework
_____ the bed
_____ friends
_____ a mistake
_____ sure
_____ well at something
_____ a decision
_____ an effort
_____ you good
_____ money
_____ the shopping
_____ a meal

3 Write sentences with three of the phrases from exercise 2. In groups, compare your sentences.

Magic metaphors

4 When we talk about *problems*, we sometimes use words or phrases that have a connection with *illness*. Complete the sentences with the words from the box.

headache • unhealthy • recover • get over

1 Samantha's been having a few problems at school lately, but she should _____ them before her exams.
2 Trying to organise a wedding is a real _____ ! There are just so many problems to deal with.
3 The company is in a(n) _____ financial situation and it doesn't look like things are going to get any better.
4 It took me a long time to _____ from failing my exams, but in the end I decided to take them again.

Listening

1 🎧 **2.11** Listen to an interview with a woman who is on a diet. Decide whether each statement is true (T) or false (F).

1 Judy thinks that she is too fat. _____
2 Judy can eat fast food during the diet. _____
3 Judy has to think about different types of food. _____
4 Judy gets points when she doesn't eat something. _____

2 Listen again. For questions 1–5, choose the best answer (A, B or C).

1 Judy started the diet after
  A she realised she had to lose weight.
  B she decided she needed more energy.
  C someone at a gym recommended it.
2 With the diet, you need to
  A know some facts about what you eat.
  B understand that chips are bad for you.
  C learn that junk food makes you fat.
3 Judy says we should eat
  A more fruit and vegetables.
  B all types of food.
  C more fatty foods.
4 Cream is in
  A the 'Enjoyment' group.
  B the same group as pasta.
  C the same group as eggs.
5 How many points does Judy try to get each day?
  A five
  B nine
  C ten

Soundbite /ɑː/, /ɔː/ and /uː/

🎧 **2.12** Look at the vowel sounds that are underlined in the words. In each group of four, one word has a different vowel sound. Circle the odd one out. Listen and check.

1 c<u>a</u>r   f<u>a</u>t   f<u>a</u>ther   c<u>a</u>n't
2 w<u>o</u>rd   sw<u>o</u>rd c<u>ou</u>rt   b<u>o</u>red
3 b<u>oo</u>t l<u>oo</u>k   t<u>oo</u>   sh<u>oo</u>t

Speaking

Useful Phrases

1 Complete the answer with words and phrases from the box.

Of course • so • To begin with
but • Secondly • For example

Do you think we are healthier than people 50 years ago?

Yes, we are. _____ , we have a better diet. _____ , people today eat more fruit and vegetables. _____ , we also eat more fast food, _____ generally our diet is better. _____ , doctors can cure more illnesses, _____ we live longer. Yes, we're definitely healthier today.

Useful Phrases

2 In pairs, talk about the following questions. Use the phrases from exercise 1 to help you.
• Do you think we are healthier today than people were 50 years ago?
• What are the main health problems young people face?
• Do you think all medical care should be free?
• What is a healthy diet?

I can see that there are arguments on both sides. As far as I'm concerned, …

`Teenagers face many health problems, including ...`

Absolutely. Yes. People today …

From what I've heard, I think people need …

◆ Look at *Speaking database - Giving/Asking for opinion* on page 165.

Use of English

Infinitives of purpose

👁 Look at *Grammar database* page 192 before you do the exercises.

1 Rewrite the sentences using the phrase in bold. The first one has been done as an example.
1 I thought I should ask the doctor about going on a diet so I went to the surgery. **in order**
   I went to the surgery in order to ask about going on a diet.
2 I had to lose some weight, so I went on a strict diet. **in order** _____
3 She doesn't want to get ill, so my mum takes vitamin tablets. **in order** _____
4 Because they want to keep fit, many people take up sports. **so as** _____
5 I want to stay healthy, so I try to eat lots of fruit. **in order** _____
6 I didn't want to catch a cold, so I wore a warm coat and a scarf. **in order** _____

Word patterns

2 Complete the sentences using the words in the box. You may need to change the form of the words.

> object • approve • prevent • capable
> congratulate • afraid • succeed • manage

1 Some people don't _____ of smoking because it's bad for your health.
2 When you're seriously ill, you're not really _____ of working.
3 If they _____ to find a cure for cancer, it'll be a great discovery.
4 Some people believe that eating garlic can help _____ you from getting ill.
5 We rang my brother to _____ him on passing his medical degree.
6 In order to _____ in becoming a doctor, you need to work very hard.
7 If I was a doctor, I'd constantly be _____ of catching something from my patients!
8 Dr Frankenstein was surprised to discover that some people _____ to his medical experiments.

3 Choose three of the words and write sentences. In groups, compare your sentences.

4 For questions 1–10, read the text below and think of the word which best fits each gap. Use only one word in each gap. There is an example at the beginning (0). Write your answers IN CAPITAL LETTERS.

ALTERNATIVE MEDICINE

What do you do when you're ill? You probably call your doctor, (0) __WHO__ examines you, makes a diagnosis and then gives you (1) _____ prescription. These days, more and more people are asking themselves (2) _____ this is the best way of dealing with illness. They object (3) _____ taking too many pills and look around in (4) _____ to find other cures.
Most cultures practise some form (5) _____ traditional medicine. This is often based (6) _____ plants, or other natural ingredients. They are usually prepared in some way (7) _____ as to make them more effective, for example by drying them and making them (8) _____ a powder.
The Chinese, in particular, have a large number of traditional medical techniques. One of them is acupuncture, (9) _____ involves sticking needles into the patient! It might sound a little strange, but many people have used acupuncture for everything (10) _____ giving up smoking to dealing with pain.
So, the next time you're ill, maybe you should look for an alternative before you send for the doctor!

12 Writing

A report

👁 Look at *Writing database - reports* on page 151 before you do the exercises.

1 It's important to think about the purpose of your writing. Match the types of writing to the purposes for writing.

1 story _____
2 report _____
3 review _____
4 letter of application _____
5 informal letter/email _____
6 formal letter/email _____
7 essay _____
8 article _____

a to be offered a job or to get an interview for a job
b to exchange information with someone you don't know well, or someone in a position of authority
c to interest the reader by giving your opinion about a book you've read, film you've seen, place you've visited, etc
d to entertain and inform your readers by writing on a subject that will interest them
e to present information and recommendations in a clear, well organised and formal way
f to entertain your readers with interesting descriptions and characters
g to gossip and swap news or information in a friendly, chatty way
h to present an argument in a clear, logical way

2 Read this writing task. Who is going to read your report?

> You work for a local tourist office and your manager has asked you to write a report on health facilities in the area. The report will be used to produce a leaflet for tourists coming to your area.

Write a **report** of between **120** and **180** words in an appropriate style.

Working model

3 Read the answer to the writing task.

4 This report was written by Sharon Gilmore. Her manager is Elizabeth Watson. Correct the first part of the report.

To: **My manager**
From: **Me**
Subject: **What you asked me to do**

Introduction
As requested, I have done some research into health facilities in this area. There is a hospital, an eye clinic and a large number of doctors' surgeries. This is very good for such a small town.

Westford Hospital
Westford Hospital is modern, with beds for about 1,000 patients. They deal with illnesses and accidents, although people who are seriously ill are moved to Pentonfield, 20 miles away. Tourists are treated at the hospital for free.

Westford Eye Clinic
Westford has very good facilities for eye problems. The eye clinic takes patients from all over the world and the doctors and surgeons are very highly trained. It is unlikely that tourists would need the eye clinic.

Doctors' surgeries
There are about 30 GPs' surgeries in Westford. They deal with minor illnesses and accidents. Most of them charge for treating people who are not local residents.

Conclusion
In conclusion, it is clear that Westford has excellent medical facilities for a small town. Tourists are welcome at the hospital and eye clinic, although they may have to pay to see a local GP.

5 Decide if the statements about the report on page 110 are true (T) or false (F).
1. The language used is generally informal. ☐
2. Each paragraph has its own heading. ☐
3. It presents information in a clear way. ☐

Ready to write!

6 Look at this writing task. Who is going to read your report?

> You work for a sports shop and the manager is thinking of starting a new gym. He has asked you to write a report on gym facilities in the area. Your manager wants to know what you recommend.

Write a **report** of between **120** and **180** words in an appropriate style.

7 Make a plan of your answer. Use your imagination.

- How are you going to start your report?
  To: ....
  From: ....
  Subject: ....

- What have you done / who have you spoken to in order to write your report?

- What is the name of the first gym you are going to write about?
  What are you going to say about it?

- What is the name of the second gym you are going to write about?
  What are you going to say about it?

- What is the name of the third gym you are going to write about?
  What are you going to say about it?

- What recommendations are you going to make in your conclusion?

Now complete *Writing Planner 12* on page 160.

Now write!

8 You are now ready to write your report for your manager. Use formal language. Keep your purpose in mind.

Check it out!

9 Check your work. Tick (✓) what you have done.

- I have started the report in the right way. ☐
- I have used clear paragraphs with appropriate headings. ☐
- I have used formal language. ☐
- I have made appropriate recommendations. ☐
- I have described the main activities. ☐
- I have checked my spelling and my grammar. ☐
- My report is between 120 and 180 words long. ☐

◀ Look Back

Can you answer these questions? If you can't remember, look through the unit for the answers.

1. Which phrasal verb means 'exercise'?
2. If something is 'too big', is that a good thing or a bad thing?
3. What does a doctor give you to take to the chemist?
4. Which of these is wrong?
   *do some exercise   make a mistake
   do a suggestion*
5. Which preposition do we use with 'congratulate'?

Revision
Units 11-12

1 Choose the correct option.

1 I'm going to try to get _____ shape before the summer holidays.
   A off   B on   C over   D in

2 The doctor gave me a _____ for some medicine for my throat.
   A recipe   B diagnosis   C prescription   D cure

3 Both my parents work in _____ education, teaching at a college.
   A higher   B greater   C bigger   D larger

4 Maths is definitely my least favourite _____ .
   A lesson   B term   C subject   D timetable

5 If you ever _____ truant again, you'll be in big trouble.
   A are   B play   C do   D make

6 I think the baby's ill. Maybe we should call the _____ .
   A PG   B DC   C GP   D MA

7 A boy in my class was _____ for three days for fighting.
   A suspended   B qualified   C expelled   D troubled

8 Our school year is divided up into three _____ .
   A periods   B stages   C terms   D halves

9 We're going on a school _____ to a local museum next week.
   A excursion   B journey   C travel   D trip

10 Try not to get _____ trouble so much this term!
   A on   B in   C at   D out

2 Choose the correct option.

1 Everybody _____ meets John thinks he's a really nice person.
   A who   B which   C whom

2 The Town Hall, _____ was built in 1875, has been damaged in a fire.
   A who   B that   C which

3 This is the restaurant _____ Peter took me on our first date.
   A which   B that   C where

4 Everybody passed the test with top marks, _____ was a little surprising.
   A which   B that   C who

5 Stan Laurel, _____ partner was Oliver Hardy, was born in 1890.
   A which   B whose   C whom

3 Circle *make* or *do* to complete the phrases.

1 *make/do* a suggestion
2 *make/do* the shopping
3 *make/do* a mess
4 *make/do* some exercise
5 *make/do* a mistake
6 *make/do* up your mind
7 *make/do* friends
8 *make/do* a complaint
9 *make/do* you good
10 *make/do* a meal

4 Complete the letter using the correct form of the phrasal verbs in the box.

get over • break up • take over • run over • work out

Dear Kelly,

Hi! I haven't heard from you for ages. How are you? I'm fine. We (1) _____ for the Easter holidays last week so I decided to join a gym at last! I'm really out of shape and I wanted to start (2) _____ before the summer comes.

The first day at the gym was terrible, though! I was almost (3) _____ by a car on my way there! I managed to jump out of the way just in time but I fell and hurt my ankle. I couldn't do any exercise at all! The trainer got someone else to (4) _____ his aerobics class while he examined my ankle. It wasn't broken, and I (5) _____ it in the end, but it was a bit frightening, I can tell you.

Now I'm off to the gym to try again. Take care and write soon.

Love,
Sandy

5 Circle the correct preposition to go with each word.

1 capable *of*/*on*
2 complain *in*/*about*
3 approve *to*/*of*
4 afraid *on*/*of*
5 concentrate *to*/*on*
6 aware *about*/*of*
7 keen *on*/*of*
8 succeed *to*/*in*
9 prevent *on*/*from*
10 refer *in*/*to*

6 Complete the sentences using the correct form of the phrases in exercise 5.

1 You should put your car in the garage overnight to _____ it _____ getting stolen.
2 A number of customers _____ the service to the manager.
3 With all this noise, I can't _____ my homework!
4 I remember being very _____ the dark when I was little.
5 Who do you think the head teacher was _____ when she said 'a star student'?
6 By now, most people must be _____ the damage that smoking can do.
7 This mobile is _____ running for a month without you charging the battery!
8 My grandparents don't _____ young people having a tattoo.
9 I don't like tomatoes much, but I am really _____ pizza – and that has tomatoes on it!
10 I'd like to be a doctor, if I _____ getting into university.

7 Circle the correct word in each sentence.

1 I can't wait until I'm old *so*/*such*/*enough* to ride a motorbike.
2 My dad's *so*/*such*/*too* forgetful that sometimes he can't find the car!
3 There were *so*/*such*/*too* many people at the party that there was nowhere to dance.
4 Tommy is *so*/*such*/*enough* a good runner that he might be in the next Olympics®!
5 My grandparents have always wanted to live in Spain, but they're *so*/*such*/*too* old to do it now.

8 Complete the definitions with one word. You have been given the first letter to help.

1 If you have to do something, it is c_____ .
2 A doctor's office is called a s_____ .
3 A person who advises you about fitness is a t_____ .
4 The parts of your body that give you strength are your m_____ .
5 If you have letters such as 'MA' after your name, it tells people what q_____ you have.

Score ____ /60

13

Art Attack

Start thinking!

Have you ever been to an art gallery?
Which of these works of art do you prefer? Why?
Can you name any famous artists?
Do you like to paint or draw?

Reading

1 🎧 **2.13** Quickly read the short story. Ignore the gaps for now. Describe briefly what happens.

The competition

'Sadie, you're creative,' said Sadie's mum, handing her the newspaper. 'Here's something that'll keep you busy for five minutes.'

'Why are you giving me the crossword, Mum?' said Sadie.

'You know I don't like crosswords.'

'Not that,' said her mum. 'This!'

Sadie's mum pointed to a small advertisement on the same page as the crossword. Sadie read it aloud. 'Are you an artist? Painting competition. Free entry. Open to all amateur artists. The top fifty paintings received by August 15th will be displayed at an exhibition in an art gallery in London.' Sadie sat there thinking. 'Yeah, maybe,' she said at last, but her mind was racing. 'August 15th,' she thought to herself. 'That gives me three weeks. **1** All my friends are on holiday. But what am I going to paint?'

Sadie was too excited to sleep that night. 'I know I can do a good picture if I really try,' she thought. 'An art gallery in London! Wouldn't that be great?' For hours, she ran through the options. 'I'm not doing an abstract, that's for sure. **2** It's got to be something with detail. A still life picture, like a bowl of fruit? Maybe, but it's a bit boring. A landscape? I could do the view of the hill from my bedroom window. No – it's got to be something that will stand out. Something that expresses real emotion. Something that shows that I can paint.' As Sadie finally drifted off to sleep, she whispered the words to herself over and over again: 'A portrait. I'm going to paint a portrait …'

Sadie got to work. She had it all planned out. Base it on a photograph. Do a sketch first. And then when she was happy with that, do the full painting. She spent hours each day up in her room. Whenever her mum asked her how it was going, all she'd say was 'Fine.' When her mum asked her if she needed any help, all she'd say was 'No, thanks.' When, two weeks later, the painting was finished, and Sadie's mum said 'Can I see it now?' Sadie replied 'Not now. I'll send it off. **3** If I don't, then it's not worth seeing, anyway.'

August 15th, August 16th and August 17th came and went, and there was no news from the competition judges. 'Don't worry, love,' said Sadie's mum. **4** 'You'll hear one way or the other in time. I've got my fingers crossed for you.'

'Sadie!' shouted her mum, up the stairs. 'There's a phone call for you!' It was September 5th, and Sadie had convinced herself that her painting hadn't been chosen. 'Who is it?' she asked as she came down the stairs. Her mum just handed her the phone.

'Hello?' said Sadie.

'Hello, is that Sadie Taggart?' said the voice at the other end.

2 Decide what each paragraph is about.

Paragraph 1 ____	a working alone
Paragraph 2 ____	b reading the advertisement
Paragraph 3 ____	c being at the event
Paragraph 4 ____	d not understanding
Paragraph 5 ____	e trying to make Sadie feel better
Paragraph 6 ____	f getting good news
Paragraph 7 ____	g having different options

3 Read the story again. Six sentences have been removed from the story. Choose from the sentences A–G the one which fits each gap (1–6). There is one extra sentence which you do not need to use.

A They might look good, but they don't show off your talent.
B It'll take them a bit of time to choose the winners.
C Sadie's heart started beating faster than it had ever beaten before.
D That's enough time, and I've got nothing else to do.
E I always knew you were a genius, Sadie.
F They were both nervous and needed to collect their thoughts for a moment before entering.
G If I win, you can come and see it at the exhibition.

'Yes,' said Sadie.

'Hi, Sadie,' said the voice. 'I'm calling about the painting competition you entered.' **5**

'We've judged all the paintings now and I'm very pleased to tell you that your painting has been selected. I was one of the judges and, I have to tell you, considering your age, I thought it was a real work of art. Very well done! I do hope you'll be able to make it to London to the exhibition.'

Four weeks later, Sadie and her mum were standing on the pavement outside the Shoreham Gallery. **6** While they were standing there in silence, looking at each other, the front door opened. A man came out. 'I recognise you,' he said to Sadie's mum, smiling.

'Me? But we've never met before!' said Sadie's mum with surprise.

'Ah, but I've seen you before. In Sadie's picture. Yes, yes, a very good likeness. Very good indeed. Do come in. Everyone's talking about Sadie's wonderful picture.'

WORD BOX

4 Match the words or phrases in the box with the correct definitions.

creative • portrait • talent • art gallery
sketch • work of art • genius • abstract

1 _____ natural ability to do something well
2 _____ place where paintings, etc are displayed
3 _____ painting, etc of high quality
4 _____ painting of a real person
5 _____ draw something quickly, without adding a lot of detail
6 _____ (of art) showing areas of colour instead of objects or people
7 _____ person who is naturally extremely good at something
8 _____ having new ideas and a good imagination

Have your say!

- Did you enjoy reading this story?
- Would you ever consider entering a competition like the one Sadie entered?

Grammar clinic

The causative

👁 Look at *Grammar database* page 193 before you do the exercises.

1 Read this sentence and choose the correct option.

My mum's going to have her portrait painted.

1 Who is going to paint the portrait?
   a the speaker's mother   b an artist
2 What is the object of the sentence?
   a my mum   b her portrait
3 What verb is used here to form the causative?
   _____ + object + past participle

   What other verb could be used?

2 Read the sentences. Choose one other sentence which means the same.

1 We are paying an artist to paint a new picture for the living room.
   a We are having an artist painted for the living room.
   b We are having a new picture painted for the living room.
2 Dad has asked someone to do a sculpture for our garden.
   a Dad is having a sculpture done for our garden.
   b Dad has done a sculpture for our garden.
3 Our art teacher arranged for our pictures to be hung in the local art gallery.
   a The local gallery got our pictures hung by our art teacher.
   b Our art teacher got our pictures hung in the local gallery.
4 A local architect has been asked to design a new restaurant for *McBurger's*.
   a *McBurger's* are having their new restaurant designed by a local architect.
   b A local architect is having a new restaurant designed by *McBurger's*.

3 Correct the sentences that have mistakes in them. One sentence has no mistakes. Which one?

1 Why don't you have cut your hair before you have taken your photo?
2 You should get your new house designed by a professional.
3 Not many people their portrait have had painted by a famous artist.
4 My dad has had published a book about the history of art.
5 Many companies have created for them new works of art.

4 Complete each sentence so that it means the same as the first sentence. Use the words given without changing them. Use no more than five words.

1 They hope the Queen will open the new gallery.   **opened**

   They hope to _____ by the Queen.

2 Thieves have stolen 10 paintings from the museum in the last four months.   **had**

   The museum _____ in the last four months.

3 A famous graffiti artist is going to come and paint a school wall for us.   **painted**

   We are going to _____ by a famous graffiti artist.

4 We have asked someone to write some music especially for our wedding.   **written**

   We are _____ especially for our wedding.

5 Jen got a friend to design her poster.   **got**

   Jen _____ a friend.

6 Someone was redecorating their hall when I went round.   **having**

   They _____ when I went round.

V Vocabulary builder

Art and artists

1 Use the words in the box to describe the pictures.

easel • frame • brush • statue • sculptor • composer

2 Complete the sentences using the correct form of the words from the box in exercise 1.

1. Beethoven was one of the greatest _____ who ever lived.
2. I bought myself a new poster yesterday and now I need to get a(n) _____ for it.
3. Henry Moore was a famous _____, whose works of art can be seen all over the world.
4. Most towns put up _____ of local people who everyone respects.
5. When painting with oils, it's very important that you remember to clean your _____ .
6. I've got a small wooden _____ that I can take with me when I want to do some painting outside.

Word formation: suffixes

3 Use the suffixes (endings) to create as many adjectives derived from these words as you can. Write the negative adjectives where appropriate. Be careful with spelling.

act • addition • anxiety • believe • comfort • create
desire • effect • end • expense • fame • finance
harm • help • industry • nerve • profession • reason
recognise • success • use • value

Magic metaphors

4 When we talk about *descriptions*, we sometimes use words or phrases that have a connection with *painting and drawing*. Complete the sentences with the words from the box.

image • colourful • outline • picture

1. In this chapter, the writer gives a very _____ description of his early childhood.
2. He was the _____ of his grandfather at the same age.
3. In this book, Dickens paints a detailed _____ of the poor people of London.
4. I'd like to _____ for you the company's plans for next year.

-ous	-ful	-less	-al	-able	-ive
nervous	successful	helpless	financial	desirable	expensive

13 Art Attack

Listening

1 🎧 **2.14** You are going to listen to five conversations in an art gallery. As you listen, decide what the relationships between the people are.

Conversation 1 ____   a two friends who are at college
Conversation 2 ____   b two friends who live together
Conversation 3 ____   c an artist and the gallery owner
Conversation 4 ____   d two friends who work together
Conversation 5 ____   e a guide and a visitor to the gallery

2 You will now hear the conversations again. For questions 1–5, choose the best answer (A, B or C).

1 What does the woman say about Picasso?
  A He was important in the development of art.
  B He used light colours in all his paintings.
  C He started painting around 1905.

2 What does the man say about their manager?
  A He doesn't understand modern art.
  B He doesn't like works of art in the office.
  C He has traditional tastes in art.

3 What do the women have different opinions about?
  A what to get for the living room
  B the artist's other paintings
  C who the painting is by

4 Why are these two men visiting the gallery?
  A to help them decide what furniture to get
  B to look at other works of art to get ideas
  C to pass some time before their lectures

5 Why did the owner choose this position for the artist's work?
  A His work is similar to another artist's.
  B It was one of the artist's demands.
  C She wanted two different works next to each other.

Soundbite — silent letters (2)

🎧 **2.15** Circle the words where you think the 'h' is silent. Listen and check.

1 hour
2 hello
3 himself
4 heir
5 handkerchief
6 honour
7 heel
8 humour

Speaking — Useful Phrases

1 Circle the correct words to complete the phrases.
- spend time *to do/doing*
- make time *to do/doing* something
- spend time *on/at* something
- waste time *to do/doing* something
- be *short/small* of free time
- have enough time *to do/doing* something

2 In pairs, ask and answer the questions. Try to say as much as you can. Use the phrases from exercise 1 to help you.
- Do you have any hobbies?
- How much time do you spend on them each week?
- Do you feel you have enough free time? Why? / Why not?
- What else do you do in your free time?
- What kind of music do you like?
- Do you play any musical instruments? Would you like to?
- Are there any hobbies or free time activities you'd like to take up?

Useful Phrases

Well, I don't really have much free time, but when I do, I …

Yes, I have a few hobbies. I like …

Actually, I think I have quite a lot of free time. I enjoy ...

👁 Look at *Speaking database - Giving personal information* and *Expressing preferences* on page 165.

Use of English

Gradable and ungradable adjectives and adverbs

👁 Look at *Grammar database* page 193 before you do the exercises.

1 Circle the correct word or phrase in each sentence.
1. My mum loves *absolutely/really* expensive modern works of art.
2. I find it *completely/a little* difficult to get the colours right.
3. I think Roy Lichtenstein's art is *absolutely/fairly* brilliant.
4. I've made a few mistakes because I drew it *totally/a bit* quickly.
5. Trying to paint like van Gogh is *totally/very* impossible.
6. It's *completely/quite* hard to produce something that other people like.

... totally, absolutely, completely, fantastic!

Synonyms

2 Match the words and expressions which mean the same.
1. demolish
2. take a look at
3. take someone for someone else
4. not accept
5. succeed in doing
6. be employed by
7. put up with

a. think someone is someone else
b. turn down
c. examine
d. work for
e. pull down
f. tolerate
g. manage to do

3 Rewrite the words in bold using phrases from exercise 2.
1. The old gallery's going to be **demolished** tomorrow.
2. An expert **examined** the painting.
3. Sorry! I **thought you were** a famous painter!
4. They **didn't accept** my offer so I didn't buy the sculpture.
5. You've **managed to create** a real work of art!
6. How long **were you employed by** that interior designer?
7. I don't know how you **tolerate** all that criticism!

4 For questions 1–6, complete the second sentence so that it has a similar meaning to the first sentence, using the word given. Do not change the word given. You must use between two and five words, including the word given. Write the missing words IN CAPITAL LETTERS.

1. I have a cousin who works for a local record company. **by**
   I have a cousin who _____ a local record company.
2. Walking round museums all day was extremely tiring. **exhausted**
   We _____ after walking round museums all day.
3. U2 were offered a fee to perform a concert and they refused to accept it. **down**
   U2 _____ they were offered to perform a concert.
4. I'm hoping that I can afford to pay a professional artist to paint my portrait. **painted**
   I'm hoping that I can afford _____ by a professional artist.
5. The school has said it will tolerate graffiti art on certain walls. **put**
   The school has decided _____ graffiti art on certain walls.
6. Why don't you pay a professional decorator to decorate your living room? **decorated**
   I suggest _____ by a professional decorator.

13 Writing

A review

👁 Look at *Writing database - reviews* on page 152 before you do the exercises.

1 Read this writing task. What different kinds of books would be suitable to write about? What could you say about them? Use the words in the box to help you.

autobiography • biography • dictionary
encyclopaedia • fiction • full-colour photographs
handbook • history • non-fiction

You recently saw this notice in an English-language magazine called *Art World*.

> ### Reviews needed!
> Have you read a book about art or artists recently? If so, could you write us a review of the book? Include information on what kind of book it is, what it's about, and say whether you would recommend the book to other people.
> The best reviews will be published next month.

Write a **review** of between **120** and **180** words in an appropriate style.

2 Circle the correct word to complete these phrases we can use to make recommendations.

1 I'd **strongly/greatly** recommend reading/seeing/etc …
2 I would **advice/advise** anyone who likes … to read/see/etc …
3 Don't **lose/miss** the chance/opportunity to read/see/etc …
4 If you get the chance to read/see/etc … , **do/make** it!
5 This would **create/make** the perfect present for anyone who likes …

Working model

3 Read the answer to the writing task.

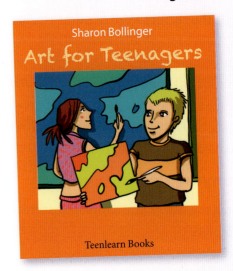

Art for Teenagers

'Art for Teenagers', written by Sharon Bollinger and published by Teenlearn Books, is a wonderful handbook with over two hundred different activities for teenagers interested in art. From doing a simple sketch to making a mask out of newspaper, 'Art for Teenagers' shows you how to do it.

The book is divided into four sections: 'Drawing things', 'Painting things', 'Making things' and 'Know your materials'. This final section shows things like the difference between oil paints and water-based paints, and the different kinds of pencils available.

For each activity, Sharon Bollinger takes us step-by-step through the process. There are full-colour photos of actual teenagers doing the activities, and the results are impressive. I've already tried several of them, and they're as easy to do as she says. I can't wait to do more of them!

I'd strongly recommend this book to any teenager who is creative and likes painting, drawing or making things. It would make the perfect Christmas or birthday present too!

4 Decide if the statements are true (T) or false (F).
1. The writer has given the review a title.
2. The writer has given each paragraph a heading.
3. The review contains the most important facts about the book.
4. The writer only expresses their opinion in the final paragraph.
5. The writer has used a very formal style and hasn't used any contractions (*it's*, etc).

Ready to write!

5 You are going to write a review in answer to the same writing task. Use your imagination to complete the chart.

Title of book	
Type of book	
Written by	
Published by	

6 Make a plan of your answer. Use your imagination.

- What's the title of your review?

- Paragraph 1: What key information about the book will you include here?

- Paragraphs 2 and 3: You'll go into detail here about two main aspects of the book. What points will you make in each paragraph?

- Paragraph 4: Are you going to recommend the book? If so, who to? If not, why not?

Now complete *Writing Planner 13* on page 161.

Now write!

7 You are now ready to write your review. Use your plan from exercise 6 to help you. Write between 120 and 180 words.

Check it out!

8 Check your work. Tick (✓) what you have done.

- I have given my review a title.
- I have said who the book was written and published by.
- I have written four main paragraphs.
- I have said whether I recommend this book or not.
- My review is friendly and interesting rather than formal.
- I have checked my spelling and my grammar.
- My review is between 120 and 180 words long.

◀ Look Back

Can you answer these questions? If you can't remember, look through the unit for the answers.
1. What do we call a painting of a real person?
2. Which verbs do we use to form the causative?
3. What adjectives come from the word 'reason'?
4. Which of these is incorrect? *an honour   an handkerchief   an hour*
5. Why is 'very perfect' not right?

Game, Set and Match

Start thinking!

How many Olympic® sports events can you name? Quickly make a list.

Reading

1 🎧 **2.16** Read the magazine article. Which of the sports mentioned do you prefer watching?

2 Decide in which paragraph the writer does these things.

a introduces the idea of athletes competing in many events   Paragraph ____

b presents one athlete's reasons for doing the decathlon   Paragraph ____

c tells the reader where to find further information   Paragraph ____

d raises the question of why athletes choose the decathlon   Paragraph ____

e presents useful advice for young athletes   Paragraph ____

Ten Events, One Champion:
THE DECATHLON

Fay Webster takes a look at the world of athletics and finds out what it takes to be a true champion.

1 The Olympic Games™ have changed a lot since their origins in Ancient Greece. Today, athletes from countries all over the world take part and the Olympics® are big business, watched by millions on television. Some things, though, have stayed the same. The athletes then could make a lot of money from winning, just like today's competitors. In the ancient Games, a great champion might have received as much as a year's pay for winning a race.

2 Another thing that hasn't changed is the search for an all-round champion, somebody who can defeat their opponents at a number of different sporting events. In the ancient Olympics®, athletes competed in the pentathlon. This consisted of the long jump, the discus, the javelin, a running race and wrestling. The first winner, in 708 BC, was Lampis of Sparta, who must have been a great athlete to beat so many others from all over the Hellenic world. The pentathlon was an important part of the Olympics® until Emperor Theodosius of Rome banned the Games in 393 AD.

3 The Stockholm Olympics® of 1912 brought back this tradition of the search for all-round greatness. The modern pentathlon was included (shooting, swimming, fencing, riding and running) and so was the modern decathlon (ten events), with the heptathlon (seven events) for women being introduced later. So what drives someone to take on this running, throwing, jumping challenge and push their body to its limits? I met American decathlete Bruce Thorpe in New York and told him he must have been crazy to take up the decathlon. He laughed.

4 'Yes, I think I probably was. I could have done lots of different sports, but I chose the decathlon. It's very tough and it demands a lot of different skills. You have to train just as hard as other athletes, only you have to do it in ten different events! I think we're probably all a little crazy, but it's very satisfying in the end,' he said. I asked him to explain what happens in the decathlon.

3 Read the article again. For questions 1–6, choose the answer (A, B, C or D) which you think fits best according to the text.

1. The writer says that athletes today
   A are more popular than in ancient times.
   B are much better than in ancient times.
   C treat the Olympics® like a business.
   D can become wealthy through sport.

2. The ancient pentathlon **didn't** test athletes' abilities to
   A throw things.
   B jump high.
   C run fast.
   D jump far.

3. According to the passage, the heptathlon for women
   A is much easier than the decathlon.
   B is similar to the ancient pentathlon.
   C tests the ability to ride a horse.
   D became an Olympic® event after 1912.

4. What do you have to do to win a gold medal in the decathlon?
   A Score more points than all the other competitors.
   B Beat the other competitors in at least three events.
   C Finish each event in the top three.
   D Complete the events in the right order.

5. What does Bruce say about the events?
   A The 1500 metres should be on the first day.
   B The first day is tougher than the second.
   C The 1500 metres is different from the other events.
   D It looks easier than it actually is.

6. What is Bruce's advice for people thinking of becoming decathletes?
   A Get a trainer to guide you.
   B Get up early to start training.
   C Take up the heptathlon instead.
   D Try to get a good time in all the events.

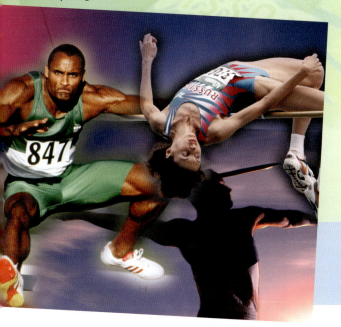

5 'The way it works is you complete each event and you get points, depending on how well you do in that event. At the end of two days, the person with the most points is the champion and takes the gold medal, the second person gets the silver and the third the bronze medal. We start with the 100 metres, the long jump, the shot put, the high jump and the 400 metres. The second day, it's the 110-metre hurdles, the discus, the javelin, the pole vault and the one that we all dread, the 1500 metres.' I asked him what made the 1500 metres such a struggle. 'All the other events demand speed or strength. With the long race, it's stamina. Really, decathletes aren't built for that event.'

6 So what tips does Bruce have for those of you thinking of taking up the decathlon? 'Start as early as you can and join a good club,' he said. 'It takes a long time to master ten different events, or seven for the heptathlon, and you need expert help. And don't expect to have much free time!'

7 Ten events, one champion. Think you might be the one? If you're interested in finding out more about the decathlon, contact your local athletics club.

WORD BOX

4 Use words from the article to complete the definitions. You've been given the first letter to help you.

1. The sport involving different events like running around a track, throwing or jumping is known as a _____ .
2. Someone taking part in a sports competition is called a c_____ .
3. The people you are competing against are your o_____ .
4. S_____ is the ability to keep going for a long time.
5. A c_____ is made up of a group of people who are all interested in a sport or hobby.

Have your say!

- Do you think you'll follow the decathlon during the next Olympics®?
- Would you ever consider taking part in a decathlon? Why? / Why not?

G Grammar clinic

Modals (2): modal perfect

👁 Look at *Grammar database* page 194 before you do the exercises.

1 Read this sentence and circle the correct word.

'You must have been very pleased to win the decathlon.'

1 This refers to the *past/present*.
2 This sentence expresses *certainty/possibility*.

Find other examples of the modal perfect in the article. Answer the questions above for each example you find.

2 What do the sentences express? Choose the correct option.

1 You should have asked Tim what time the race starts when he called.
 a I think you probably did this.
 b You didn't do this and I think that was wrong.
2 Look at Wendy's face! They must have lost the match.
 a I am (almost) certain this happened.
 b This didn't happen, but it was a possibility.
3 Be careful! You could have hit me with that javelin!
 a I am (almost) certain you hit me with the javelin.
 b You didn't hit me with the javelin, but it was a possibility.
4 Patrick might have forgotten about our arrangement to play basketball.
 a I am (almost) certain he has forgotten about it.
 b It is possible that he has forgotten about it.
5 You ought to have let your dad win when you were playing tennis.
 a I am (almost) certain you did this.
 b You didn't do this and I think that was wrong.
6 They should have shown the match in the evening, not the morning!
 a It is possible that they did this.
 b They didn't do this and I think that was wrong.

3 Correct the sentences that have mistakes in them. One sentence has no mistakes. Which one?

1 Britney might has heard about the competition from Sarah last week.
2 Look out! You should have killed someone playing like that!
3 Oh, he's missed! He really must have scored from that position!
4 Thinking about it now, we should play better in last week's match.
5 But Lauren is hopeless! She can't have beaten Oscar at tennis!

4 What would you say in these situations? Complete the sentences using a modal perfect and the verbs in brackets.

1 Will has left his football behind. The only explanation is that he forgot it. (**forget**)

 'Will _____ his football.'

2 George is very bad at football. You don't believe he scored a goal. (**score**)

 'George _____ a goal!'

3 Your mum says she tried to call your sister an hour ago. You are almost certain that your sister was playing volleyball then. (**play**)

 'She _____ when you called.'

4 Your friend complains to the referee during a match. Afterwards, you tell her/him that you thought her/his behaviour was wrong. (**complain**)

 'You _____ during the match.'

V Vocabulary builder

Sport

1 Complete the sentences with words from the box.

umpire • spectator • trainers • defeat • individual
trainer • referee • team • medal • victory

1 The _____ blew his whistle and the footballers started the game.
2 Simpson's _____ means that he is now the European heavyweight boxing champion.
3 The ball went into the crowd and a(n) _____ was injured.
4 The volleyball team I belong to has got a new fitness _____ .
5 The winner felt very proud when the _____ was placed around her neck.
6 My mum has promised to get me a brand new pair of Adibok _____ !
7 You learn to work with others by taking part in _____ sports, such as football and basketball.
8 The _____ shouted. 'Play!' and the tennis match started.
9 I prefer _____ sports, such as running, where you don't have to rely on other people.
10 Porttown City will find it difficult to recover from their _____ on Saturday.

2 Match each of the sports to the correct picture.

basketball • cricket • volleyball
rugby • tennis • football • squash
hockey • badminton

Collocations

3 Decide whether the sports in exercise 2 are played on a court or on a pitch.

Phrasal verbs with other particles

4 Match the phrasal verbs in the sentences with the correct definitions.

1 Could you please **put** me **through** to the manager of the club?
2 United's dream **turned into** a nightmare when they lost 8-0.
3 Mark **takes after** his father. They're both mad about running.
4 The match is going to be **brought forward** to this Saturday.
5 The thieves managed to **get away with** a lot of expensive sports equipment.
6 The police are **looking into** the crowd violence at the match last Friday.
7 These trainers were really expensive so my mum said I have to **look after** them.

_____	to escape	_____	to keep in good condition
_____	to become	_____	to move to an earlier date or time
_____	to investigate	_____	to be like an older relative
_____	to connect somebody on the phone		

Listening

1 🎧 **2.17** Listen to a short extract from an interview with a snooker player. Write a number or short phrase to answer each question.

1 What is the programme called?
2 How old is Angela Oliver?
3 How old was Angela when she started playing snooker?
4 When did Angela win the Lancashire Amateur Snooker Championship?
5 What does she want to be when she's older?

2 🎧 **2.18** Listen to the interview. For questions 1–7, complete the sentences.

Angela's father was both excited and **1** _____ when she won.
A snooker game requires a table, a snooker cue, a white ball, six coloured balls and **2** _____.
You get five points if you successfully pot the **3** _____ ball.
Once the red balls have been potted, the aim is to pot the remaining balls **4** _____.
If a player accidently pots the black, **5** _____ are given to the opponent.
A 'snooker' is when you are unable to **6** _____ the ball you want to hit next, because of an obstruction.
The side of the table you can hit a ball against is called **7** _____.

Speaking

1 Write down three things that football and the high jump have in common.

1 *They are both sports.*
2 _____
3 _____

2 Write down three differences between football and the high jump.

1 *Football is a team sport while/whereas the high jump is an individual sport.*
2 _____
3 _____

3 Answer the questions.

Which sport do you prefer to watch, football or the high jump? Why?

4 Work in pairs. One of you should read the instructions and the other should talk for one minute. Then swap.

Which sport do you prefer to watch?
I'd like you to compare and contrast the two photos and say which sport you prefer to watch.

Soundbite stress (2)

 2.19 Underline the syllable you think is stressed most in the words in each set. Listen and check.

The first word is an example.
1 <u>pho</u>tograph   pho<u>to</u>grapher   photo<u>gra</u>phic
2 athlete   athletic
3 victory   victorious
4 famous   infamous
5 science   scientific
6 concentrate   concentration

👁 Look at *Speaking database - Comparing* and *Expressing preferences* on page 165.

Use of English

The unreal past

👁 Look at *Grammar database* page 194 before you do the exercises.

1 Circle the correct form in each sentence.
1. It's about time the team **starts/started** working better together.
2. I would rather **watch/watched** water polo than volleyball.
3. I wish I **have/had** enough money to go and see my team play tonight.
4. I would rather you **play/played** for our side than for theirs.
5. Paul thinks it's high time you **take/took** athletics seriously.
6. I'd rather you **don't/didn't** tell everyone that you beat me at tennis.

2 Use the notes to make complete sentences.
1. I wish I/am better/football.
2. Laurence would rather you/not come/watch him play this weekend.
3. It is about time we/get ready/the match.
4. Joanne/wish/she/not have to play handball this weekend.
5. Instead of a theatre, I'd rather the town/spend the money/a new stadium.

Common mistakes

3 Circle the correct word in each sentence.
1. I'm really looking forward **at/to/for** the competition.
2. You need **both/and/also** strength and determination to be a good long-distance swimmer.
3. My parents would **better/like/rather** I didn't talk about football all the time!
4. I **wish/want/hope** I was as fast a runner as Diane is.
5. It's time he **join/joins/joined** our team.

4 For questions 1–12, read the text below and think of the word which best fits each gap. Use only one word in each gap. There is an example at the beginning (0). Write your answers IN CAPITAL LETTERS.

Tug – of – war

Every year, on (0) ___THE___ last Saturday of July, our village has its Annual Tug-of-war Day. Everyone (1) _____ forward to it because it's great fun – (2) _____ if it's pouring with rain!

We (3) _____ the whole afternoon watching and taking (4) _____ in tug-of-war competitions. In tug-of-war, you have two teams – usually with eight people in each team – trying to pull a rope across a line. In our village, we have four categories of teams: men's, women's, under 16s and mixed, (5) _____ is men, women and children together.

You need both strength (6) _____ determination to be good at tug-of-war. Last year, our team (7) _____ second in the under 16s category. I think we could (8) _____ won – we were strong enough – but it was very muddy because it had (9) _____ raining and we all kept falling over!

This year, my dad's going to be in one of the men's teams (10) _____ the first time. I'm really pleased, because it's about time he (11) _____ up a sport. His team's going to practise hard throughout the winter, so it should keep him fit! My mum says she (12) _____ rather he did something less physical, like fishing, because she doesn't want him to hurt himself!

14 Writing

An article

👁 Look at *Writing database - articles* on page 153 before you do the exercises.

1 Read this writing task. Who is going to read this article?

Your school magazine has asked you to write an article to encourage people to join the school athletics club. The editor has sent you this note:

> The school athletics club is looking for more people to get involved. Do you think you could write an article for the magazine? Mr Richards (he's the teacher in charge) told me they meet twice a week (Monday and Thursday, 5pm-7pm) and they do all kinds of athletics. I don't know anything about it so I thought I'd ask you.
> Thanks.
> Anna.

Write an **article** of between **120** and **180** words in an appropriate style.

2 Decide if the statements are true (T) or false (F).

1. This article should be formal because it is going to be in a magazine.
2. This article should be formal because teachers might read it.
3. This article should be quite informal because students will read it.
4. You should not use contractions (*it's*, *don't*, etc) in this kind of article.
5. Your main aim is to criticise students for being too lazy.
6. You can add relevant information that is not mentioned in the question.
7. You should never use direct speech in an article.
8. You should never use exclamation marks (!) in an article.

Working model

3 Read the answer to the writing task.

WHY YOU SHOULD THINK ABOUT JOINING
THE SCHOOL ATHLETICS CLUB
WHICH IS RUN BY MR RICHARDS

We all know that we should get more exercise. We all know that sport is a great way to enjoy yourself and meet new friends. We all know that winning is a great feeling. So why aren't we all in the athletics club?

'It's perfect for students who want to take up a new sport,' says Mr Richards, the teacher in charge, and he's right! You can do almost anything at the club, including running, the pole vault and the javelin. In fact, there's everything you need to become the next Olympic® decathlon champion!

The members of the club meet every Monday and Thursday evening between 5pm and 7pm. I spoke to one of them to find out what she gets out of being a member. 'Well, it's a lot of fun,' says Tracy Jones, who's been a member for two years. 'It can be hard work, but you see your friends and you keep in shape. Oh, and it's completely free!'

Why not try it? If you're interested, ask Mr Richards for more details.

4 Underline where the writer does these things in the article on page 128.
1 asks their readers a question
2 tells their readers what someone says
3 agrees with someone
4 makes a suggestion
5 tells their readers what to do next

5 Does the model have a good title? Can you think of a better one?

Ready to write!

6 You are going to write a similar article about an athletics club for the school magazine. Here is the note the editor has sent you. Who does he suggest you could speak to?

> Mrs West (she runs the club) wants to encourage more people to join the athletics club. Could you write an article for us? She said you could ask her about it, and you might ask James Edwards a few things. He's been a member for three years, I think. They meet on Tuesdays and Fridays, 6pm–8pm.
> Thanks a lot.
> Adam

7 Make a plan of your answer. Use your imagination.
- What title are you going to give your article?
- Why should people join the club? Think of three reasons.
- What did Mrs West tell you?
- What did James Edwards tell you?
- When does the club meet?
- What sports can you do at the club?
- What should your readers do if they want more information?

Now complete **Writing Planner 14 on page 161**.

Now write!

8 You are now ready to write your article for the school magazine. Use the information you have been given. Use at least one example of direct speech. Your article shouldn't be very formal. Write between 120 and 180 words.

Check it out!

9 Check your work. Tick (✓) what you have done.

- I have given my article an appropriate title.
- I have included the information about the club.
- I have used fairly informal language.
- I have used some direct speech.
- I have checked my spelling and my grammar.
- My article is between 120 and 180 words long.

◀ Look Back

Can you answer these questions? If you can't remember, look through the unit for the answers.
1 What do women do instead of the decathlon?
2 What do you get for coming third in the Olympics®?
3 In which event do athletes jump as far as they can?
4 What tense follows *It's about time …*?
5 Does tennis have a referee or an umpire?

Revision
Units 13-14

1 Choose the correct option.

1. I prefer _____ art to traditional art.
   A abstract   B shape   C sketch   D gallery

2. We should get a _____ for the painting that your Aunt Michelle bought you for your birthday.
   A brush   B frame   C portrait   D sketch

3. The _____ blew his whistle, the players kicked the ball, and the Cup Final began.
   A umpire   B trainer   C spectator   D referee

4. I always look forward to the Olympics® because I like watching _____ .
   A tracks   B clubs   C athletics   D trainers

5. The local _____ all cheered when the home side scored a goal.
   A viewers   B audience   C spectators   D witnesses

6. The key to winning at tennis is to be fitter than your _____ .
   A umpire   B opponent   C competitor   D trainer

7. I was always much better at _____ sports than at team sports.
   A personal   B singular   C individual   D lonely

8. It takes a lot of skill to be a _____ and make works of art out of stone.
   A statue   B composer   C painter   D sculptor

9. If we can win this match against the champions, it would be a great _____ .
   A medal   B victory   C competitor   D prize

10. Some members of the crowd got onto the _____ at the end of the football match.
    A court   B surface   C earth   D pitch

2 Complete each sentence so that it means the same as the first sentence. Use the words given without changing them. Use no more than five words. You will get two marks for each correct answer.

1. We're thinking of asking a professional decorator to do our new house.   **having**
   We're thinking of _____ by a professional decorator.

2. 'Why don't you get somebody to clean your car before you sell it?' said Mike.   **cleaned**
   Mike suggested _____ before I sold it.

3. You can't read that sign? You should ask the optician to test your eyes!   **get**
   You should _____ if you can't read that sign.

4. The dentist had removed a tooth, which meant Megan couldn't speak properly.   **had**
   Megan couldn't speak properly because she _____ removed.

5. I am going to the hairdresser's tomorrow morning, so I can't meet you at nine.   **cut**
   I _____ tomorrow morning, so I can't meet you at nine.

6. I suggest you ask someone to fix your bike so we can go for a ride.   **fixed**
   Why don't you _____ so we can go for a ride?

3 Circle the correct word or phrase in each sentence.
1. Our teacher made us **write/to write** four tests last week!
2. Police say the young woman **which/who** disappeared has been found.
3. I hope **that/so that** Jack asks me to go out with him!
4. It's about time you **learned/have learned** to be a little more polite.
5. I'll meet you at the pool and we'll go **swimming/for swimming**.

4 Complete the sentences using the verbs in brackets.
1. Is this Sally's bag? She _____ (**must/forget**) it when she left.
2. Pete's very sensitive. You really _____ (**should not/say**) those things to him last night.
3. The evidence showed that the accused man _____ (**could not/kill**) the victim.
4. I'm sorry. I think we _____ (**might/meet**) before. At Bill's party?
5. You _____ (**can't/clean**) your room. Just look at it!
6. My dad thinks I _____ (**ought to/call**) to tell them I was going to be late.

5 Complete the sentences using *very* or *absolutely*.
1. I thought the concert was _____ wonderful.
2. When you stand next to an elephant you realise that they are _____ huge.
3. Theresa is a(n) _____ difficult person to get on with.
4. Lady Gaga's latest CD is _____ terrible.
5. Try this soup. It's _____ delicious!
6. It's _____ tiring spending hours in the art gallery.
7. This knife is _____ useless! It won't cut anything.

6 Read this text. For questions 1–10, use the word given at the end of each line to form a word that fills the gap. There is an example at the beginning (0). You will get two marks for each correct answer.

The key to being a (**0**) _professional_ artist is to understand what the	PROFESSION
art world wants and then produce it. The (**1**) _____ artist	SUCCESS
needs to have a (**2**) _____ style and to make works of art	RECOGNISE
that other people find (**3**) _____ . It takes an artist	DESIRE
(**4**) _____ practice to develop their own style, but the	END
(**5**) _____ rewards can be amazing. People don't just want	FINANCE
art. They want (**6**) _____ art because they think that the	EXPENSE
more (**7**) _____ a painting is, the better it is. Often, that is	VALUE
true, but sometimes bad art sells for a(n) (**8**) _____ price.	BELIEVE
Many (**9**) _____ artists made very little money from their	FAME
art, but now we can see how important their (**10**) _____ really are.	CREATE

Score _____ /60

15

Up in Smoke

Start thinking!

What are the main threats to the environment today?

How can ordinary people help protect the environment?

Do you do anything to protect the environment?

Reading

1  2.20 Quickly read the article. Ignore the gaps for now. Why should we care about the Amazon rainforest?

2 Find the words in bold in the article. What do they refer to?
1 It (line 13)
2 it (line 19)
3 their (line 29)
4 more (line 30)
5 That (line 31)
6 them (line 35)

Think about words like *that*, *this* and *these* to help you with exercise 3.

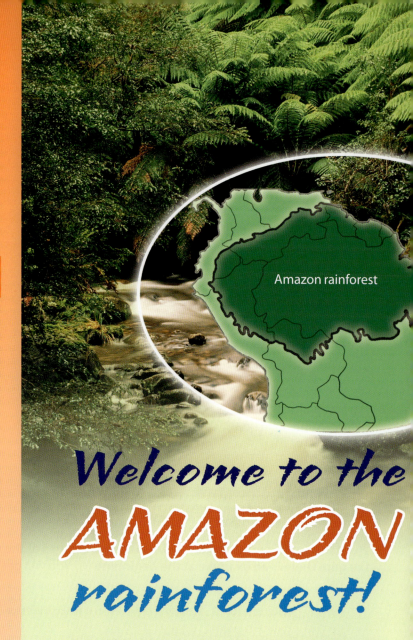

Amazon rainforest

Welcome to the AMAZON rainforest!

Do you know how big the Amazon rainforest is? It's big! It covers 5.5 million square kilometres. That's about ten times the size of France. It's the largest tropical rainforest in the world. Approximately 60% of the rainforest is in Brazil, the rest being in Bolivia, Columbia, Ecuador, French Guiana, Guyana, Peru, Suriname and Venezuela.

The Amazon rainforest is home to more than a third of all the world's species of plants, birds and animals. Twenty per cent of all the birds in the world live in the rainforest. Scientists have discovered thousands of types of plant and animal that can only be found there. **1** ▭ There are at least 2.5 million species of insect there. Imagine

13 what would happen if they all lost their home. **It** couldn't happen, could it? Unfortunately, it's happening right now. Yes, the rainforest is big. But it's getting smaller. Every day. The problem is that people are cutting down the trees, mainly to make room for cows. **2** ▭ This process of cutting down trees is called 'deforestation'.

19 The good news is that **it** is slowing down. In 2004, for example, more than 27,000 square kilometres were cut down. That's an area bigger than Wales. In 2006, because of all the campaigns to save the rainforest, it had dropped

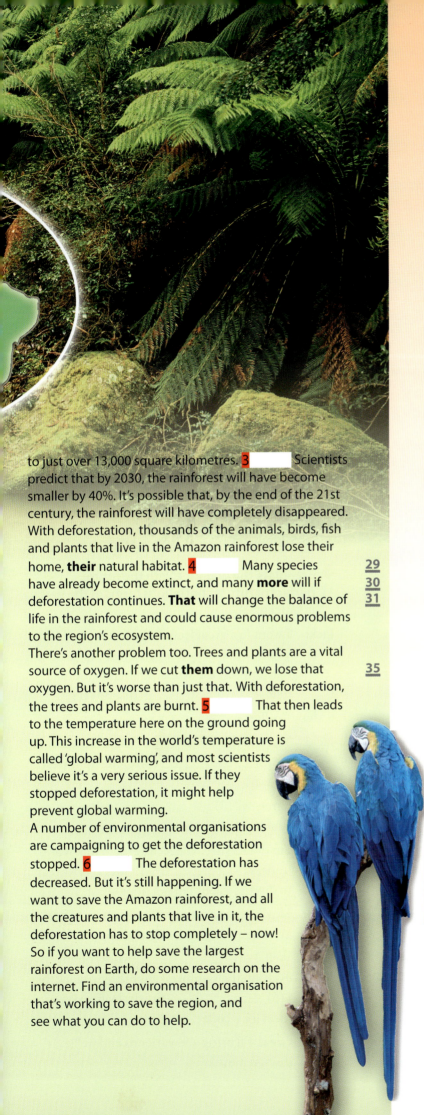

3 Read the article again. Six sentences have been removed from the article. Choose from the sentences A–G the one which fits each gap (1–6). There is one extra sentence which you do not need to use.

A The bad news is that it's not enough.
B These provide meat and make money for their owners.
C This sends gases into the Earth's atmosphere, which stop some of the Earth's heat escaping.
D As we've seen, they have been partly successful.
E Some of them move to other areas, but most of them die.
F How many new medicines are actually found in the rainforest each year?
G There are thousands – probably millions – more that we haven't discovered yet.

to just over 13,000 square kilometres. **3**_____ Scientists predict that by 2030, the rainforest will have become smaller by 40%. It's possible that, by the end of the 21st century, the rainforest will have completely disappeared. With deforestation, thousands of the animals, birds, fish and plants that live in the Amazon rainforest lose their home, **their** natural habitat. **4**_____ Many species have already become extinct, and many **more** will if deforestation continues. **That** will change the balance of life in the rainforest and could cause enormous problems to the region's ecosystem.

There's another problem too. Trees and plants are a vital source of oxygen. If we cut **them** down, we lose that oxygen. But it's worse than just that. With deforestation, the trees and plants are burnt. **5**_____ That then leads to the temperature here on the ground going up. This increase in the world's temperature is called 'global warming', and most scientists believe it's a very serious issue. If they stopped deforestation, it might help prevent global warming.

A number of environmental organisations are campaigning to get the deforestation stopped. **6**_____ The deforestation has decreased. But it's still happening. If we want to save the Amazon rainforest, and all the creatures and plants that live in it, the deforestation has to stop completely – now! So if you want to help save the largest rainforest on Earth, do some research on the internet. Find an environmental organisation that's working to save the region, and see what you can do to help.

WORD BOX

4 Use words or phrases from the article to complete the sentences. You've been given the first letter to help you.

1 How many s_____ of insect live in the rainforest?
2 I'd love to go on holiday to a t_____ country to see what it's like during the rainy season.
3 A tiger's natural h_____ is the jungle.
4 Every animal is a v_____ part of its environment and its disappearance could be an environmental disaster.
5 G_____ w_____ is a real problem and it could lead to changes in the weather all over the world.

Have your say!

- What are the biggest environmental problems facing your country?
- What solutions can you suggest?

G Grammar clinic

The future (2)

👁 Look at *Grammar database* page 195 before you do the exercises.

1 Read this sentence from the article on pages 132 and 133 and answer the question.

> … *by the end of the 21st century, the rainforest will have completely disappeared.*

Which of these is the correct order of events?

a now ➡ the 21st century ends ➡ the rainforest completely disappears

b now ➡ the rainforest completely disappears ➡ the 21st century ends

Find another example of *will* + *have* + past participle in the article and underline the sentence. Write the events the sentence refers to in the correct order.

now ➡ _____ ➡ _____

2 Choose the event which happens first.

1 By the year 2100, we will have solved the problem of the rainforest.
  a The year 2150 comes.
  b We solve the problem of the rainforest.

2 We will have lost 10% of the rainforest by the end of the decade.
  a We lose 10% of the rainforest.
  b The decade ends.

3 Many species of animal will have disappeared by the time we wake up to this problem.
  a Many species of animal will disappear.
  b We wake up to this problem.

4 By eight o'clock, I'll have finished reading the article.
  a It is eight o'clock.
  b I finish reading the article.

3 Look at today's calendar for Jack, a student. Write sentences using the future continuous as in the example.

all-day	
8am	breakfast at Mike's
9am	meeting with Charlie
10am	
11am	attend lecture on the rainforest
12pm	
1pm	lunch with Kate
2pm	
3pm	write essay on the rainforest
4pm	
5pm	
6pm	dinner with Harry

At 8:30am, Jack will be having breakfast at Mike's.

1 At 9:30am, _____.
2 At 11:30am, _____.
3 At 1:30pm, _____.
4 At 3:30pm, _____.
5 At 6:30pm, _____.

4 Complete the dialogue with the future perfect or future continuous forms of the verbs in brackets.

Jack: I went to a great lecture this morning. Did you know that by this time next year an area of rainforest the size of 30 million football fields (1) _____ (**disappear**)?

Kate: Really?

Jack: Yes, and that's every year! Before we know it, we (2) _____ (**lose**) the rainforest forever!

Kate: Surely we (3) _____ (**solve**) the problem before that happens.

Jack: I'm not so sure. The lecturer said that world leaders (4) _____ (**meet**) next year to discuss it, but I'm not hopeful.

Kate: Maybe there's something we can do to help. What are you doing this afternoon?

Jack: Well, I (5) _____ (**work**) on my essay on the rainforest after three o'clock, but I (6) _____ (**finish**) by five. We can meet for a coffee.

Kate: Great. I'll bring a few friends and we'll discuss it then.

V Vocabulary builder

The environment

1 Complete the definitions using the words in the box.

survive • extinct • green • countryside • litter
endangered • fumes • pollution • farmland

1 If you _____ , you continue to exist in spite of difficulties.
2 If a species is _____ , there is a possibility that it could disappear.
3 The _____ is made up of the natural areas outside towns and cities.
4 Cars produce _____ , which are gases that damage the environment.
5 If you are _____ , you care about the environment and try to help protect it.
6 The areas where plants are grown and animals are raised for food are known as _____ .
7 If an animal becomes _____ , it disappears forever from the world.
8 Chemicals that damage the environment are known generally as _____ .
9 Rubbish that people drop in the streets is called _____ .

2 Complete the phrases with a word from the box.

friendly • lover • bank • bin • species • acid

1 a place to leave your bottles to be recycled: **bottle** _____
2 a kind of animal that is threatened with extinction: **endangered** _____
3 not damaging the environment: **environmentally** _____
4 someone who cares about the natural world: **nature** _____
5 a kind of rain that carries harmful chemicals: _____ **rain**
6 a small container in the street for people to put rubbish in: **litter** _____

Confusable words

3 Circle the correct word in each sentence.

1 You can't wear your favourite sweater because it isn't *clear/clean*.
2 We could see for miles because it was such a *clear/clean* day.
3 Do you think you could *bring/take* me to the bottle bank?
4 Could you *bring/take* my books with you when you come to my house?
5 My cousin is *giving/taking* a biology exam this afternoon.
6 I hope I *pass/take* the First Certificate with a good grade.

Magic Metaphors

4 When we talk about *ideas*, we sometimes use words or phrases that have a connection with *plants*. Complete the sentences with the words from the box.

grow • grow on • roots • fruitful

1 I didn't really like the idea of recycling plastic at first, but it's beginning to _____ me.
2 The idea of writing protest letters had its _____ in a discussion we had in class.
3 We had a very _____ discussion about the local environmental problems and we came up with a lot of ideas.
4 Lisa suggested recycling everything we use at home and the idea seemed to just _____ from there, really!

15 Up in Smoke

🎧 Listening

1 🎧 **2.21** You are going to listen to five people talking about different aspects of the environment. Decide what each speaker's purpose is.

Speaker 1 is *explaining/denying* something.

Speaker 2 wants to *persuade/entertain* people.

Speaker 3 is *denying/complaining about* something.

Speaker 4 is trying to *persuade/entertain* people.

Speaker 5 wants to *explain/deny* something.

2 🎧 **2.22** Listen to the speakers again, in a different order. For questions 1–5, choose from the list (A–F) what each person says about the environment. Use the letters only once. There is one extra letter which you do not need to use.

A The destruction of different habitats is increasing. Speaker 1 _____

B Some people's appearance was surprising. Speaker 2 _____

C Changes in the law are to blame for causing the problem. Speaker 3 _____

D There are things ordinary people might do. Speaker 4 _____

E There are problems we can't see. Speaker 5 _____

F There is a lack of facilities.

Soundbite /ɒ/ and /əʊ/

🎧 **2.23** Look at the words. The vowel in each underlined syllable is pronounced /ɒ/ (like *hot*) or /əʊ/ (like *hope*). Put the words into the correct boxes. Listen and check.

h<u>o</u>tel   n<u>o</u>t   w<u>o</u>ke   forg<u>o</u>tten
sh<u>o</u>pping   l<u>o</u>ck   b<u>oa</u>t   wr<u>o</u>te
st<u>o</u>p   h<u>o</u>le   b<u>o</u>mb   c<u>o</u>mb

like 'hot'	like 'hope'

🎤 Speaking

Useful Phrases

1 Match to make ways of expressing your opinion.

1 I believe   a my opinion, …
2 In   b my mind, …
3 As far as   c that …
4 My personal   d view is that …
5 I tend   e I'm concerned, …
6 To   f to think that …

2 Work in pairs. Use the phrases from exercise 1 to help express your opinions.

- Discuss how big these environmental problems are in the area where you live.
- Decide which one is the biggest threat to your local environment.

industrial pollution

traffic pollution

rubbish

deforestation

👁 Look at *Speaking database - Giving/Asking for opinion* on page 165.

Use of English

Transferred negation

👁 Look at *Grammar database* page 195 before you do the exercises.

1 Use the notes to make complete sentences about each person. There is an example to help you.

1 Hanna (think): 'The rainforests won't survive another 50 years.'
Hanna doesn't think the rainforests will survive another 50 years.
2 Jacob (think): 'I'm not going to join Greenpeace.'
3 Mr Hussain (believe): 'The rainforests are not my problem.'
4 I (imagine): 'Environmental problems won't be solved easily.'
5 My parents (think): 'Recycling isn't such a good idea.'
6 People in the Amazon (hope): 'The rainforest won't be completely destroyed.'
7 Local people (believe): 'The council won't solve the litter problem.'

Word formation

2 Make people nouns derived from each of the words. Be careful with your spelling. Where there is a second gap, write another noun.

direct	*director* / *direction*
inspect	_____ / _____
create	_____ / _____
protect	_____ / _____
science	_____
biology	_____
environmental	_____
campaign	_____
protest	_____
vote	_____
visit	_____
politics	_____
survive	_____ / _____

3 For questions 1–10, read the text below. Use the word given in capitals at the end of some of the lines to form a word that fits in the gap in the same line. There is an example at the beginning (0). Write your answers IN CAPITAL LETTERS.

Mass Protest in City Centre

Many (**0**) _____VISITORS_____ to the city yesterday were surprised to find the roads blocked by (**1**) _____ . Around ten thousand people took to the streets to try to persuade (**2**) _____ to take seriously recent warnings from (**3**) _____ . The protesters claim that unless something is done urgently about the (**4**) _____ of our coastline, it is highly likely that many (**5**) _____ species of bird will disappear. Among those facing (**6**) _____ is the rare puffin, which has seen its numbers reduced enormously over the past 50 years. Some (**7**) _____ say that unfortunately it may already be too late for this bird, but immediate action is needed to ensure the (**8**) _____ of other rare birds. The (**9**) _____ of habitats all along our shores and the effects of (**10**) _____ warming have been blamed.

VISIT
PROTEST

POLITICS
ENVIRONMENT

PROTECT
DANGER
EXTINCT

SCIENCE

SURVIVE
DESTROY
GLOBE

Up in Smoke 15

Writing

A formal letter/email

👁 Look at *Writing database - formal letters/emails* on page 150 before you do the exercises.

1 Decide whether the points are necessary, not necessary but relevant, or irrelevant for the writing task in exercise 2.

1. Mrs Collins' party didn't help Greenpeace with their advertising costs.
2. Her party has around five million members across the country.
3. Tourists are put off by the pollution of the sea.
4. The river is no cleaner than it was two years ago.
5. Tourism has not increased due to pollution of the sea.
6. The local park is often full of litter.

2 Read this writing task. How formal should your letter be? Why?

> You have read an article in your local newspaper in which your local MP talks about environmental problems. Read the extract from the article, on which you have made some notes. Then write a letter to the editor of the newspaper, using all your notes.

Write a **letter** of between **120** and **150** words. You must use grammatically correct sentences with accurate spelling and punctuation in a style appropriate for the situation. Do not write any addresses.

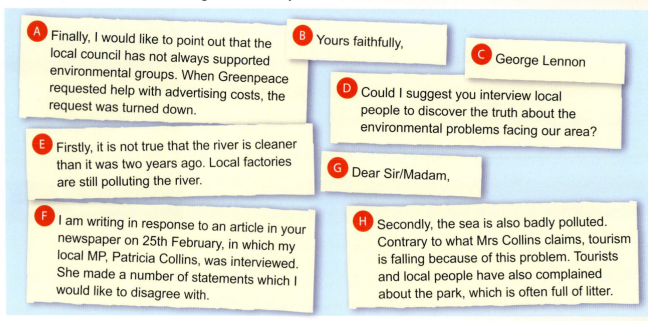

didn't help Greenpeace with advertising costs

I then asked Mrs Collins about the environmental problems in her local area. 'We have made a lot of progress recently,' *not true* she replied. 'Our local river, for example, is now much cleaner than it was two years ago. We have made a real effort to support local environmental groups, and we help them in whatever way we can. Our beach-cleaning scheme has also been a great success, with local young people helping to attract tourism. My party is proud of our record on these problems in my area.'

tourism still falling – sea dirty!

Working model

3 Read the answer to the writing task. Put the parts in the correct order.

A Finally, I would like to point out that the local council has not always supported environmental groups. When Greenpeace requested help with advertising costs, the request was turned down.

B Yours faithfully,

C George Lennon

D Could I suggest you interview local people to discover the truth about the environmental problems facing our area?

E Firstly, it is not true that the river is cleaner than it was two years ago. Local factories are still polluting the river.

F I am writing in response to an article in your newspaper on 25th February, in which my local MP, Patricia Collins, was interviewed. She made a number of statements which I would like to disagree with.

G Dear Sir/Madam,

H Secondly, the sea is also badly polluted. Contrary to what Mrs Collins claims, tourism is falling because of this problem. Tourists and local people have also complained about the park, which is often full of litter.

Correct order: 1 ___ 2 ___ 3 ___ 4 ___ 5 ___ 6 ___ 7 ___ 8 ___

4 Find formal phrases in the letter on page 138 that mean the same as these informal phrases.

1. to reply to
2. She said many things …
3. … I think are wrong.
4. Disagreeing with what Mrs Collins says …
5. Why don't you …?
6. Lots of love,

Ready to write!

5 You are going to write a similar letter. You have seen this interview with a local businessman in your local paper. What information do you have to include?

not true – still lots of litter!

Mr Frank Yates, a local businessman, agrees. 'The local council have done a lot in our area. They've done a very good job of cleaning up the city centre. They've also done all the work they promised to do on the local park, including building a new basketball court. I'm sure young people will welcome that. They have also worked very closely with local people to plan for the future.'

they promised a new youth club but didn't build it

they only organised one meeting

6 Make a plan of your answer. Use your imagination.

- How are you going to start your letter?
- When did you see the article?
- Which point are you going to talk about first? What are you going to say about it?
- Which point are you going to talk about second? What are you going to say about it?
- Which point are you going to talk about third? What are you going to say about it?
- Are there any other relevant points to add?
- How are you going to close your letter?
- What will be the final thing you write?

Now complete *Writing Planner* 15 on page 162.

Now write!

7 You are now ready to write your letter to the editor of the newspaper. Use formal language. Include all the information you have to. Use the model to guide you. Write between 120 and 150 words.

Check it out!

8 Check your work. Tick (✓) what you have done.

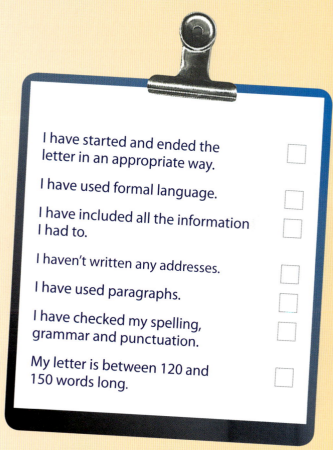

- I have started and ended the letter in an appropriate way.
- I have used formal language.
- I have included all the information I had to.
- I haven't written any addresses.
- I have used paragraphs.
- I have checked my spelling, grammar and punctuation.
- My letter is between 120 and 150 words long.

Look Back

Can you answer these questions? If you can't remember, look through the unit for the answers.

1. Which country is most of the Amazon rainforest in?
2. Where do we put bottles that we want to recycle?
3. What does a species of animal or plant become when it dies out completely?

16

On the Run

Start thinking!

How many different kinds of crime can you name?

Have you or anyone you know ever been the victim of a crime?

What do you think would be the worst thing about being in prison?

Reading

1 🎧 **2.24** Read this magazine article about a crime. Do you feel any sympathy for the criminal?

THE MANY SIDES OF A CRIME

When a crime is committed, many people are involved. We took one crime and spoke to everybody it affected to see what really happens when somebody breaks the law.

A THE CRIMINAL

Carl Maxwell is currently in prison, serving a six-month sentence. In July of last year, he was arrested and a TV, a video recorder and a DVD player were found in his car. He admits now that he stole them, although at the time he claimed that he was innocent. He says he has no regrets about the burglary.

'I come from a very poor family. We never had anything. We couldn't afford much and we never went on holiday when I was a child. If my childhood had been different, I would have got a proper job. But as I grew up, I realised that I could get things easily just by stealing them. Well, if people are so stupid that they leave their windows unlocked, it's not my fault. I've never hurt anyone, so I think it's unfair that I'm in here. Still, I'll be out in another four months.'

B THE VICTIM

Olivia Norton lives in a quiet suburb, alone apart from her two cats. She says that what happened that night in July has had a long-lasting effect on her.

'You can always replace the things you own, and I had insurance, but it takes a long time to feel safe in your own home again. If I'd known what was going to happen, I'd have been more careful, but you never know, do you? The crime rate around here is increasing and there just aren't enough police officers. Their failure to prevent crime means that many people are afraid to leave their own homes.'

Olivia believes that poverty can push people into crime but that it isn't an excuse. 'My parents never had much money, either. But they worked hard and saved what they could. If I'd decided to turn to crime, I could have got lots of things for free. I didn't, though, because I believe that honesty is important.'

C THE POLICE OFFICER

'It wasn't the first time I'd stopped Maxwell,' says Wendy Holmes, the police officer who made the arrest. 'I recognised him as soon as I saw him and I knew he'd been in prison

2 Find the answers to the questions. Do not read the article in detail.
1. How long is Carl Maxwell's sentence?
2. When did the crime take place?
3. How much of his sentence is left?
4. Who does Mrs Norton live with?
5. What made Officer Holmes suspicious?
6. How long has George Blackwell been a judge?

3 Read the article again. For questions 1–9, choose from the people (A–D). The people may be chosen more than once.

Which person(s) makes the following points?

Putting people in prison doesn't solve everything.	1 ____
Burglars try to find houses that are unlocked.	2 ____
Criminals who aren't violent shouldn't be in prison.	3 ____
The victims of crime are to blame for their situation.	4 ____
Losing your things is not the worst effect of a crime.	5 ____
The police were told about the crime by the victim.	6 ____
People who turn to crime are frequently out of work.	7 ____
It wasn't Maxwell's first crime.	8 ____ 9 ____ 10 ____
There are more crimes in this area than in the past.	11 ____

before. Even if I hadn't known who he was, I would have searched his car because he looked very suspicious. He had a mask and a torch on the seat beside him. When I opened the boot of the car, it was obvious that he'd been on a burglary. When Mrs Norton reported the crime, we knew that Maxwell was guilty, and we soon got a few fingerprints from the house to prove it.'

Officer Holmes has some good advice for people who are afraid of this sort of crime. 'Make sure you lock all your doors and windows at night. Most burglars are just out looking for an opportunity. Don't give it to them. If Mrs Norton had locked all her windows, Maxwell would have found another house. If we are going to lower the crime rate in this area, people have to start being more careful.'

D **THE JUDGE**
George Blackwell, QC, has seen all kinds of criminal pass through his court in his ten years as a judge. He says that Carl Maxwell is no different from hundreds of young men he sees every year. 'Maxwell is quite typical. Most burglars are young men, often unemployed, who think that it's an easy route to the lifestyle that other people work hard for. It isn't. Crime destroys people's lives. Like so many others, Maxwell pleaded not guilty at the trial, but the police evidence was very clear. It only took the jury a few minutes to decide he was guilty, and, in my opinion, it was clearly the correct verdict. It wasn't his first offence, and I sentenced him to six months inside. Prison isn't a perfect solution, but at least it keeps people like him off the streets.'

WORD BOX

4 Use words or phrases from the article to complete the definitions. You've been given the first letter to help you.

1. s_____ the punishment given to a criminal, usually time in prison
2. i_____ not having committed a crime
3. b_____ the crime of stealing things from a house
4. c_____ r_____ a measure of how much crime is committed
5. g_____ having committed a crime
6. f_____ marks we leave behind when we touch something
7. c_____ the place where decisions are made about who committed a crime

Have your say!

- How big a problem is crime in your local area?
- What do you think could be done about the problem?

16 On the Run

G Grammar clinic

Conditionals (2): third

👁 Look at *Grammar database* page 196 before you do the exercises.

1 Look at this sentence from the article and decide if the statements are true (T) or false (F).

If my childhood had been different,	I would have got a proper job.
condition	result

1 This sentence refers to the past. ☐
2 The condition is impossible. ☐
3 The result actually happened. ☐

Look through the article again and find other examples of sentences like the one above. Underline them.

2 Choose the sentence which expresses the same idea.
1 If I hadn't been caught, I wouldn't have been sentenced to prison.
   a I wasn't caught and I wasn't sentenced to prison.
   b I was caught and I was sentenced to prison.
2 The burglar wouldn't have got in if I had locked the windows.
   a I didn't lock the windows and the burglar got in.
   b I locked the windows and the burglar didn't get in.
3 If the police hadn't found fingerprints, they wouldn't have had enough evidence.
   a The police found fingerprints and they had enough evidence.
   b The police didn't find fingerprints and they didn't have enough evidence.
4 If I hadn't had a mask in the car, the police officer wouldn't have been suspicious.
   a I had a mask in the car and the police officer was suspicious.
   b I didn't have a mask in the car and the police officer wasn't suspicious.

3 Correct the sentences that have mistakes in them. One sentence has no mistakes. Which one?
1 I would have escaped if I hadn't had a faster car.
2 I hadn't been sent to prison if I had committed a burglary.
3 He wouldn't have become a thief if he has had more money when he was a child.
4 If there would be more police officers, the crime rate wouldn't have been so high.
5 If I hadn't noticed the unlocked window, I would have tried to find another house.

4 Decide what the people would/wouldn't have done if the past had been different.
1 Barbara stole a diamond ring so she was arrested.
2 Joe ended up in prison because he attacked someone in the street.
3 The criminal was guilty so I sentenced him to six months in prison.
4 The evidence was very clear so the jury took only a few minutes to decide.
5 Your car was stolen because you didn't lock it.
6 My father was a police officer so I became one.

5 Make true sentences about your past. In groups, compare your sentences.

If I had worked harder I would have passed the test.

V Vocabulary builder

Crime and punishment

1 Complete the definitions using the words in the box.

shoplifting • murder • assault
robbery • blackmail • arson

1 If you kill somebody illegally, you are guilty of _____ .
2 If you deliberately start a fire, you are guilty of _____ .
3 If you steal items from shops, you are guilty of _____ .
4 If you attack someone physically, you are guilty of _____ .
5 If you steal things, eg money from a bank, you are guilty of _____ .
6 If you make somebody give you money so that you don't tell people their secrets, you are guilty of _____ .

2 Match each punishment to the description.
1 You don't go to prison. If, however, you commit another crime in the near future, you will be sent to prison.
2 You have to pay some money to the court.
3 You have to do something for your local area. The work you are given might be connected to the crime you committed.
4 You are sent to prison for a very long time for committing a serious crime.

a a life sentence **b** a fine **c** community service
d a suspended sentence

Word formation: irregular forms

3 Complete the sentences with the correct form of the word in bold.

1 Most _____ are eventually caught by the police. **crime**
2 There was an investigation into the _____ of the police to catch the robbers. **fail**
3 The woman was able to give a very detailed _____ of her attacker to the police. **describe**
4 I accept that _____ is connected to crime, but not all poor people become criminals. **poor**
5 The accused man walked free from the court because there was no _____ that he had committed the crime. **prove**
6 The government are trying to _____ the age at which young people can be sent to prison. **low**

Word patterns

4 Complete the word patterns with words from the box.

accuse • charge • suspect
apologise • get away • let off
sentence • blame

1 _____ somebody with a crime
2 _____ somebody _____ with a warning
3 _____ somebody of (doing) something
4 _____ somebody of (doing) something
5 _____ with a crime
6 _____ somebody for a crime
7 _____ somebody to time in prison
8 _____ for (doing) something

5 Write a word or phrase from exercise 4 in the correct form in each gap. Add any other words you need.

It isn't easy to (1) _____ a crime and the police often have an idea of who might have committed an offence. If the police (2) _____ committing a crime, they usually question that person and collect evidence. If it's an unimportant or minor offence, the police might (3) _____ with a warning. If it's not a minor offence, the police might (4) _____ with the crime and then they are taken to court. If they are guilty, the judge might give them a fine or (5) _____ some time in prison.

143

16 On the Run

Listening

1 **2.25** You are going to listen to a man being interviewed about crime. Answer the questions.
1. Why has Robert White been invited onto the show?
2. What scheme is he on the show to talk about?

2 Listen to the interview again. For questions 1–6, complete the sentences.

> Local crime is increasing because crime is increasing in **1** _____.
>
> Many young people have time to get involved in crime because of **2** _____.
>
> People don't know **3** _____ because they travel to see friends or to work.
>
> The crime that causes most problems in the area is **4** _____.
>
> Fewer cars are stolen because of improved **5** _____.
>
> People should visit their **6** _____ for further information about Neighbour Power.

Soundbite weak forms (2)

 2.26 Listen to how we say the underlined words in the sentences.

<u>Do</u> you always lock your doors and windows at night?

My purse has been stolen <u>from</u> my bag!

I think we need <u>some</u> advice about crime prevention.

The crime rate has increased by more <u>than</u> 10 per cent.

Now try saying the sentences in the same way.

Speaking

1 Look at the different ways of asking people to make something clear. Cross out the ones that are not polite.

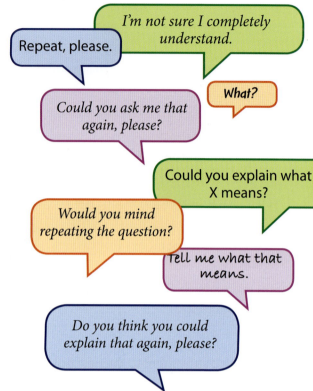

2 In pairs, choose four or more of the questions to talk about. Use the phrases from exercise 1 to check anything you don't understand.
- Do you think prison helps to prevent crime?
- Why do people become criminals?
- What problems of crime does your local area face?
- Would you like to work as a police officer?
- Why? / Why not?
- Apart from prison, what other ways of dealing with crime are there?

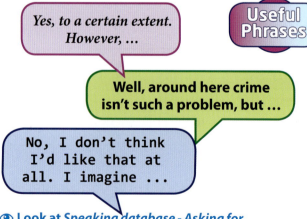

👁 Look at *Speaking database - Asking for clarification* and *Giving/Asking for opinion* on page 165.

Use of English

Wishes and regrets

👁 Look at *Grammar database* page 196 before you do the exercises.

1 Correct the sentences.

1 I wish my new watch hasn't been stolen from my bag yesterday.
2 Don't you wish now you locked your windows last night?
3 I'm sure everybody wishes they can prevent crime in their area.
4 I wish we didn't get burgled when we go on holiday this summer.
5 I wish I didn't mention the fact that Kelly's dad's in prison when I saw her last week.

2 Write what the people might say in each situation. Use *wish* or *if only*.

1 Emily wants to become a police officer. She isn't tall enough.
   'I _____ to become a police officer!'
2 I stole sweets from my local shop. I regret doing it now.
   'If _____ sweets from my local shop!'
3 The thief wasn't careful enough and he got caught.
   'If _____, I wouldn't have got caught.'
4 I'm taking a law exam next week. I don't want to do it.
   'I _____ a law exam next week.'
5 There's a crime thriller on at the cinema but I can't afford to go.
   'If _____ to the cinema to see the crime thriller!'

Parts of speech

3 Complete the phrases on the right so that they mean the same as the words and phrases on the left using the verbs in the box. Use some of the verbs more than once.

| pay • make • have • find |

1 find it difficult to do   _____ difficulty in doing
2 be worried about something   _____ something worrying
3 not regret   _____ no regrets about
4 complain   _____ a complaint about
5 visit someone   _____ someone a visit
6 suggest   _____ a suggestion

4 For questions 1–5, complete the second sentence so that it has a similar meaning to the first sentence, using the word given. Do not change the word given. You must use between two and five words, including the word given. Write the missing words IN CAPITAL LETTERS.

1 'I'm sorry I didn't let the police know about it sooner,' said Larry. **wished**
   Larry _____ the police about it sooner.
2 My neighbours make so much noise that I complained to the police. **complaint**
   I _____ my noisy neighbours to the police.
3 'I regret starting the fire deliberately,' said Alex. **wished**
   Alex _____ arson.
4 Mack doesn't regret robbing the bank. **regrets**
   Mack _____ robbing the bank.
5 'Why don't we visit your uncle in prison tomorrow?' said Mum. **paying**
   Mum suggested _____ in prison the following day.

Writing

A story

👁 Look at *Writing database - stories* on page 152 before you do the exercises.

1 Tick (✓) the correct statements about writing stories.

1. Spelling and punctuation are less important in stories.
2. It's best to have lots of characters in a story.
3. You should know what is going to happen before you write.
4. Stories usually have a beginning, a middle and an end.
5. A simple plot is better than a complicated plot.
6. It's good to use direct speech for the things people say.

2 Read this writing task. What do you think 'an appropriate style' would be?

> A website for young people is holding a story competition. The winning stories will be published on the website. The competition rules state that all stories must have the following title:
> **The Missing Diamonds!**

Write a **story** of between **120** and **180** words in an appropriate style.

Working model

3 Read this entry to the competition. Use slashes (/) to divide the story into paragraphs. Compare your choices with a partner and see if you agree.

The Missing Diamonds!

Jake Johnson, the detective, was at a party being given by Mrs Spender, the richest woman in the area. It was a gorgeous evening and the guests were chatting in the garden. Suddenly, there was a scream and Mrs Spender rushed out of the house. 'My diamonds have been stolen!' she cried. Jake immediately took control. He ordered the guests not to leave and he took Mrs Spender inside. He asked her what exactly had been stolen. 'My diamond necklace!' she replied. 'I placed it on the table while I fed the cat. And the next time I looked, it was gone!' Jake told her to rest and then he questioned all the guests. It seemed that everyone had been in the garden at the time the crime was committed. Jake suddenly heard a sound like glass. He looked up and outside the window was Mrs Spender's cat, with a diamond necklace around its neck! He picked up the cat and went into Mrs Spender's room. 'I think I've solved the mystery of the missing diamonds!' he said, laughing.

4 Read the story again and find words that mean the same as these words and phrases but which are more descriptive.

1 nice   _____
2 talking   _____
3 loud shout   _____
4 ran   _____
5 shouted   _____
6 told   _____
7 said   _____
8 put   _____

Ready to write!

5 You are going to write your own story to enter the competition. Make a plan of your answer. Use your imagination.

- Where does your story take place?
- Who are the main characters?
- Describe them.
- Who do the missing diamonds belong to?
- When do they go missing?
- Does someone look for them? Where?
- Have they been stolen?
- Does someone find the diamonds? How?
- Describe the plot of your story in one or two sentences.

Now complete *Writing Planner 16* on page 162.

Now write!

6 Your are now ready to write your story. Make sure you write in paragraphs. Use good descriptive language and use direct speech for the things people say. Write between 120 and 180 words.

Check it out!

7 Check your work. Tick (✓) what you have done.

- I have used the title given and I haven't changed it. ☐
- I have used some good descriptive language. ☐
- I have written in paragraphs. ☐
- I have used direct speech at least once. ☐
- My story has a simple but interesting plot. ☐
- I have checked my grammar and spelling. ☐
- My story is between 120 and 180 words long. ☐

◀ Look Back

Can you answer these questions? If you can't remember, look through the unit for the answers.

1 What is the opposite of 'innocent'?
2 What is the third conditional used to talk about?
   the present   the past   the future
3 Which of these is a kind of stealing?
   arson   blackmail   shoplifting
4 Write a noun that comes from 'poor'.
5 What can you say if you don't understand someone's question?

Revision
Units 15-16

1 Choose the correct option.

1 Many people feel that _____ warming is a major problem.
  A global   B earth   C world   D worldwide

2 The criminal's _____ were all over the stolen money.
  A fingermarks B fingertips   C fingerprints D fingernails

3 The 12 members of the _____ reached agreement after a long discussion.
  A court   B jury   C judge   D verdict

4 I'm a real nature _____ and I enjoy long walks in the countryside.
  A carer   B follower   C lover   D friend

5 The Prime Minister announced new laws to deal with the rising crime _____ .
  A amount   B rate   C speed   D total

6 Don't just drop your rubbish! Put it in the litter _____ .
  A box   B bank   C tidy   D bin

7 I wonder why all the dinosaurs _____ extinct at the same time.
  A did   B made   C became   D went

8 The giant panda faces extinction due to the destruction of its _____ .
  A habitat   B habit   C inhabitant   D habitation

9 The accused man shouted, 'I am _____ ! I didn't do it!'
  A guilty   B pure   C innocent   D faultless

10 The woman was _____ with murder and placed in a police cell.
  A accused   B suspected   C sentenced   D charged

2 Write one word to answer these questions.

What crime have you committed if you …

1 steal things from a shop? _____
2 deliberately set fire to things? _____
3 kill somebody on purpose? _____
4 steal money from a bank? _____
5 attack someone physically? _____
6 steal things from a house? _____
7 threaten to reveal a secret unless someone gives you money? _____

3 Choose the correct option.

1 I wish I _____ with you to the zoo tomorrow.
  A came   B will come   C could come

2 Don't you wish you _____ Ed to your wedding?
  A invited   B had invited C would invite

3 Look what the dog's done! If only I _____ him outside when I went out earlier!
  A put   B would put   C had put

4 Mary told me she wishes you _____ about her all the time.
  A gossip   B wouldn't gossip C won't gossip

5 I wish we _____ pizza for lunch instead of beans – again!
  A were having B are having C have

6 If only I _____ the bill, they wouldn't have cut the phone off!
  A was paying B can pay   C had paid

7 Jackie hopes that she _____ to university next year.
  A went   B will go   C was going

148

4 Complete the patterns with the correct prepositions.

1 sentence somebody _____ time in prison
2 accuse somebody _____ committing a crime
3 charge somebody _____ a crime
4 blame somebody _____ something
5 suspect somebody _____ doing something
6 apologise _____ something
7 get away _____ committing a crime

5 Complete the sentences using the correct form of the words in brackets. You will get two marks for each correct answer.

1 My father says that you should never trust _____ . (**POLITICS**)
2 Apparently, _____ have discovered a new species of ape in Africa. (**SCIENCE**)
3 Thousands of _____ filled the city centre today and demanded new laws to control pollution. (**PROTEST**)
4 The _____ shouted 'Action!' and the actor started running towards the burning house. (**DIRECT**)
5 Rescue teams searched the area of the plane crash, but there were no _____ . (**SURVIVE**)
6 Government _____ checked the factory and decided that levels of pollution were unacceptable. (**INSPECT**)

6 Complete each sentence so that it means the same as the first sentence. Use the words given without changing them. Use no more than five words. You will get two marks for each correct answer.

1 I've got your school report here and I'm a little worried about it, George. **find**
I've got your school report here and I _____ , George.
2 We could go and visit Hilary this weekend, if you like. **pay**
We could go and _____ this weekend, if you like.
3 I'd like to suggest something, if you'd let me. **make**
I'd like to _____ , if you'd let me.
4 My dad gave up his career to look after us kids, but he says he doesn't regret it at all. **regrets**
My dad says he _____ giving up his career to look after us kids.
5 As I left, two hotel guests who wanted to complain were demanding to see the manager. **make**
As I left, two hotel guests who _____ were demanding to see the manager.

7 Match to make complete sentences.

1 If I had known there was a problem,
2 If you had invited Neil,
3 If we'd seen the weather forecast,
4 If the weather had been bad,
5 If we hadn't discovered America,
6 If you had told me you needed money,
7 If Lisa had said that to you,

a we would have known it was going to rain.
b we wouldn't have started eating potatoes.
c I would have given you some.
d the concert in the park would have been cancelled.
e you would have been annoyed with her too!
f I would have done something about it.
g he would have really enjoyed the party.

Score _____ /60

Writing database

Each piece of writing you do is different, but there are a few general pieces of advice you should remember every time you write something.

First of all, you have to know who your reader is. This tells you how formal your writing should be. In general, use formal language with strangers and people who are in authority (managers, teachers, etc). Use informal language with people you know personally (family members, friends, pen friends, etc).

Secondly, you have to know why you are writing. Your purpose affects what you write. Read the question carefully and make sure you understand why you are writing.

Thirdly, you have to know what type of text you are writing. Look at the following descriptions of each text type. Follow this guide when you write. Your writing should look like the examples here. An article should look like an article, a letter should look like a letter, etc. Make sure you have everything in the right place.

Dear Ms Lawson,

Thank you for agreeing to be interviewed. I am writing to give you further information and to arrange the time and date of the interview.

Firstly, I would like to suggest we hold the interview at five o'clock on either the 11th or 12th. Since you are staying at the Hotel Rex, it might be best if we met there.

The interview should last half an hour, and I am planning to ask you for a description of your tour. Our readers will also be interested in why you came on the tour and whether you have met any interesting people or other travellers.

I wonder if you could bring any photos you have of places you have visited. We would also like to take photographs during the interview, so I hope you do not mind if I arrange that.

I look forward to hearing from you soon.

Yours sincerely,

Jan Merton

formal letters/emails

Formal letters/emails are letters/emails you write to someone you do not know well. You might write one to make a complaint, make arrangements, give or request information, etc. When you are asked to write one, you will be given a situation and some information which you have to include. You should use formal language and start and end the letter/email in an appropriate way.

Key things to remember:
- make sure you understand the situation
- make sure you understand who you are writing to
- decide whether your letter should be formal or informal
- start and end your letter/email in an appropriate way
- use paragraphs to separate key points
- include all the information you are given
- use indirect questions
- ◄ This is what a formal letter/email should look like.

reports

A report is a way of giving information to somebody clearly. They are usually formal and consist of separate paragraphs. It is a good idea to give your paragraphs headings to make your information clear. You are given a situation and asked to write a report for your employer, your manager, etc. You are often asked to give your opinion/suggestions/recommendations.

Key things to remember:

- make sure you understand the situation
- make sure you know who you are writing the report for
- start your report with
  To: (the name of the person the report is for)
  From: (your name)
  Subject: (what your report is about)
- use separate paragraphs for each main point
- use clear headings for your paragraphs
- use reported speech for things people said
- use formal language

This is what a report should look like. ➤

To: Thomas Edwards
From: Claire Eliot
Subject: Camping in this area

Introduction
As requested, I have researched camping facilities in the local area to help the group of students who intend to visit. The results are presented below, together with my recommendations.

Campsites
There are two main campsites locally, Camping World and Sunshine Campsite. While Camping World is cheaper, the facilities are also more basic. Sunshine Camping is slightly more expensive, but it does have excellent shower and cooking facilities.

Time of year
Both campsites are open all year round. Prices are lower during the winter, but the weather in this part of the world can get very cold. The campsites can be very busy during July and August.

Clothing
This depends on the time of year. However, even in summer the evenings and nights can be quite cold, so warm clothing is needed, particularly when camping.

Recommendations
I would recommend staying at Sunshine Campsite because of the excellent facilities. In my opinion, the best time to visit would be September, when the weather is still good, but the campsites are not as busy as they are earlier in the summer.

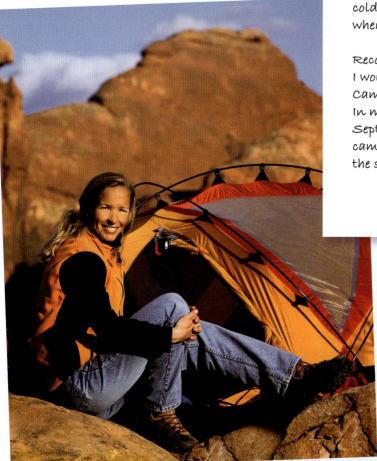

stories

Stories are meant to be entertaining and you need to use good descriptive language. A simple plot with few characters is usually better than a complicated plot with lots of characters. You are often given a sentence that you should start or end your story with.

Key things to remember:
- give your story a title
- if you are given a sentence, use it in the right place without changing it
- have a clear beginning, middle and end to your story
- keep your plot simple
- don't have too many characters
- use good adjectives and adverbs
- use direct speech for what your characters say

This is what a story should look like. ▶

The Message

Suddenly, a message appeared on the computer screen. I had been surfing the internet and was surprised to be interrupted. I looked around the room, but everybody was working.

'Hello. How are you, Greg?' Who could it be? I started typing.

'Hello. Who are you?' I waited for the answer, which appeared a few seconds later.

'A friend. Be careful. You are in great danger.' I felt cold. I asked the mysterious stranger what kind of danger I was in.

'Somebody is planning something.' Nervously, I tried to remember if I had upset anyone recently. As I sat there, wondering what to do next, another message appeared.

'Look out! Behind you!' I turned, my heart beating quickly. Standing there was a ghost! I jumped up, closed my eyes and screamed!

Then, I heard laughter. I opened my eyes and standing in front of me was my friend, Michael, with a white sheet. On the other side of the room another friend, Simon, was typing and laughing. I looked at the computer screen and another message appeared.

'April Fool! Ha, ha!'

---

reviews

In a review, you give your opinion of something you have seen (a play, a TV programme, etc) or read (a book, a story, etc) or a place you have visited (a restaurant, a hotel, etc). You should describe the most important features, explaining why you think they are positive or negative things. A review often ends with a suggestion or recommendation. The formality depends on who your readers are, but usually you should use a neutral style (neither too formal nor too informal).

Key things to remember:
- give your review a title
- explain what you are reviewing
- decide what key features your readers are interested in
- describe the key features in separate paragraphs
- give your opinions and the reasons for them
- make relevant suggestions/ recommendations

This is what a review should look like. ▶

'The Perfect Crime' by Alison Greene

'The Perfect Crime' is Alison Greene's second novel. In it, she describes what happens when a work of art is stolen from a museum. The police have no luck finding the criminal until Detective Paul Milligan solves the crime.

Although Detective Milligan is a strong character, many of the others are very similar to each other. Greene is a good descriptive writer, but the dialogues between her characters seem unnatural and old-fashioned. It's not always easy to remember who is speaking and I often had to go back a few pages to check.

The plot's quite complicated, which is not surprising for such a long thriller. When Detective Milligan finally solves the crime, it's a complete surprise to learn that the thief was the museum director. However, he seems to solve it by luck instead of skill, which spoils the ending of the book.

I would recommend this book for fans of crime fiction, who will find that there's lots of action to keep them interested. However, many people will find the book too long and difficult to follow.

articles

You are often asked to write articles for magazines. Make sure you know who you are writing for because that tells you how formal your article should be. An article for other students should be lively, interesting and not too formal. You can use questions to interest your readers.

Key things to remember:
- give your article a title
- make sure you know who your readers are
- use questions to interest your readers
- use the right level of formality
- use exclamation marks to give a lively feel
- use direct speech for things people said

◀ This is what an article should look like.

A Magical World

Have you ever watched a DVD and thought it was disappointing? Some films just don't seem to work on the small screen, do they? For today's action films, there's only one way to see them: in a modern cinema.

Everything about most films, from the picture to the sound, is designed for the big screen. Special effects that look ordinary on a TV screen suddenly come to life in the cinema. There's nothing like the excitement of watching a scene, hearing the sound all around you and really feeling like you're there, in the middle of the action.

Apart from that, going to the cinema is a special occasion. The smell of the popcorn, the feel of the seats and the excitement in the voices of the audience all make a visit to the cinema feel like entering a magical world.

A DVD is something you watch to pass the time. A film at the cinema is an escape into a dream. So, for me, it's the cinema every time!

---

essays

Essays are formal and usually written for your teacher. You usually have to explain whether you agree or disagree with a statement, what the advantages and disadvantages of something are, etc. You should use a new paragraph for each main point and use good connectors to link your sentences together.

Key things to remember:
- use formal language
- use good connecting words and phrases
- present your argument clearly
- use a new paragraph for each main point
- only make points that are relevant to the question
- make sure you do what the question asks you to do

◀ This is what an essay should look like.

It has often been suggested that only someone who makes music can enjoy other people's music. While all of us can enjoy music in our own way, it is true that playing a musical instrument helps you to understand a piece of music.

To begin with, it takes long hours of practice to become a musician. If you play an instrument, you understand how much hard work it has taken for the musician to become so good. You enjoy the music more because you know how difficult it is to produce. You also recognise the ability of a talented musician.

Secondly, music expresses emotions. If you have tried to express yourself through music, you have a better idea of what a musician is trying to do. You understand the meaning of the music and that increases your enjoyment.

To sum up, I would argue that the ability to play an instrument helps you to appreciate music in many ways. Understanding the effort and the emotion behind the music makes listening to it more enjoyable.

informal letters/emails

Informal letters/emails are written to a friend or to a member of your family. You should use informal language and be friendly. Even though the letter/email is informal, you still need to use paragraphs and include whatever information the questions ask you to.

Key things to remember:
- use informal language
- start and end your letter/email in an appropriate way
- ask about a piece of news in the first paragraph
- use exclamation marks to give a friendly feel
- use separate paragraphs for each main point
- use direct questions

This is what an informal letter/email should look like. ▶

Dear Sanjay,

Hi! How are you? I hope everything is okay. How were your exams? I bet you passed them all!

Thanks for your letter. I can't believe you've been offered two summer jobs at the same time! You said that one of them was in a restaurant and the other in a museum. If I were you, I would definitely take the one in the restaurant.

The first thing is that you'll be there in the summer. The last thing you want to do is spend the summer in a museum! Imagine how boring that would be! In a restaurant, you'll meet people. It might be hard work, but it'll be worth it. I've got a cousin who works in a restaurant and he says it's quite tiring, but he really enjoys it.

The second thing is that you can probably eat at the restaurant. You said the pay was the same, but you might save money by eating there, so you'll be better off!

Good luck with it, and I hope you make the right decision.

Write soon!
Love,
Elaine

Formal and informal language

Once you have decided how formal your writing should be, you need to decide what language you can use. Here are a few things you should remember about formal and informal language.

formal language

- We don't use contractions (*I've*, *it's*, etc) in formal writing.
  Most people do not agree with this position.
- We start and end letters in a formal way.
  Dear Sir,
  Dear Madam,
  Dear Sir/Madam,
  Dear Mr Smith,
  Dear Mrs Jones,

  Yours sincerely, (after *Dear* + surname)
  Yours faithfully, (after *Dear Sir*, etc)
  (+ your full name)

- We always write in complete sentences.
  I hope that you will be able to come to speak to the students on the 14th December.
- We use formal vocabulary.
  accommodation instead of *a place to stay*
- We use indirect questions.
  I would be grateful if you could provide further information about the salary.
- We use the passive voice more.
  A new law has been introduced to reduce crime.
- We use formal connecting words and phrases.
  Moreover, it is clear from statistics that more people are getting divorced than ever before.
- We don't use exclamation marks in formal writing.

informal language

- We use contractions (*I've*, *it's*, etc) in informal writing.
  I've just seen the film you mentioned. It's great!
- We start and end letters in an informal way.
  Dear + first name

  Lots of love,
  Take care,
  (+ your first name)

- We don't always write in complete sentences.
  Sorry to hear about your dog.
- We use informal vocabulary.
  cool instead of *impressive*
- We use direct questions.
  Did you pass your Spanish exam?
- We use the active voice more.
  They're pulling down the old theatre across the road.
- We use informal connecting words and phrases.
  Anyway, what I wanted to tell you about was the party last night.
- We use exclamation marks.
  I can't wait to see you!

Laser Writing Planner 1 — Informal letter/email

Complete the chart. Be careful! Do NOT write your letter until your teacher has seen your notes here.

	purpose	notes	useful expressions
first line	greeting	Dear _____ , or Hi _____ !	
first paragraph	say hello and ask about your brother's news		How are you? / I hope you're well. / Did you … ? / What happened about … ? / I hope you …
second paragraph	tell your brother in general about where you are and whether you're having a good time		So, here I am in … / The family I'm staying with are really nice/friendly/etc
third paragraph	describe the member of the family		Dan's dad is a doctor and … / His sister Elaine is two years older than him …
fourth paragraph	say what you've done so far and what you're going to do during the rest of your visit		Last weekend we went to … / I haven't … yet / Tomorrow, I think we're going to …
ending the letter	end the letter in an informal way		That's all for now! / Have to go! / Write soon! / Love, / Lots of love,
final line	give your first name		

Laser Writing Planner 2 — Essay

Complete the chart. Be careful! Do NOT write your essay until your teacher has seen your notes here.

	purpose	notes	useful expressions
first paragraph	introduce the subject		It is clear that … / Some people claim that … / I would like to argue that …
second paragraph	present your first main points agreeing or disagreeing with the statement		Firstly, … / The evidence shows that … / In addition, … / As a result, …
third paragraph	present further main points		Another important point is that … / We should also bear in mind that …
fourth paragraph	come to a conclusion		In conclusion, … / My view is that … / Finally, …

Laser Writing Planner 3 — Informal letter/email

Complete the chart. Be careful! Do NOT write your email until your teacher has seen your notes here.

	purpose	notes	useful expressions
first line	greeting	Dear _____ , *or* Hi _____ !	
first paragraph	say hello and ask about your friend's news		How are you? / I hope you're well. / Did you … ? / What happened about … ? / I hope you …
second paragraph	check when he is leaving		I know you're arriving on … but I just wanted to check something. When … ?
third paragraph	offer Tom choices and give your opinion; explain why money isn't a problem		So, I've got two choices … / The first one is … / I think … / If you ask me, … / Don't worry about … because …
fourth paragraph	ask him to let you know his choice		Let me know … because …
ending the email	end the email in an informal way		That's all for now! / Have to go! / Write soon! / Love, / Lots of love,
final line	give your first name		

Laser Writing Planner 4 — Report

Complete the chart. Be careful! Do NOT write your report until your teacher has seen your notes here.

	purpose	notes	useful expressions
report heading	say who the report is to, who it is from and what the subject is	To: _____ From: _____ Subject: _____	
first paragraph	describe the background to the report and what you have done	**Introduction**	To prepare for this report, … / As requested, … / My main sources of information were …
middle two or three paragraphs	present your main points	_____ (heading) _____ (heading)	The usual daily routine of a(n) … consists of … / A(n) … is also responsible for … / The salary is generally … / However, …
fourth paragraph	conclude and present your own opinion	**Conclusion**	In conclusion, … / As far as I'm concerned, … / I would rather … than …

Laser Writing Planner 5 — Story

Complete the chart. Be careful! Do NOT write your story until your teacher has seen your notes here.

	purpose	notes	useful expressions
title			
first one or two paragraphs	say where and when the story happened		I was watching TV, and suddenly … / I called my mum and said '…'
middle paragraph	say what happened after seeing yourself on the news and how you felt; say what happened after that		I immediately … / '…,' said … / I decided to … / I couldn't believe … / I felt …
final paragraph	say what happened in the end; describe how you felt		Finally, … / I realised that … / I was relieved that …

Laser Writing Planner 6 — Article

Complete the chart. Be careful! Do NOT write your article until your teacher has seen your notes here.

	purpose	notes	useful expressions
title			
first paragraph	ask a question to get your readers' attention; introduce the subject		Have you ever … ? / Where I live, we have / there are … / I live …
second paragraph	describe the first kind of weather and the problems it causes		In the winter, we often/sometimes have … and that can cause … / We also sometimes have … / It also sometimes … / This can lead to … / People find it very difficult to …
third paragraph	describe the second kind of weather and the problems it causes		
fourth paragraph	describe the third kind of weather and the problems it causes		
fifth paragraph	conclude your article		X is a beautiful country, but … / The summer in X is wonderful but in the winter, you need … / Come and visit us in the … when …

Laser Writing Planner 7 — Formal letter/email

Complete the chart. Be careful! Do NOT write your email until your teacher has seen your notes here.

	purpose	notes	useful expressions
first line	greeting	Dear _____ ,	
first paragraph	reason for writing		Thank you for agreeing to … / I am writing to …
second paragraph	tell him about the interview		We would like the interview to take place … / We would like to interview you about …
third paragraph	ask him to prepare recipes and ask about photos		I wonder if you could … / I'm sure our readers … / Do you think we could … ?
ending the email	end the email in a formal way		I look forward to hearing from you. / Yours sincerely,
final line	give your full name		

Laser Writing Planner 8 — Review

Complete the chart. Be careful! Do NOT write your review until your teacher has seen your notes here.

	purpose	notes	useful expressions
title			
first paragraph	describe the place in general		one of the most popular … / open all year/summer/etc / a number of things/activities for …
second paragraph	say where it is, how to get there, and how much the entrance fees cost		a short/long walk/drive from … / Tickets cost … / The entrance fee is …
third paragraph	describe the main facilities and activities		there's a(n) … / the main attraction is … / most people … / such as / Another thing you can do there is …
fourth paragraph	recommendation		I'd definitely recommend … / I wouldn't recommend … / X will really enjoy …

Laser Writing Planner 9 — Informal letter/email

Complete the chart. Be careful! Do NOT write your email until your teacher has seen your notes here.

	purpose	notes	useful expressions
first line	greeting	Dear _____ , or Hi _____ !	
first paragraph	say hello and ask about your friend's news		How are you? / I hope you're well. / Did you … ? / What happened about … ? / I hope you …
second paragraph	talk about the first kind of technology and say how you and/or your family use it		You asked me for/about … / Well, I've got a smartphone/netbook/ etc and I use it … / My dad doesn't often … / In the kitchen, we've got … / Another piece of equipment I/we often use … / It's really useful for …
third paragraph	talk about the second kind of technology and say how you and/or your family use it		
fourth paragraph	talk about the third kind of technology and say how you and/or your family use it		
ending the email	end the email in an informal way		That's all for now! / Have to go! / Write soon! / Take care! / Love, / Lots of love,
final line	give your first name		

Laser Writing Planner 10 — Essay

Complete the chart. Be careful! Do NOT write your essay until your teacher has seen your notes here.

	purpose	notes	useful expressions
first paragraph	introduce the subject		It is clear that … / Some people claim that … / I would like to argue that …
second paragraph	present your first main points agreeing or disagreeing with the statement		Firstly, … / The evidence shows that … / In addition, … / As a result, … / However, …
third paragraph	present further main points		Another important point is that … / We should also bear in mind that … / Finally, …
fourth paragraph	come to a conclusion		To conclude, … / In conclusion, … / To sum up, … / My view is that …

Laser Writing Planner 11 — Informal letter/email

Complete the chart. Be careful! Do NOT write your letter until your teacher has seen your notes here.

	purpose	notes	useful expressions
first line	greeting	Dear _____,	
first paragraph	say hello and ask about your friend's news		Hi! I hope you are well. / Oh, what happened with … ? / I hope you managed to …
second paragraph	tell your friend about nursery and primary education		Well, young children go to nursery at the age of … / Then we start primary school … / Some children might …
third paragraph	tell your friend about secondary school		Most people start secondary school at … / We are there for … years and … / At the end, we take … exams …
fourth paragraph	tell your friend any other points		Some schools have uniforms, while … / We also have private schools, but …
ending the letter	end the letter in an informal way		That's all for now! / Have to go! / Write soon! / Love, / Lots of love,
final line	give your first name		

Laser Writing Planner 12 — Report

Complete the chart. Be careful! Do NOT write your report until your teacher has seen your notes here.

	purpose	notes	useful expressions
report heading	say who the report is to, who it is from and what the subject is	To: _____ From: _____ Subject: _____	
first paragraph	describe the background to the report and what you have done	**Introduction**	To prepare for this report, … / As requested, … / My main sources of information were …
middle two or three paragraphs	present your main points about each gym in turn	_____ (name of gym) _____ (name of gym) _____ (name of gym)	The facilities included … / I noticed that there were no … / The cost of membership was quite … / Generally, this gym seemed to be …
final paragraph	conclude and present your recommendations	**Recommendations**	In conclusion, … / In my opinion, … / I would like to recommend that … / I would also suggest that …

Laser Writing Planner 13 — Review

Complete the chart. Be careful! Do NOT write your review until your teacher has seen your notes here.

	purpose	notes	useful expressions
title			
first paragraph	give key information about the book		written by … / published by … / is a wonderful/lovely/fantastic/etc handbook/guide/etc …
second paragraph	describe the first main aspect of the book		One great feature of the book is … / Readers will love … / This shows us how to … / This presents … / Another great feature is … / I was particularly impressed by …
third paragraph	describe the second main aspect of the book		
fourth paragraph	recommendation		I'd definitely recommend … / I wouldn't recommend … / X will really enjoy … / It would be perfect for …

Laser Writing Planner 14 — Article

Complete the chart. Be careful! Do NOT write your article until your teacher has seen your notes here.

	purpose	notes	useful expressions
title			
first paragraph	introduce the topic; give three reasons why someone should join the club		Have you ever thought about …? / We all know that … / … is a great/fantastic way to …
second paragraph	describe the club activities and say what Mrs West told you		'…,' says Mrs West, who … / You can do … / There's also …
third paragraph	say when the club meets and say what James Edwards told you		The club meets … / I spoke to … / '…,' says …
fourth paragraph	conclude your article and tell readers how to get further information		Why not …? / If you'd like more information, contact …

Laser Writing Planner 15 — Formal letter/email

Complete the chart. Be careful! Do NOT write your letter until your teacher has seen your notes here.

	purpose	notes	useful expressions
first line	greeting	Dear _____ ,	Dear Sir/Madam, / Dear Editor,
first paragraph	reason for writing		I am writing in response to … / I would like to …
second paragraph	respond to the first point in the article		First of all, Mr Yates claims that … / However, …
third paragraph	respond to the second point in the article		He also states that … / This is not true, because …
fourth paragraph	respond to the third point in the article		Finally, he says that … / I would like to disagree because …
ending the letter	end the letter in a formal way		Yours faithfully,
final line	give your full name		

Laser Writing Planner 16 — Story

Complete the chart. Be careful! Do NOT write your story until your teacher has seen your notes here.

	purpose	notes	useful expressions
title		The Missing Diamonds!	
first one or two paragraphs	say where and when the story happened		One day last summer, … / It was early winter and I was at … / Mr Jones, the detective, was …
middle two paragraphs	say what happened at first and how the story developed		It seemed that … / '…,' said … / She looked pale and worried. / I felt … / After speaking to her, I … / Mr Jones decided to …
final paragraph	say what happened in the end; describe how you felt		Finally, … / We realised that … / We were all shocked and amazed.

Word pattern database

(sb = somebody, sth = something)

able	be able to do
account	take into account
accuse	accuse sb of -ing
add	add sth to sth
admit	admit (to) -ing, admit that …
advise	advise sb to do, advise sb on, advise (sb) against sth
afraid	afraid of
agree	agree with sth/sb, agree on sth, agree to do
apologise	apologise for sth
apply	apply for, apply in writing
approve	approve of
argue	argue about sth, argue with sb
ask	ask sb sth, ask sb to do sth, ask sb about sth
bad	bad at sth, bad for sb
believe	believe sth/sb, believe in sth/sb (God)
blame	blame sb for sth
capable	capable of doing
care	care about, care for
claim	claim to be, claim that …
complain	complain about
congratulate	congratulate sb on
continue	continue doing, continue to do
deal	deal with
decide	decide on, decide to do, decide that …
demand	demand that …, demand sth, a demand for sth
deny	deny -ing, deny that …
depend	depend on sth/sb
despite	despite sth/-ing, despite the fact that …
difference	make a difference
difficulty	have difficulty in doing
do	do your best/homework/the ironing/the housework/the cooking/an experiment/research/do you good
dream	dream of -ing
encourage	encourage sb to do sth
enjoy	enjoy yourself, enjoy sth/-ing
exam	take/do/have/fail/pass an exam, sit (for) an exam
explain	explain sth to sb, explain that …
fond	be fond of sth/-ing
forget	forget (about) sth, forget to do, forget doing
fun	be/have fun, make fun of
good	good at sth, good for sb
have	have a party/a good time/a meal/a bath/a plan/an idea/an argument/a family
help	help sb (to) do, help sb with sth
homework	do your homework, have homework to do
insist	insist on sth/-ing, insist that …
in spite of	in spite of sth/-ing, in spite of the fact that …
interest	have/take/express an interest in sth
interested	interested in
keen	keen to do, keen on -ing
know	know about sth, know how to, be known as
let	let sb do sth
listen	listen to (music)
look	look after, look for, look at, look forward to -ing
make	make sb do, make the beds/a mess/a decision/a difference/a complaint/a fortune/a mistake/a noise/a phone call/a suggestion/friends/make fun of
manage	manage to do
object	object to
occasion	on this occasion
part	take part in, be a part of sth
pay	pay for sth, pay sb
persuade	persuade sb to do, persuade sb that …
prefer	prefer to do sth rather than (to) do sth else, prefer sth/-ing to/rather than sth/-ing
prevent	prevent from -ing
protect	protect from
recommend	recommend (that) sb do
refer	refer to sth/sb
refuse	refuse to do
regret	regret (not) -ing, regret sth, regret to inform you …
rely	rely on
remind	remind sb of sth/sb, remind sb about sth
say	say sth (to sb), say that …
sentence	sentence sb to
share	share sth with sb
stop	stop to do, stop -ing, stop sb from -ing
succeed	succeed in
suggest	suggest sth/-ing (to sb), suggest that …
suspect	suspect sb of, suspect that …
think	think about, think of
time	spend time -ing, spend time on sth, in time, on time, it's (about/high)time
touch	in touch with sb
work	work as/on/in sth

Phrasal verb database

bring up	to care for a child until they become an adult
bring up	to mention or start discussing a subject
call off	to decide to stop something that is planned
carry on	to continue doing something
carry out	to do something such as research, an experiment, an investigation, etc
come across	to find something or meet someone unexpectedly
come down with	to become ill, usually with an illness that is not serious
come on	start to be shown on television
come up	(of problems, difficulties) appear suddenly
come up with	to think of something such as an idea or a plan
cut out	to remove or not include
fall out	to stop being friends because you have had an argument
find out	to discover, to learn
get away	to escape
get down	to make someone feel sad or depressed
get on	if people get on, they like each other and are friendly to each other
get on	if you get on with something, you continue working on it
get over	to recover from an illness, a shock, etc
give up	to stop doing something you do regularly
go about	to do something, particularly something difficult
go off	to explode
go off	to stop liking something or somebody you used to like
go on	to continue happening or continue doing something
grow on	if something or someone grows on you, you start to like them after some time
grow up	to become older and bigger, to become an adult
hurry up	to go somewhere or do something more quickly
keep on	to continue doing something
let down	to disappoint by not doing what you are expected to do
let off	to give someone little or no punishment for something they did wrong
let off	to make something (such as a bomb) explode
look after	to take care of somebody
look after	to keep something in good condition
look down on	to consider someone to be of less value than you
look into	to investigate, to try to discover the facts about something
look over	to have a view of from above
look up	to try to find something (a word, etc) in a source of information (a dictionary, etc)
make off	to escape (with something stolen)
make out	to see, hear, or understand someone or something with difficulty
make up	to become friends with someone again after an argument
make up	to invent a story, an excuse, a lie, etc
pick on	to keep treating someone badly or unfairly
plug in	to connect a piece of equipment to another piece of equipment, or to an electric socket
put down	to kill an animal because it is very old, ill, or dangerous
put off	to delay doing something
put on	to start showing a programme on television
put out	to make something (a fire, etc) stop burning
put through	connect on the telephone
run out of	to use all of something and not have any left
run over	to hit someone or something with a car
stand out	to be easy to see or notice
take after	to be or behave like an older relative
take off	to remove something you are wearing
take off	(of a plane, etc) to leave the ground
take over	to replace someone in a position (of authority)
take up	to fill a particular amount of space or time
take up	to start doing something regularly as a habit, etc
think up	to invent, to have the idea for the first time
throw away	to get rid of something that you don't want
turn down	to refuse to accept an offer or request
turn into	to become
turn off	to stop a machine, eg a television
turn on	to start a machine, eg a television
turn out	to develop in a particular way or have a particular result
turn over	to change to another channel on television
turn over	to turn something so that the other side shows
turn up	to appear unexpectedly

Speaking database

Greetings and farewells
- Hello.
- Good morning/afternoon.
- How do you do?
- Pleased to meet you.
- Nice to have met you.
- Goodbye.

Giving personal information
- My name is …
- I'm … years old.
- I'm still at school and I go to …
- I come from a big/small family. There are … of us.
- I'm the eldest / youngest / second eldest / etc.
- I've got … brothers and sisters.
- My dad's a(n) … and my mum's a(n) …
- I enjoy …-ing and …
- When I have free time, I like …-ing and …

Comparing
- A is good, whereas/while B isn't.
- A is much better/etc than B.
- A is far better/etc than B.
- A is not as good as B.
- A is not nearly as good as B.
- A is almost as good as B.
- On the one hand, …
- On the other hand, …

Expressing preferences
- I prefer …-ing to …-ing because …
- I would rather … than …
- I find … more interesting than … because …

Agreeing/Disagreeing
- I completely/totally agree.
- Yes, you're right.
- I agree with you up to a point.
- That's true, but …
- I'm not sure I agree with you.
- I'm afraid I disagree with you.
- I completely/totally disagree.

Giving/Asking for opinion
- In my opinion, …
- As far as I'm concerned, …
- If you ask me, …
- My view is that …
- What do you think?
- Do you agree?
- We should … , shouldn't we?
- What do you think of …?
- How/What about …?

Asking for clarification
- Could you say that again, please?
- Could you explain it again, please?
- Could you say that again more slowly, please?
- I'm sorry. Would you mind repeating that?
- Do you mean …?

Grammar database

1 Present simple and present continuous

Present simple:

'to be'

Positive			Negative			Question		
I	am ('m)		I	am not ('m not)		Am	I	
You We They	are ('re)	late.	You We They	are not ('re not) (aren't)	late.	Are	you we they	late?
He She It	is ('s)		He She It	is not ('s not) (isn't)		Is	he she it	

regular verbs

Positive			Negative			Question		
I You We They	work.		I You We They	do not (don't)	work.	Do	I	work?
						Do	you we they	
He She It	works.		He She It	does not (doesn't)		Does	he she it	

⚠ BE CAREFUL!

I have – he/she/it **has**
I go – he/she/it **goes**
I do – he/she/it **does**

The present simple is used to talk about …

- habits
  My father **drives** to work.

- how often things happen
  It **rains** almost every day in the rainforest.
  (or don't happen)
  It never **snows** in the Sahara desert.

- permanent situations
  I **live** in North London.

- general truths and facts
  Water **boils** at 100° C.

- general abilities
  I **play** the piano.

- states
  I **know** him and his brother.

- the future in timetables
  My train **leaves** in an hour. (see page 179)

- the future in time clauses
  I'll tell Carrie when I **see** her. (see page 179)

❗ BE CAREFUL!

When we want to emphasise an action or situation in the present, particularly to emphasise that it actually happens, or that it's different to what someone else thinks, we can use the *emphatic present simple*, with *do* or *does*.

'Your brother plays the piano, doesn't he?'

'No, but **he does play** the guitar.'

'I know you don't like peanut butter.'

'No, you're wrong. **I do like** peanut butter.'

(We don't use the *emphatic present simple* with the verb *to be*.)

Present continuous:

Positive			Negative			Question		
I	am ('m)	working.	I	am not ('m not)	working.	Am	I	working?
You We They	are ('re)		You We They	are not ('re not) (aren't)		Are	you we they	
He She It	is ('s)		He She It	is not ('s not) (isn't)		Is	he she it	

The present continuous is used to talk about …

- actions in progress at the moment of speaking
  Come inside – it**'s raining**.
- temporary series of actions
  I **am learning** to drive.
- temporary situations
  We **are staying** at the Grand Hotel.
- changing situations
  This city **is getting** bigger every year.
- annoying habits (usually with *always*)
  Oh! You **are** always **losing** your keys!
- definite arrangements and plans for the future (see page 179)
  We **are having** a test tomorrow.

❗ BE CAREFUL!

Some people use the term *present progressive* instead of *present continuous*. They mean the same thing.

✅ QUICK CHECK

1. Which tense do we use to talk about scientific facts?
2. Which tense do we use with phrases like 'once a month'?
3. Which tense do we use to talk about temporary situations?

Stative verbs

Some verbs are not normally used in continuous tenses because they don't describe actions. These are called 'stative verbs'. For example, we say 'I love you', **not** 'I am loving you'. Some of these verbs **can** be used in continuous tenses, but the meaning changes.

Stative verbs often refer to …

thinking
  eg believe, imagine, understand, know

emotions
  eg love, hate, like, prefer, want, satisfy

the human senses
  eg hear, see, smell, taste, sound

appearance
  eg seem, resemble, appear, look

relationships between things
  eg belong to, own, consist of, include, involve

Look at how the meaning changes when we use some of these verbs in the continuous form.
  The milk **smells/tastes** funny.
  I **am smelling/tasting** the milk to see if it is okay.
  I **see** much better with my new glasses.
  I **am seeing** Debbie tomorrow about the car.
  But Elvis Presley is dead! I must **be seeing/hearing/imagining** things!

I **think** you're wrong. (That is my opinion.)
I **am thinking** of a famous person. Guess who! (I have a picture in my mind.)
He **looks** just like his father. (He resembles his father.)
He **is looking** at me in a funny way.

! BE CAREFUL!

With *hear*, *see* and *smell*, we often use *can* to describe what is happening now. For example:

I **can hear** a strange noise coming from the kitchen.

✓ QUICK CHECK

1 Which of these is a stative verb?
   play/hate/come

2 Which is correct?
   You seem worried./You are seeming worried.

3 Which of these is **not** a stative verb?
   understand/prefer/leave

2 Past simple and past continuous

Past simple:

'to be'

Positive			Negative			Question		
I He She It	was	late.	I He She It	was not (wasn't)	late.	Was	I he she it	late?
You We They	were		You We They	were not (weren't)		Were	you we they	

regular verbs

Positive		Negative			Question		
I You We They He She It	worked.	I You We They He She It	did not (didn't)	work.	Did	I you we they he she it	work?

! BE CAREFUL!

A number of verbs form their past tense in an irregular way.

The past simple is used to talk about …

- single completed actions
  I **walked** to school yesterday morning.
- repeated actions which don't happen now
  My father **walked** to school every day when he was a boy.
- past states
  I **knew** her when we were at primary school.

When we want to emphasise an action or situation in the past, particularly to emphasise that it actually happened, or that it was different to what someone else thinks, we can use the *emphatic past simple*, with *did*.

'You lived in Oxford, didn't you?'
'No, but I **did stay** there once.'
'I bet you didn't ask Mary to go out.'
'No, you're wrong. I **did ask** her and she said yes.'

(We don't use the *emphatic past simple* with the verb *to be*.)

⚠ BE CAREFUL!

The past simple can also refer to the present in conditional sentences (If I **had** more money, …) and after certain phrases (It's high time we **left**/I'd rather you **came** at five o'clock). This is called the *unreal past* because it refers to now, not the past (see page 194).

Past continuous:

Positive			Negative			Question		
I He She It	was	working.	I He She It	was not (wasn't)	working.	Was	I he she it	working?
You We They	were		You We They	were not (weren't)		Were	you we they	

Most uses of the past continuous are like the uses of the present continuous, but in the past.

For example, the past continuous is used to talk about …

- actions in progress at a point in the past
  I **was reading** a book at 10 o'clock yesterday morning.
- temporary situations in the past
  I **was staying** in a hotel until my flat was ready.
- changing situations in the past
  At that time, unemployment **was getting** worse.
- annoying past habits
  When I was a child, my parents **were** always **criticising** me.
- arrangements and plans for the future in the past
  I was worried on Monday night because we **were having** a test the next day.

We also use the past continuous to talk about …

- actions in progress over a period of time
  I **was reading** a book all morning.
- two actions in progress at the same time
  Mum **was washing** up while I **was doing** my homework.
- background information in a story
  The sun **was shining**. The birds **were singing**. Suddenly, a bomb exploded.

The past simple and the past continuous are often used together to show that one action happened (past simple) during the time defined by another action (past continuous). For example, imagine I started watching TV at 5pm and the phone rang at 6pm. I can say:

'I **was watching** TV when the phone **rang**.'

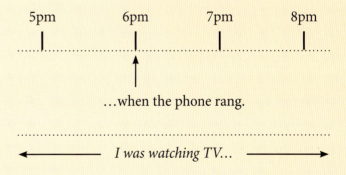

Sometimes this means the action in progress is interrupted or stopped.

> I **was reading** when suddenly all the lights **went** out.

! BE CAREFUL!

Some people use the term *past progressive* instead of *past continuous*. They mean the same thing.

Compare the uses of the past continuous with those of the present continuous (see page 167). Often, it is used in the same way, but in the past.

✓ QUICK CHECK

1 Which tense do we use for a single completed action?
2 Which tense do we use for background information in a story?
3 *It's time you went to bed.* Does this refer to the present or the past?

Would, used to, be used to

Would and *used to* can be used to talk about past habits, especially for the distant past. *Would* can be used like this:

> When I was a child, my grandma **would** read to me every night.

Used to can be used in the same way:

> When I was a child, my grandma **used to** read to me every night.

The difference between them is that *used to* can be used to talk about **states** in the past, but *would* can't.

> I **used to** like tomato soup, but now I hate it. (✓)
> I ~~would like tomato soup, but now I hate it.~~ (✗)

We don't use *would* or *used to* in the negative or in questions very often. The negative of *would* is *would never* or *would not*. The most common negative form of *used to* is *never used to*.

> I **never used to** be very good at languages.

You might also see these negative forms.

> I **didn't use to** be very good at languages.
> I **used not to** be very good at languages.
> (This is quite formal.)

Used to has this question form.
> **Did** you **use to** live abroad?

Be used to is used to talk about something that is familiar to you, or that isn't strange to you any more. It is followed by a noun or an *-ing* form.

> I didn't like this town at first, but now I **am used to** it.
> I'm **used to** studying every day, but I found it hard at first.

Be used to can be used to talk about the past like this:

> I found studying every day hard at first because I **wasn't used to** it.

When we want to talk about the process of becoming familiar with something, we use *get used to*.

> It's hard at first, but you'll soon **get used to** it.

! BE CAREFUL!

Used to and *be used to* are pronounced differently from the verb *use*.

> I *used* an opener to open the bottle. (/juːzd/)
> I *used to* live around here. (/juːstə/)
> I *am used to* working hard. (/æmjuːstə/)

✓ QUICK CHECK

1 Which of these is **not** used for past habits?
would/used to/be used to
2 What is the most common negative form of *used to*?
3 Which of these can be used to talk about past states?
would/used to

3 Present perfect and present perfect continuous

Present perfect:

Positive			Negative			Question		
I You We They	have ('ve)	been … done … worked …	I You We They	have not (haven't)	been … done … worked …	Have	I you we they	been …? worked …? done …?
He She It	has ('s)		He She It	has not (hasn't)		Has	he she it	

In general, present perfect tenses are used to connect the past with the present.

The present perfect is used to talk about …

- actions and situations continuing up to now
  I've **known** him for about 10 years.
- a series of actions continuing up to now
  I've **played** chess every Friday for two years now.
- completed actions at a time in the past
  We've **seen** that film before.
- completed actions where the important thing is the present result
  Julian **has broken** his arm.

❗ BE CAREFUL!

A number of verbs form their past participle in an irregular way.

The present perfect is used with words and expressions like: *just, yet, already, This is the first time …, ever, never, for, since, so far, up to now*, etc.

Rachel has **just** left.
Have you seen the new James Bond film **yet**?
I've **already** told you once that you can't go to the party!
This is the first time I've used a computer.
Have you **ever** met a famous person?
John has **never** eaten Indian food.
I've known Michael **for** seven years.
I've been at this school **since** 2002.
We've received over a hundred applications **so far/ up to now**.

❗ BE CAREFUL!

We don't say: ~~I have six months to see Tara.~~ (✗)

Instead, we say: I haven't seen Tara for six months. (✓)

The present perfect can also be used to refer to the future in time clauses after *when, as soon as*, etc.

I'll call you when I've **finished** my homework.

When you want to say exactly when something happened, you should use the *past simple*.

I **saw** that film last week at the cinema. (✓)
~~I have seen that film last week at the cinema.~~ (✗)

❗ BE CAREFUL!

With the verb *go*, we sometimes use *been* as the past participle. Compare:

John's **gone** to Paris. (= He's there or on his way there.)

John's **been** to Paris. (= He went there and now he is back.)

Present perfect continuous:

Positive				Negative				Question			
I You We They	have ('ve)	been -ing		I You We They	have not (haven't) ('ve not)	been -ing		Have	I you we they	been -ing?	
He She It	has ('s)			He She It	has not (hasn't) ('s not)			Has	he she it		

The present perfect continuous is used to talk about …

- (temporary) actions and situations continuing up to now
  I'**ve been working** here for six months.

- (temporary) actions over a period of time that has recently ended
  I'm out of breath because I'**ve been running**.

The present perfect continuous is often used with words and phrases like *all morning/day/week/etc*, *just, for, since*, etc. It can often mean that the action is not complete.

  I'**ve been reading** a great book about dinosaurs. (I haven't finished it.)

Sometimes, you have to look at the context to decide:

  I've been working all morning and now I'm going to watch TV. (I finished recently.)

  I've been working all morning and I've only done half of it. (I haven't finished.)

! BE CAREFUL!

We don't normally use ever or never with the present perfect continuous.

  ~~I've never been reading any of his books.~~ (✗)
  I've **never** read any of his books. (✓)

! BE CAREFUL!

Some people use the term *present perfect progressive* instead of present *perfect continuous*. They mean the same thing.

✅ QUICK CHECK

1 Which auxiliary verb is used to make the present perfect?
  _____ + past participle

2 Which is correct?
  I did it yesterday./I have done it yesterday.

3 Which word is missing?
  Have you _____ cooking all morning?

Articles

There are three articles in English: *a*, *an* and *the*. *A* and *an* are called 'indefinite articles' and both mean the same thing. *An* is used with words which begin with a vowel sound: an umbrella, an orange, an hour. Notice that we say '**a** uniform' and '**a** US citizen' because these begin with a 'y' sound. *The* is called the 'definite article'.

We use the indefinite article (*a*, *an*) to talk about …

- single countable nouns (not particular ones)
  I saw **an** accident yesterday.

We use the definite article (*the*) to talk about …

- single countable nouns (particular ones)
  There's **the** man I mentioned yesterday.

- single countable nouns (in general)
  The lion is a very fierce animal.

- plural countable nouns
  Where are **the** children?

- uncountable nouns
  The weather is quite warm.

We don't use an article when we are talking about …

- plural countable nouns in general
  Lions are very fierce animals.

- uncountable nouns in general
  Coffee is generally bitter.

Notice how we use articles in the following phrases:

- entertainment, media and sport
  ➡ '**the** television' = the piece of equipment
  ➡ Turn on **the** TV.
  ➡ watch television, on television
  ➡ but: listen to **the** radio, on **the** radio
  ➡ go to **the** cinema/**the** theatre
  ➡ listen to music
- no article for games and sports
  ➡ I love tennis.
- for years, usually no article
  ➡ in 2002
  ➡ but: in **the** 1990s, in **the** 20th century, etc
- for seasons, with 'in' and 'during' the meaning is usually the same either with or without article
  ➡ in winter or in the winter
- for months and days, no article
  ➡ in March, on Friday, on Sunday morning
  ➡ in **the** morning/**the** afternoon/**the** evening
  ➡ at night
- geographical areas use *the* with: seas, mountain groups, rivers, island groups, regions
  ➡ **the** Mediterranean, **the** Alps, **the** Thames, **the** Bahamas, **the** Arctic
- don't use *the* with: planets, continents, countries, towns/cities, streets, lakes, most mountains, individual islands
  ➡ eg Mars, Europe, Germany, London, Carnaby Street, Lake Superior, (Mount) Everest, Crete
  ➡ but: **the** Earth, **the** world, **the** Moon, **the** Sun, **the** UK, **the** USA
- jobs usually with *a* or *an*
  ➡ She is **an** engineer.
- use *the* with positions of authority
  ➡ **the** Mayor
- organisations usually use *the*
  ➡ **the** army, **the** navy, **the** police, etc
- public buildings usually use *the*
  ➡ **the** bank, **the** post office, **the** Theatre Royal, etc
  ➡ but: go to prison/hospital, be in prison/hospital

❗ BE CAREFUL!

*He's gone to **the** prison/**the** hospital* is possible when the person is only visiting.

- nationalities, no article for particular people
  ➡ She's Nigerian.
- but: use *the* when talking about nationalities in general
  ➡ **The** French drink a lot of wine.
- travel
  ➡ go home
  ➡ on **the** bus, in **the** car, etc
  ➡ but: go by car/bus/bike/plane, etc
- education
  ➡ go to school/university, etc
  ➡ be at school/university, etc
  ➡ be in Class 5

❗ BE CAREFUL!

*He's gone to **the** school* is possible when the person is only visiting.

- for subjects, usually no article
  ➡ I love chemistry.

❗ BE CAREFUL!

We put *an* before singular countable nouns with a vowel sound. It doesn't depend on spelling. So, we say '**an** umbrella' but '**a** university', '**an** hour' but '**a** holiday', etc.

✅ QUICK CHECK

1. Which is incorrect?
   an umbrella/an uncle/an uniform
2. Which of these is correct?
   the Britain/the USA/the China
3. Which is incorrect?
   in the morning/at the night/on Tuesday morning

4 Past perfect and past perfect continuous

Past perfect:

Positive			Negative			Question		
I You We They He She It	had ('d)	been … done … worked …	I You We They He She It	had not (hadn't)	been … done … worked …	Had	I you we they he she it	been …? done …? worked …?

When we are talking about the past and we want to talk about something earlier in the past, we can use the past perfect.

The past perfect is used to talk about …

- actions and states before the main time in the past we are interested in
  I **had heard** about Alicia before I met her.
- what somebody said in reported speech
  (see pages 181–182)
  Emma said she **had** never **been** to Morocco.
- a hypothetical past in conditional sentences
  (see page 196)
  If **I'd known** you were coming, I would have bought a cake.
- wishes about the past (page 196)
  I wish I **had studied** harder for the test.

❗ BE CAREFUL!

The past perfect is used with words and expressions like: *before, after, when, already, as soon as, It was the first time …*, etc. A number of verbs form their past participle in an irregular way.

❗ BE CAREFUL!

The past perfect can sometimes be used with *before* to talk about an action which didn't happen or wasn't completed in time.

Joel called before I **had finished** my homework.
(= I **hadn't finished** my homework when Joel called.)

Past perfect continuous:

Positive			Negative			Question		
I You We They He She It	had ('d)	been … -ing	I You We They He She It	had not (hadn't)	been … -ing	Had	I you we they he she it	been … -ing?

The past perfect continuous is used to talk about …
- longer actions which continued up to the main time in the past we are interested in

I **had been running** so I was out of breath when I got home.

- what somebody said in reported speech (see pages 181–182)

Mrs Collins said she **had been doing** the garden.

The past perfect continuous is often used with words and phrases like *all morning/day/week/*etc, *just, for, since,* etc. It can often mean that the action was not complete.

! BE CAREFUL!

We don't normally use *ever* or *never* with the past perfect continuous.

~~I'd never been thinking of doing French until my mum suggested it.~~ (✗)
I'd never thought of doing French until my mum suggested it. (✓)

! BE CAREFUL!

Some people use the term *past perfect progressive* instead of *past perfect continuous*. They mean the same thing.

Compare the uses of the past perfect continuous with those of the present perfect continuous (see page 172). Often, it is used in the same way, but in the past.

! BE CAREFUL!

We can often use the past (simple or continuous) instead of the past perfect (simple or continuous), particularly if *after* or *before* make the order of the actions clear:

I ate my lunch after my friend left.
(=I ate my lunch after my friend had left.)

✓ QUICK CHECK

1 Which tense do we use after *It was the first time …*?
2 *I wish I hadn't spent my money.* Does this refer to the past or the present?
3 Which word is missing?
   Lena _____ been working all morning and was very tired.

Comparatives and superlatives

When we want to compare two or more things, we can use the comparative and superlative forms of adjectives and adverbs. We use the comparative to compare things or people that are different and separate from each other:

The blue book is **bigger** than all the red ones.

We use the *superlative* to compare one member of a group with the whole group:

This book is the **biggest** one on the shelf.

one-syllable adjectives

- With most one-syllable adjectives, add *-er, -est.*
  black – blacker – blackest,
  young – younger – youngest
- If the adjective ends in *-e,* add *-r, -st.*
  late – later – latest, brave – braver – bravest
- If the adjective has one vowel followed by one consonant, double the final consonant, then add *-er, -est.*
  big – bigger – biggest, thin – thinner – thinnest

two-syllable adjectives

- If the adjective ends in *-y,* replace the *-y* with *-ier, -iest.*
  happy – happier – happiest, lovely – lovelier – loveliest
- Otherwise, use *more* and *the most* (or *less* and *the least*).
  boring – more boring – the most boring

! BE CAREFUL!

With some two-syllable adjectives, there is a choice: *clever – cleverer – cleverest* or *clever – more clever – the most clever.* We usually use the forms with *more* and the *most.*

adjectives with three or more syllables

- Use *more* and *the most* (or *less* and *the least*).
  interesting – more interesting – the most interesting
- If the adjective is formed from a two-syllable adjective ending in *-y,* then use either *more – the most* or *-ier – -iest.*
  unhappy – more unhappy – the most unhappy or
  unhappy – unhappier – unhappiest

adverbs

- Use *more* and *the most* (or *less* and *the least*).
  quickly – more quickly – the most quickly
  (Superlative adverbs like this are not used in English very much.)

A number of adjectives and adverbs, and one or two other words, form the comparative and the superlative in an irregular way:

irregular adjectives
- *good – better – best*
- *bad – worse – worst*

irregular adverbs
- The adverbs *early, late, fast, hard* and *often* follow the rules for adjectives.
- *early – earlier – earliest*
- *often – more often – the most often*
- *far – farther/further – farthest/furthest*
- *badly – worse – worst*

irregular determiners
- *little – less – the least*
- *much/many – more – the most*

With the comparative, we usually use *than*:
Rachel is older **than** all her cousins.

When you want to emphasise the difference, you can use *much*:
My dad is **much** older than yours.

When you want to say that two things are or aren't the same, you can use
as … as:

My computer is **as fast as** yours.
(= My computer is the same speed as yours.)

My computer isn't **as fast as** yours.
(= My computer is slower.)

! BE CAREFUL!

When we want to talk about the result of something increasing, we can use *the* + comparative, *the* + comparative:

The older my grandfather becomes, **the slower** he gets.
The more you exercise, **the fitter** you become.

✓ QUICK CHECK

1 What is the comparative form of *bright*?
2 What is the comparative form of *comfortable*?
3 Which word is missing?
   My bag isn't as big _____ yours.

5 The passive

We make the passive by using an appropriate form of the verb *to be* and the past participle of the main verb:

This castle **was built** in 1450.

Your papers **will be collected** at the end of the exam.

A good way to think about the passive is to start with an ordinary active sentence:

They **took** the young man to hospital.

This sentence is in the past simple, with 'They' as the subject and 'the young man' as the object. To make it passive, we put the object first, then the verb *to be* in the right tense (here, past simple), then the past participle of 'take':

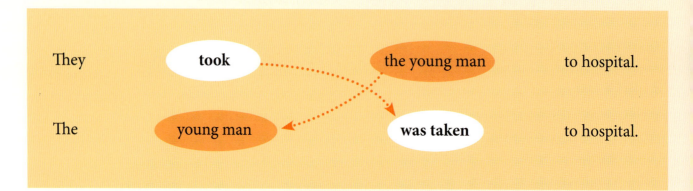

Notice that the verb 'was' is in the same tense as 'took' in the first sentence (past simple). Also notice that we do not need to say who did the action. When we do want to say who did it, we normally use *by*. We normally only do this when it is important information. For example:
   Gunpowder was invented **by the Chinese**.

When we want to say that the action was done using something, such as a tool, we use *with*:
   The dead man had been shot **with a pistol**.

We use the passive …

- when we don't know who does/did something
   The bank **has been robbed**!

- when we aren't interested in who does/did something, or it's obvious
   A man **was arrested** at the airport as he got off the plane.

- for emphasis
   The radio **was invented** by Marconi. (We are mainly interested in the radio, not Marconi.)

Some verbs are not normally used in the passive. They include intransitive verbs (without objects) and verbs such as *have, let, lack, seem, appear, resemble, fit* and *suit*.

Some verbs can take two objects: a direct object and an indirect object. For example:
   Our teacher gave **us some photographs**.

There are two possibilities in the passive. The first is probably more common.

   We were given **some photographs**
   (by our teacher).
   Some photographs were given **to us**
   (by our teacher).

Some sentences have a clause as the object.
   People think/say/believe **that the economy is in trouble**.

There are two possibilities in the passive. The first is probably more common.
   The economy **is thought/said/believed to be** in trouble.
   It is thought/said/believed that the economy is in trouble.

QUICK CHECK

1 Which word is missing?
   The lottery _____ won by a man from London.

2 Which of these is not normally used in the passive?
   appear/break/make

3 Write one reason for using the passive voice.

Countable and uncountable nouns

There are different kinds of nouns: those we can count (*a book, two books*) and those that we can't count (*information, advice*).
   Please pass me those **pencils**, would you? (countable)
   The **news** was a bit of a shock. (uncountable)

Uncountable nouns often refer to collections of things, materials and other things we think of as 'masses' rather than individual objects. You have to be careful because nouns that are countable in your language might be uncountable in English. Here are some common uncountable nouns.
   information, advice, luggage, baggage, knowledge, money, news, travel, furniture

We use a singular verb with these nouns.
   Your advice **was** really useful.

Some nouns can be countable with one meaning and uncountable with another (*coffee, a coffee*). This often happens when we talk about a material or substance and a thing made out of it.

For example:
   Chocolate is made using cocoa beans.
   (uncountable, refers to the substance)

   Would you like **a chocolate**?
   (countable, refers to one from a box of chocolates)

   You really should get your **hair** cut.
   (uncountable)

   There's **a hair** in my soup!
   (countable)

We often use different words with countable and uncountable nouns. Here are some.

Countable nouns: *many, how many, a lot of, lots of, some, a few, few, a number of, a, an, one, two, three, etc, the*

Uncountable nouns: *much, how much, a lot of, lots of, some, a little, little, an amount of, a piece of, the*

! BE CAREFUL!

Use *many* and *much* before a noun in negative statements and in questions. In positive statements (and also in negative statements and questions) use *a lot of*, *lots of*, or *a large number/amount of*. (You can use *much* or *many* in positive statements, but it's very formal.)

Few/little and *a few/a little* mean different things.

few (countable nouns)
  I have **few** friends. (= not many)

a few (countable nouns)
  I have **a few** days off work. (= some)

little (uncountable nouns)
  They gave us **little** information. (= not much)

a little (uncountable nouns)
  Let me give you **a little** advice. (= some)

The phrase *only a few …* means 'not many' and *only a little …* means 'not much'.

Sometimes, you might want to use a countable noun instead of an uncountable noun. With many of them, you can do that by using the phrase *a piece of …*, eg
  Let me give you **a piece of** advice.

There are some uncountable nouns which are plural and which take a plural verb. They do not have a singular form. These include: *jeans, trousers, spectacles, scissors, groceries*, etc.
  ~~We need a new scissors.~~ (✗)
  We need some new scissors. (✓)
  We need a new pair of scissors. (✓)

✓ QUICK CHECK

1 Which of these is countable?
  money/advice/question

2 Which is correct?
  The news was shocking./The news were shocking.

3 Which is incorrect?
  informations/trousers/jeans

6 The future (1)

There are a number of different ways of talking about the future in English. It can be confusing because often more than one of them could be correct. Sometimes you have to think about which is more natural. It helps if you think about what you want to express.

making predictions

When we make predictions that we are sure of based on our own judgement or knowledge, we often use *will*.
  I think United **will** win the Championship this year.

When we make predictions based on evidence we can see now, we often use *be going to*.
  Look out! You**'re going to** drop the drinks!

In general, *be going to* is more informal than *will* and is mainly used in conversation. Often, we can talk about predictions using both of them with no difference in meaning.
  Do you think we**'ll** see Tom at the party?
  Do you think we**'re going to** see Tom at the party?

When we predict the future but we are not so sure of our predictions, we can use other modal verbs (see page 188).
  Be careful! You **might** have an accident.
  Do you think we **might** see Tom at the party?
  I think United **could** win the Championship this year.

making decisions

We often use *will* when we are making a decision.
  Oh, I don't know. Mmm … I**'ll** have an omelette, please.
  I'm really tired. I think I**'ll** stay in tonight.

But we can also use *be going to* if we want to emphasise the intention.
  I'm really tired. I think I**'m going to** stay in tonight.

talking about plans, intentions and arrangements

When we want to tell somebody about our plans or intentions, we often use *be going to*.

> I'**m going to** apply for a job at that new factory.
>
> I'**m going to** be a teacher when I finish university.
> (**Not**: I'm being a teacher…)

When we have made some arrangements (bought a ticket, agreed to meet, etc), we often use the present continuous.

> I'**m meeting** Helen tomorrow outside the library.
>
> We'**re flying** to Paris and then **staying** in a great hotel.

We don't normally use the present continuous for talking about intentions. However, the difference between an intention and an arrangement can be quite small, so you could use *be going to* in both of these situations. It depends on what you want to emphasise.

> I'**m going to** meet Helen tomorrow outside the library.
>
> We'**re going to** fly to Paris and then stay in a great hotel.

making offers, promises, suggestions, refusals

When we make offers, promises or suggestions, we generally use *will* or *shall*. In modern English, *shall* is quite rare and is usually used in questions. When we refuse to do something, we can use *won't*, the present continuous or *be going to*.

- offers
  I'**ll** help you, if you like.
  Shall I open the window for you?
  (**Not**: Will I …)

- promises
  I'**ll** return your book as soon as I've read it.

- suggestions
  Shall we try that new Chinese restaurant?

- refusals
  No, I **won't** do your homework for you.
  No, I'**m not doing** your homework for you.
  No, I'**m not going to** do your homework for you.

talking about timetabled future events

The time or date when some things happen is decided in advance, usually by something like a timetable or the calendar. When we want to talk about things like this, we can use the present simple.

> Our plane **leaves** at four in the morning.
>
> Our exams **start** on 20th May.
>
> Next year, my parents **celebrate** their 50th wedding anniversary.
>
> Christmas Day **falls** on a Friday this year.

These ideas can often be expressed using either the present continuous (for arrangements), *be going to* (for intentions and predictions) or *will* (for predictions).

> Our plane **is leaving** at four in the morning.
>
> Our exams **are going to** start on 20th May.
>
> Next year, my parents **are celebrating** their 50th wedding anniversary.
>
> Christmas Day **will fall** on a Friday this year.
>
> Christmas Day **is going to** fall on a Friday this year.

! BE CAREFUL!

The present simple is also used to talk about the future in clauses after words like *when, until, if, what,* etc, as well as in conditional sentences (see page 185).

> I hope we see Mike when we **are** in York.
> (**Not**: … when we will be in York.)
>
> I can't call Mary until she **gets** home from school.
>
> If I **go** to university, I'll probably study maths.

✓ QUICK CHECK

1 Which is more informal?
   will/be going to

2 Which tense do we use to talk about future arrangements?

3 Which word is missing?
   _____ we go to the cinema this evening?

Question tags

In sentences with the verb *be* as a main verb, we make question tags using *be*. We usually make the question tag positive if the verb is negative and negative if the verb is positive.

    It**'s** warm, **isn't** it?

    You**'re not** nervous, **are** you?

In sentences with an auxiliary verb, we make question tags using the auxiliary.

    You**'re** going to Greg's party, **aren't** you?

    You **haven't** forgotten, **have** you?

    I**'m** meeting you tomorrow, **aren't** I?

    (**Not**: ..., amn't I?)

    Emily **can** play the piano, **can't** she?

When the sentence doesn't have an auxiliary verb, we use the verb *do*.

    You **live** in the town centre, **don't** you?

    Phil **plays** football on Saturdays, **doesn't** he?

    Colin **has** a very big house, **doesn't** he?

We use question tags when we want to …

- ask someone to agree with us
  It's a nice day, **isn't** it?
- check whether something is true
  You've been to Paris, Sue, **haven't you**?

When we are asking someone to agree with us, our voice goes down at the end of the sentence. When we are checking whether something is true, our voice goes up at the end.

❗ BE CAREFUL!

We also use tags when we want somebody to do something, either using *let's* or an imperative.

When we want to add a question tag with *let's*, we use *shall we?*

    Let's order a pizza, **shall we**?

After a positive imperative, we use *will/would/could you?* and after a negative imperative, we use *will you?*.

    Pass me the salt, **will/would/could you**?

    Don't go out with Sandra, **will you**?

In sentences with a negative word like *never, little, no, hardly, nobody*, etc, we use a positive tag.

    You never turn up on time, **do you**?

    Nobody called while I was out, **did they**?

    There's no reason to leave now, **is there**?

In question tags where the subject is 'there', we repeat 'there' in the tag.

    There's a lot of vocabulary to learn, isn't **there**?

✔ QUICK CHECK

1 *You've met Paul, _____ you?* What is missing?
  didn't/haven't/aren't

2 What question tag do we use after *Let's …?*
  do we/will we/shall we

3 Write one reason we use question tags.

7 Reported speech

We use reported speech when we want to tell someone what someone else said. We usually have to change the tense if the reporting verb is in the past. We sometimes have to change other words as well, such as pronouns (*we*, *you*, etc) or words that refer to time and place (*now*, *here*, etc). We also have to decide which reporting verb to use, for example, *said*, *admitted*, *suggested*, etc.

This is how the tenses change …

Direct speech ➡	Reported speech
Present simple	Past simple
'I **am** hungry,' said Tim.	Tim said (that) he **was** hungry.
Present continuous	Past continuous
'I **am writing** a letter,' said Alice.	Alice said (that) she **was writing** a letter.
Past simple	Past perfect simple
'We **had** an ice cream on the beach,' said Colin	Colin said that they **had had** an ice cream on the beach.
Past continuous	Past perfect continuous
'We **were talking** about football,' she said.	She said that they **had been talking** about football.
Present perfect simple	Past perfect simple
'I **have had** a great idea!' Simon said.	Simon said (that) he **had had** a great idea.
Present perfect continuous	Past perfect continuous
'Georgia **has been waiting** all day,' my mum said.	My mum said (that) Georgia **had been waiting** all day.

(The past perfect simple and past perfect continuous tenses stay the same.)

Some modal verbs change …
  'I **can** speak three languages,' said Jerry.
  Jerry said (that) he **could** speak three languages.
  'Ben **will** be at the party,' she said.
  She said (that) Ben **would** be at the party.
  'All students **must** be on time,' said the head teacher.
  The head teacher said (that) all students **had to** be on time.

With reported questions, we use *if* or *whether* and change the tense and the word order.
  '**Have** you **finished**?' Sarah asked me.
  Sarah asked me **if/whether I had finished**.

With *wh-* questions (*what*, *who*, etc), we repeat the question word and change the tense and the word order.
  '**Who left** the fridge open?' asked Mrs Harris.
  Mrs Harris asked **who had left** the fridge open.

We also often have to change words that refer to time and place:
- *here* becomes *there*
- *today* becomes *that day*
- *now* becomes *then* or *at that moment*
- *tomorrow* becomes *the following day* or *the next day*
- *yesterday* becomes *the day before* or *the previous day*
- *ago* becomes *before*

The words *this*, *that*, *these* and *those* change as follows:
- *this/that* + noun become *the/that*
- *these/those* + noun become *the/those*
- *this/that* (as subject or object) become *it*
- *these/those* (as subject) become *they*
- *these/those* (as object) become *them*

'I hate **this** film,' said Alice.

Alice said she hated **the/that** film.

'I want **these** books,' Tony said.

Tony said he wanted **the/those** books.

'**This** is a great show,' Dad said.

Dad said **it** was a great show.

'**These** are nice candles,' said Mary.

Mary said **they** were nice candles.

'I bought **these** in town,' said John.

John said he had bought **them** in town.

'I **left** my purse **here** five minutes **ago**,' said Donna.

Donna said (that) she had left her purse **there** five minutes **before**.

'We **can** finish **these** exercises **tomorrow morning**,' our teacher said.

Our teacher said we **could** finish **the** exercises **the following morning**.

We can also report what someone said using different verbs, each with their own grammar.

'I didn't steal your money!' Peter said.

Peter **denied** stealing/having stolen my money.

'No, I won't let you go,' my mother said.

My mother **refused** to let me go.

'What about an ice cream?' my dad said.

My dad **suggested** an ice cream.

My dad **suggested** (our) having an ice cream.

My dad **suggested** (that) we (should) have an ice cream.

'I'm a great chess player,' said Will.

Will **claimed** to be a great chess player.

With imperative statements, we use a reporting verb such as *told, ordered, commanded*, etc.

'Sit still!' said the hairdresser.

The hairdresser **told** me to sit still.

'Don't say a word,' said Carol.

Carol **told** me not to say a word.

'Form a line,' said the officer.

The officer **ordered** them to form a line.

We often don't make any changes to the verb when we are reporting what somebody said very soon after they said it, when we are reporting a scientific fact or when something is still true.

'It's quite cold,' said Harry.

Harry just said (that) **it's quite cold**.

'Light from the Sun takes eight minutes to reach us,' the professor said.

The professor said (that) **light from the Sun takes eight minutes to reach us**.

'I have a niece in America,' Mr Wood said.

Mr Wood said (that) **he has a niece in America**.

We also don't make changes to the verb when we use a reporting verb in the present tense.

Mark says that he **is** staying in tonight.

✅ QUICK CHECK

1 What do we use reported speech for?

2 What do we change *ago* to in reported speech?

3 Write three reporting verbs.

Indirect questions

We use indirect questions when we want to ask questions politely. We use an introductory phrase (*Could you tell me where …*) followed by the normal word order (*… the bank is?*). We **don't** use question word order in the second part. Some indirect questions need a question mark at the end and some don't. Look at the list below.

Some introductory phrases …
with a final question mark
 Can/Could you tell me …?
 Could you let me know …?
 Do you know …?
 Do you think you could tell me …?

without a final question mark
 I wonder if you can/could tell me …
 I wonder if you could let me know …
 I wonder if you know …
 I would like to know …

Here are some example sentences. Notice the word order …

Do you know **who that man is**?
(**Not**: Do you know who is that man?)
Could you let me know where **the meeting is**?
I wonder if you know where **I can find** a chemist's.
I would like to know when **I will receive** my refund.
Do you think you could tell me how **this works**?

When the direct question is a 'yes/no' question, we use *if* or *whether*.

Direct question:
Are you going to John's dinner party?
Indirect question:
Could you let me know **if/whether** you are going to John's dinner party?

If the relative pronoun (*who, which,* etc) is the subject of the relative clause and there is no other noun or pronoun, we just add an introductory phrase:

direct question
Who is responsible?
Which is better?

indirect question
I wonder if you could tell me **who is responsible**.
Do you know **which is better**?

QUICK CHECK

1 Why do we use indirect questions?
2 Which word is missing?
_____ *you tell me what time it is, please*?
3 Do all indirect questions need a question mark at the end?
yes/no

8 Full infinitives (with *to*) and *-ing* forms after verbs

Some verbs are followed by the full infinitive and some by the *-ing* form. Some verbs can be followed by both, sometimes with a change in meaning.

Here are some common verbs that are followed by …

the infinitive	the *-ing* form	both, with no (or very little) change in meaning
afford, agree, appear, arrange, ask, attempt, be pleased/able, etc, choose, decide, expect, fail, happen, help, hope, intend, learn, manage, offer, plan, prepare, pretend, promise, refuse, seem, tend, want, wish, would like	*admit, appreciate, avoid, be capable of, good/bad at, be interested in, can't help, can't stand, consider, delay, fail, happen, help, hope, deny, discuss, dislike, enjoy, feel, like, finish, give up, imagine, involve, look forward to, mention, mind, miss, practise, succeed in, suggest, talk about, think of*	*begin, continue, hate, intend, love, prefer, start*

These verbs mean different things when they are followed by the full infinitive or the *-ing* form.

remember
- have a picture in your mind of a past event
  Do you remember **visiting** Germany when you were two?
- do something you are/were planning to do
  Did you remember **to call** Diane this morning?

forget
- not be able to remember a past event (usually *I'll never forget …*)
  I'll never forget **meeting** Paula for the first time.
- not do something you are/were planning to do
  Oh, I forgot **to ask** Donna about this evening.

try
- do something as an experiment to solve a problem
  It's hot in here! Let's try **opening** a window.
- make an effort to achieve something
  I've been trying **to open** this jar for 10 minutes!

stop
- stop an activity
  I stopped **smoking** 10 years ago.
- pause and do something else in the middle of an activity
  I was studying all evening, but I stopped **to have** a snack at seven.

go on
- continue

  After the break, our teacher went on **explaining** the grammar to us.
- stop one activity and start a new one

  After **explaining** the grammar, our teacher went on **to tell** us what the homework was.

regret
- be sorry about what has happened

  You'll regret **speaking** to me like that!
- be sorry about giving somebody bad news

  We regret **to inform** you that the flight to Berlin has been cancelled.

like
- enjoy

  I'm sure we all like **receiving** presents.
- choose to/be in the habit of/think it is a good idea

  I like **to leave** home at seven so that I get to work on time.

❗ BE CAREFUL!

When we want to use *would like/prefer* for a particular occasion, we use the *full infinitive*.

~~I would like going to the cinema this evening.~~ (✗)
I would like to go to the cinema this evening. (✓)
I would prefer to meet on Saturday, if possible. (✓)

✅ QUICK CHECK

1 Which of these is followed by the *-ing* form?
  afford/suggest/refuse

2 Which of these is followed by the full infinitive?
  deny/consider/plan

3 Which of these is correct?
  I remember to go to school for the first time./I remember going to school for the first time.

Prefer, would rather, had better

Prefer and *would rather* are both used to express preferences. *Had better* is used for saying what someone should do. Try not to confuse them. We don't say ~~would better~~. They are used like this …

prefer

I prefer basketball to football. (generally)
I prefer playing basketball, rather than football. (generally)
I prefer playing basketball to (playing) football. (generally)
I prefer to play basketball, rather than (play) football. (generally, or on this occasion)
I prefer not to play basketball during the week. (generally, or on this occasion)
I would prefer to play basketball this weekend rather than football. (on this occasion)

❗ BE CAREFUL!

We don't normally say ~~I don't prefer~~ …

would rather

I would rather play basketball than (play) football. (generally, or on this occasion)

I'd rather not play basketball. (on this occasion)

had better

You'd better see a doctor.
You'd better do your homework, rather than sit and watch TV.
You'd better do your homework, instead of sitting and watching TV.
You'd better not fail the test.

✅ QUICK CHECK

1 Which is correct?
  I would rather stay here./I would rather to stay here.

2 You _____ better see a doctor. Which word is missing?
  would/had/should

3 Which is correct?
  I wouldn't rather …/I don't rather …/I would rather not …

9 Conditionals (1): zero, first, second

There are many different kinds of sentence using *if*, and it can be a little confusing. You have to decide whether you're talking about the past, the present or the future. You also have to decide whether you're talking about a real possibility or an unreal possibility (unlikely, impossible or hypothetical).

Real possibility, present and future

Zero conditional: *if* ... present tense ... present tense

This is used to talk about general truths and scientific facts.

> If you **read** a lot, you **learn** lots of vocabulary.
>
> If you **are making** a cake, you **need** to use fresh eggs.

You can also write all conditional sentences the other way round, with the *if* clause second.

> You **learn** lots of vocabulary if you **read** a lot.
>
> You **need** to use fresh eggs if you **are making** a cake.

First conditional: *if* ... present tense ... *will* ... bare infinitive

This is used to talk about real possibilities in the present, in the future, or generally.

> If you **read** a lot, you will **learn** lots of vocabulary.
>
> You **will need** a good dictionary if you **are learning** English.
>
> If you **have studied**, you'**ll do** well in today's test.

Instead of *will*, we can also use these other modals or the imperative.

> If you are going to the party, you **can** take this cake I made.
>
> If it's too late, we **should** call them tomorrow.
>
> I **might/may** take up French if I pass my English exam.
>
> If you've finished, **do** the next exercise.

! BE CAREFUL!

When we are talking about the future, we use *if* ... present tense, **not** *if* ... *will* ...

> ~~If you will see Tina tomorrow, tell her I'm sorry.~~ (✗)
>
> If you see Tina tomorrow, tell her I'm sorry. (✓)

! BE CAREFUL!

We can use *would like* (= want) in first conditional sentences like this.

> I **would like** to study French if I pass my English exam.

✓ QUICK CHECK

1. Which kind of conditional do we use to talk about real possibilities?
2. Which of these is used for an unreal possibility? *If* ... present tense .../ *If* ... past tense ...
3. In conditionals, can you use other modals, apart from *would*?
   yes/no

Unreal possibility, present and future

Second conditional: *if* ... past tense ... *would* ... bare infinitive

This is used to talk about unreal possibilities (things that are unlikely, impossible or hypothetical) in the present and in the future.

> If I **won** the lottery, I **would move** to Hawaii.
>
> I'**d get** a new car if I **had** enough money.
>
> If you **weren't having** a lesson now, what **would** you **be doing**?

The use of the past here is called the *unreal past*, because it refers to the present or the future, **not** the past.

Instead of *would*, we can also use these other modals.

> If I won the lottery, I **could** leave my job.
>
> I **might** feel happier if I went to another school.

Instead of *If I was* ... we can also say *If I were* ..., especially in formal English.

> If I **were** Prime Minister, I would introduce new laws against pollution.

For information on talking about unreal possibilities in the past (third conditional), see page 196.

Unless, in case, as long as

Unless

Unless means 'except if'. We can use it to replace *if… not* in some sentences. When it refers to the future, it is followed by the present tense (like *if*).

I'll be there **unless** it rains.
(= I'll be there, except if it rains.)
(= I won't be there if it rains.)

We can't use *unless* to replace *if not* when *if not* **doesn't** mean *except if*.

If I wasn't ill, I'd play tomorrow. (✓)
(*if not* doesn't mean *except if* here because you are actually ill)
so we **can't** say:
~~Unless I was ill, I'd play tomorrow.~~ (✗)

in case

In case means 'because it might'. We use it to talk about things we do to prevent an unwanted result. When it refers to the future, it is followed by the present tense (like *if*).

Write down the address **in case** you forget it.
(= Write down the address because you might forget it.)

as long as

As long as means the same as *only if*. When it refers to the future, it is followed by the present tense (like if). You can also use *so long as* with the same meaning.

You can borrow my pen, **as/so long as** you give it back to me at the end of the lesson.
(= You can borrow my pen only if you give it back to me at the end of the lesson.)

✅ QUICK CHECK

1 What does *unless* mean?
2 Which phrase means 'because it might'?
3 What does *as long as* mean?

10 Modals (1)

Modal verbs are auxiliary verbs which express things like possibility, obligation, etc.

Modal verbs …

* don't change for person or tense.
  He **might** go to the cinema tonight.
  (**Not:** He mights go to the cinema tonight.)
* don't use *do* in questions.
  Can you play the guitar?
  (**Not:** Do you can play the guitar?)
* are followed by the bare infinitive (without *to*).
  I think I **will call** John.
  (**Not:** I think I will to call John.)
* can be made negative using *not* or *-n't*.
  You **shouldn't** speak to your mother like that.
  (**Not:** You don't should speak to your mother like that.)
* don't have an infinitive. You have to use another word or phrase.
  I hope to **be able to** attend the meeting.
  (**Not:** I hope to can attend the meeting.)

The modal verbs include *will, would, can, could, may, should, must, might, shall* and *ought to*. We also use the phrase *have (got) to* like a modal, although it changes like an ordinary verb.

> He **has** to go to work. (✓)
> He's **got** to go to work. (✓)
> Does he **have** to go to work? (✓)
> Has he **got to** go to work? (✓)
> Does he **have got to** go to work. (✗)

Have got to is generally more informal than *have to*.

expressing ability: *can, could*

> **Can** you open this jar? It's stuck. (present ability)
> My cousin **can** play 10 different musical instruments. (general ability)
> I **could** walk when I was just six months old. (general ability in the past)
> I wish I **could** play the violin. (hypothetical ability)

❗ BE CAREFUL!

Like other modal verbs, *can* doesn't have an infinitive, so after other modals and when we need a full infinitive we use *(to) be able to*.

> I'll **be able to** get a better job after I finish university.
> I might **be able to** see you tomorrow at six.
> I pretended **to be able to** speak Japanese.

expressing obligation: *must, have to*

Must is generally used for personal obligation (feelings of the speaker and hearer, etc) and *have (got) to* for external obligation (rules, laws, what other people tell you to do, etc). They are both used to talk about the present, the future and general obligation.

> I **must** stop eating so much fast food. (personal obligation)
> You **must** make more of an effort in class. (personal obligation)
> I **have to** be at work at nine tomorrow. (external obligation)
> Do you **have to** wear a uniform at your school? (external obligation)
> **Have** you **got to** wear a uniform at your school? (external obligation)

❗ BE CAREFUL!

To talk about the past we use *had to*.

> We all **had to** leave the building when the alarm went off.

Like other modal verbs, *must* doesn't have an infinitive, so after other modals and when we need a full infinitive we use *(to) have to*.

> If I'm late, I'll **have to** apologise to the boss again.
> I'm sorry to **have to** tell you this, but you've failed the exam.

Mustn't does **not** mean the same as *don't have to*.

> You **mustn't** speak while the teacher is speaking. (Don't do it.)
> You **don't have to** get me a birthday present. (It isn't necessary, but you can if you want to.)

Although you can form questions beginning with *must*, it's very unusual and formal.

> **Must** we argue about this all the time?

It's more common to form questions using *have to*.

Do we **have to** argue about this all the time?

asking for and giving permission: *can, could, may*

We use *can, could* and *may* to ask for and give permission now, in the future and generally.

May is more polite than *could* and *can*, and *could* is more polite than *can*.

Can I stay at Anna's this weekend, Mum?

Excuse me. **Could** I borrow your pen for a second?

May I speak to you for a moment, Mr Connors?

When talking about the past, we normally use *could*.

My parents said I **could** go to the party so I started getting ready.

(see pages 181–182 for more about reported speech)

asking for and giving advice: *should, ought to*

We use **should** and **ought to** to ask for and give advice about now, the future, or generally.

You **should** tell your teacher about your problems.

We **ought** to call if we're going to be late.

Shouldn't we start getting ready for the party?

(for criticising past actions, see page 194)

expressing possibility: *may, might, could, can*

We use *can* to talk about general possibilities.

In Russia, it **can** be quite hot in the summer.

We use *may, might* and *could* to talk about possibilities in the present, the future and generally. We sometimes use *may* to show that something is more likely to happen.

I **may** be a bit late for Friday's lesson.

Peter **might** have the right answer for number 10.

There **could** be some easy questions on the exam.

With non-stative verbs, we often use the continuous infinitive (*be -ing*) to talk about actions happening now or about possible future arrangements:

Ian **may be doing** his homework right now.

Sophia **might be playing** tennis at the moment.

I **could be going** to London this weekend.

(for deductions about past possibility, see page 194)

expressing probability: *should, ought to*

We use *should* and *ought to* to say that something is probably true or will probably happen.

Mr Davies **should** have the report by now.

(= Mr Davies probably has the report by now.)

The exam results **ought to** be on the website by now.

(= The exam results are probably on the website by now.)

With non-stative verbs, we often use the continuous infinitive (*be -ing*) to talk about actions happening now or about probable future arrangements.

They **should/ought to be having** their dinner now.

Ben **should/ought to be arriving** at about seven o'clock.

expressing certainty: *must, can't*

We use *must* when we are (almost) sure about something now, in the future or generally, often because we have seen some evidence.

Your father's late. He **must** be stuck in traffic on his way home.

Hi! You **must** be Mrs Johnson.

When we are (almost) sure that something isn't true, often because we have seen some evidence, we use *can't*.

That **can't** be the postman at the door. He's already been today.

With non-stative verbs, we often use the continuous infinitive (*be -ing*) to talk about actions happening now or about probable future arrangements.

They **must/can't be having** their dinner now.

Kelly **must/can't be going** to Athens this weekend.

(for the modal perfect, see page 194. for *will* and *shall* referring to the future, see pages 178–179. for *would* in conditional sentences, see pages 185 and 196)

✓ QUICK CHECK

1. What follows a modal verb?
   the infinitive without 'to'/the infinitive with 'to'
2. Do modal verbs have an infinitive?
   yes/no
3. Which modals do we often use for giving advice?

11 Relative clauses

Relative clauses tell us more about people and things.

> The man (who started Microsoft®) is now very rich.
>
> relative clauses
>
> Bill Gates, (who started Microsoft®), is now very rich.

In the first sentence, the relative clause identifies the man we are talking about. It is called a *defining* (or *identifying*) *relative clause*. The sentence does not make complete sense without the relative clause.

> The man is now very rich. (Which man? We don't know.)

In the second sentence, the relative clause just gives us extra information. It is called a *non-defining relative clause*. The sentence makes complete sense without it.

> Bill Gates is now very rich.

Relative clauses are often introduced by relative pronouns. We use …

which ➡ for things
Have you got the book **which** I lent you?

who ➡ for people
There's the man **who** stole my bag!

that ➡ for people, things, times and places
This is the bike **that** I got for Christmas.

whose ➡ for possession
Tony, **whose** father is a lawyer, is in trouble with the police.

when ➡ for times
I still remember the moment **when** I saw her for the first time.

where ➡ for places
England, **where** football began, has strong sporting traditions.

why ➡ for reasons
That's the reason **why** he's always late.

whom ➡ for people as the object of the relative clause (in very formal English) and after prepositions
All students **whom** the Head has invited to dinner must reply before 5pm.

That's the man **to whom** I gave the money.

In defining relative clauses, we …

- don't use commas.
  Those are the books which I told you about yesterday.

- can use *that* instead of *who* or *which* (*that* is more informal).
  Those are the books *that* I told you about yesterday.

- often leave out the relative pronoun when it is the object of the clause.
  Those are the books I told you about yesterday.

In non-defining relative clauses, we …

- separate the relative clause with commas.
  Ronald Reagan, who was the President of the United States, is ill.

- can't use *that* as a relative pronoun.
  ~~Ronald Reagan, that was the President of the United States, is ill.~~ (✗)

- can't leave out the relative pronoun.
  ~~Ronald Reagan, was the President of the United States, is ill.~~ (✗)

! BE CAREFUL!

When the relative pronoun (*which*, *who*, etc) is the subject of the relative clause, you do **not** need another subject.

> That's the girl who is going out with John. (✓)
> ~~That's the girl who she is going out with John.~~ (✗)

Which can also be used to refer to the rest of the sentence:

> He got an A in his exam, **which** impressed everybody.
>
> (This doesn't mean his exam impressed everybody. It means the fact that he got an A impressed everybody.)

QUICK CHECK

1 Which relative pronoun do we use for things?
   who/which/whom
2 *Here's the book which I borrowed from John.* Does this need any commas?
   yes/no
3 Do we use *that* as a relative pronoun in non-defining relative clauses?
   yes/no

QUICK CHECK

1 Write the missing preposition.
   This is the town _____ which my mother was born.
2 *This is the school to that my dad went.* Is this correct?
   yes/no
3 *Here's the house in where my grandma lives.* Is this correct?
   yes/no

Relative pronouns and prepositions

Where can be replaced by preposition + *which*.

   The resort **where** we spent our holiday was very quiet.

   (= The resort **in which** we spent our holiday was very quiet.)

Less formally, we can put the preposition at the end of the clause. When the preposition is at the end of the clause, we can also use *that*.

   The resort **which** we spent our holiday **in** was very quiet.

   The resort **that** we spent our holiday **in** was very quiet.

We can use other prepositions apart from *in*. The one we choose depends on the normal meaning of the preposition.

   The school **that/which** my mum went to was very traditional.

   The restaurant **at which** we met was closed.

We can do the same thing with *when*.

   The day **when** I won the lottery started badly.

   (= The day **on which** I won the lottery started badly.)

   (= The day **that/which** I won the lottery **on** started badly.)

When we use *where* and *when*, however, we don't need a preposition.

   I will always love New York, the city **where** I was born. (✓)

   I will always love New York, the city **which/that** I was born **in**. (✓)

   I will always love New York, the city **in which** I was born. (✓)

   ~~I will always love New York, the city **where** I was born **in**.~~ (✗)

12 Result *clauses: so, such, too, enough*

So, such, too and *enough* can be used to talk about results.

so

…*so*… { adjective / adverb / *many/much* + noun } …*that*…

My brother's **so handsome that** he's thinking of becoming a model.

We drove to the station **so slowly that** we missed our train.

I have to do **so much homework that** I don't have time for hobbies.

⚠ BE CAREFUL!

When *so* is used to mean *as a result*, it isn't followed by *that*.

It was very late **so** I decided to leave. (✓)
It was very late so that I decided to leave. (✗)

such

…*such*… { *a/an* + adjective +singular noun / adjective + plural noun / *a lot of* + noun } …*that*…

It was **such a boring lesson that** I fell asleep.

My cousins tell **such funny jokes that** I can't help laughing.

We've got **such a lot of homework that** I don't think I can do it all.

In all the above examples, the word *that* is optional.

My brother's so handsome he's thinking of becoming a model.

I have to do so much homework I don't have time for hobbies.

My cousins tell such funny jokes I can't help laughing.

Both *so* and *such* can be used without a *that* clause as an emphatic way of saying 'very' or 'really'.

You're **so** stupid!
It was **such** a great film!

too

…*too*… { adjective / adverb / *many/much* + noun } (+ *for* and/or full infinitive)

They told my dad he's **too old**.
They told my dad he's **too old for the job**.
They told my dad he's **too old to do the job**.
You're driving **too slowly**.
I can't come out tonight because I've got **too much work to do**.
It's **too difficult for me to do**.

⚠ BE CAREFUL!

Too is used to refer to something that is bad or negative or that prevents us from doing something.

It's **too** cold to play outside. (✓)
Don't worry! You are too popular. (✗)

When the meaning is positive, use other words and phrases, such as *really, extremely* (with adjectives or adverbs) or *lots of* (with nouns).

Don't worry! You are **really** popular.

enough

… (*not*) *enough* + noun (+ *for* and/or + full infinitive)

Yes, I've got **enough time**.
Yes, I've got **enough time** to help you.
No, I don't have **enough time** to help you.
No, there isn't **enough time for us to go** shopping.

… (*not*)… { adjective / adverb } (+ *for* and/or full infinitive)

You're **old enough to go** to school on your own now.

It's not warm **enough for us to go** swimming.

I didn't learn the vocabulary **well enough to pass** the test.

! BE CAREFUL!

Too and *enough* are not followed by a *that* clause.

~~The coffee was **too** hot that I couldn't drink it.~~ (✗)
~~The coffee was not cold **enough** that I could drink it.~~ (✗)

✓ QUICK CHECK

1 What do we use *too* to refer to?
something positive/something negative

2 *It was so hot that I got a headache.* Is this correct?
yes/no

3 *He's old enough that he can drive a car.* Is this correct?
yes/no

Infinitives of purpose

We can use a full infinitive to refer to someone's purpose.

I rang **to speak** to George.
We left early **to get** to the station on time.
~~I rang **for to speak** to George.~~ (✗)
~~We left **early for getting to** the station on time.~~ (✗)

We can also use the phrase *in order* before the full infinitive. In general, *in order* is more formal than the full infinitive alone.

I am writing **in order to request** further information.

In formal contexts, we can use the phrase *so as* before the full infinitive. *So as* isn't very common in conversation.

The Prime Minister today met MPs **so as to inform** them of his decision.

With a negative infinitive and with stative verbs, we normally use *in order not* or *so as not*. We don't normally use the full infinitive on its own.

We left early in **order/so as not** to be late.
I studied hard in **order/so as** to be ready for the test.

✓ QUICK CHECK

1 *I went home for to get my keys.* Is this correct?
yes/no

2 Which phrase means the same as *in order*?
so that/as for/so as

3 Which is correct?
I studied not to fail the test./I studied in order not to fail the test.

13 The causative

I'm having my hair cut tomorrow.
We **got our garden done** last week.
William should **have his car** cleaned. It's a mess!

We use the causative when somebody else does something for us. We often use it for things we pay other people to do. Like the passive (see pages 176–177), we use the causative when the person who does the action is unimportant or obvious or for emphasis. We form the causative using …

- *have* in the right form + object + past participle

We can also use the verb *get* instead of *have*. *Get* is less formal. As with the passive voice, we can use *by* when we want to say who does the action.

You should have your arm looked at **by a doctor**.

with when we want to refer to the tool or equipment.

You look like you've had your hair cut **with a knife and fork!**

❗ BE CAREFUL!

This structure can also be used to refer to things that other people did/have done to us but which we didn't ask them to do, for example, stealing something of ours.

I've had my bag stolen. (= My bag has been stolen.)

✅ QUICK CHECK

1 When do we use the causative?
2 Which verb can be used to form the causative, apart from *have*?
3 Which is correct?
   Get your hair cut./Get cut your hair.

Gradable and ungradable adjectives and adverbs

There are two different kinds of adjective and adverb. Words like *happy, big, angry, slowly, quickly*, etc, are gradable. This means we think of these ideas as a scale.

....▶
big   very big   extremely big   incredibly big

Words like *wonderful, impossible, perfect*, etc, are ungradable. We think of these as things you either are, or aren't. In other words you are either perfect or you aren't. We don't think of these ideas as being on a scale.

We use different words with gradable and ungradable adjectives and adverbs.

gradable adjectives and adverbs

James is .... tall.

In this sentence, we can use words that refer to degree or amount.

	very	
	a little	
	a bit	
	rather	
James is	quite	tall.
	really	
	extremely	
	incredibly	

ungradable adjectives and adverbs

The match was .... amazing.

In this sentence, we can use words that mean 'completely'.

absolutely

The match was **completely** amazing.

totally

❗ BE CAREFUL!

Quite with a gradable adjective means 'fairly'.

Quite with an ungradable adjective means 'completely'.

✅ QUICK CHECK

1 Which of these is gradable?
   perfect/cool/wonderful
2 Which of these is ungradable?
   beautiful/impossible/tall
3 Which of these do we use with ungradable adjectives?
   really/absolutely/very

14 Modals (2): modal perfect

Modal + perfect infinitive (have + past participle)

You **must have felt** great when you got your exam results.

You **shouldn't have spoken** to her like that.

You drove without a licence? You **might have killed** someone!

Paul **might have forgotten** our date.

Could you **have left** your keys at the hotel?

must, can't, couldn't

We use *must/can't* + perfect infinitive to talk about guesses about the past that we are (almost) sure of. Often, we are (almost) sure because we have some evidence.

There's John's coat. He **must have forgotten** it. Angie hates sweet things. She **couldn't/can't have eaten** the cake that was in the fridge.

should, ought to

We use *should/ought to* + perfect infinitive to criticise people (or ourselves) for things they did/didn't do.

Oh, no! I **should have called** Tony at six and I forgot! (I didn't call him.)

We **shouldn't have left** the dog at home on its own. (But we did.)

You really **ought to have invited** Maria to your wedding. (But you didn't.)

You **ought not to have copied** Rita's homework. (But you did.)

may, might, could

We use *may/might/could* + perfect infinitive to talk about things that possibly happened/didn't happen in the past.

How does Lisa know about the party? I suppose Jane **may/might/could have told** her.

The thieves **might have escaped** through the window.

Peter **might not have known** about the meeting.

⚠ BE CAREFUL!

Might/could + perfect infinitive can also be used to talk about an unreal (hypothetical) possibility, something that was a possibility in the past but which we know didn't happen.

You **might have hurt** yourself jumping off the wall like that!

Don't run across the road again! You **could have been killed**!

The modal perfect continuous can be formed using modal + *have* + *been* + *-ing* to refer to actions in progress at a point in the past or to emphasise the duration of an action.

You **can't have been doing** your homework all this time! I don't believe you!

Darren **must have been sleeping** when we called him yesterday.

✓ QUICK CHECK

1. When does the modal perfect refer to?
   the past/the present/the future

2. Which of these is used to criticise other people?
   can't have done/should have done/must have done

3. Which modal is missing?
   There's John. He _____ have got back from Canada.

The unreal past

The past simple is not always used to refer to the past. It can be used to refer to the present, or even the future, when it is used after certain phrases or in certain types of sentence. This is called the *unreal past*.

We use the unreal past …

- in hypothetical conditional sentences
  If I **won** the lottery, I'd buy a new house.
  (see page 185)

- to talk about unlikely hypothetical situations using *suppose* or *imagine*
  Imagine you **got** an A in the exam. How would you feel?

- to talk about present wishes
  I wish I **had** more money. (see page 196)

- after *would rather* when we are talking about things we want/don't want other people to do
  I'd rather you **came** at six tomorrow.

- after *it's* (*high* or *about*) time
  Don't you think it's about time we **left**?

- in polite requests and questions
  I'm sorry, Sir. **Did** you want something?

✓ QUICK CHECK

1. Does the past simple always refer to the past?
   yes/no

2. Which is correct?
   I'd rather you don't do that./I'd rather you didn't do that.

3. *Imagine you won the lottery.* Does the speaker think this is likely or unlikely?
   likely/unlikely

15 The future (2)

We have already looked at some ways of talking about the future in Unit 6 (see pages 178–179). Here are some other ways.

Future perfect: will + have + past participle

> I**'ll have finished** my homework by 8 o'clock.
> I **won't have spoken** to John by the time I see you.

We use the future perfect to show that an action will happen at some point between now and a time in the future.

now   8 o'clock

I'll have finished my homework by 8 o'clock.

I finish my homework at some point between these times.

This means that at 8 o'clock I can say: *I have finished my homework.*

So, now I can say: *I will have finished my homework by 8 o'clock.*

We can also use other modals *(might, may, should)* to talk about actions that will possibly or probably happen between now and a point in the future.

> Call me on my mobile because we **may/might have left** by midnight. (possibly)
> I **should have finished** my homework by six, so give me a ring then. (probably)

Future continuous: will + be + -ing

> This time next week, **I will be lying** on a tropical beach.

now   *This time next week ...*
(eg Wednesday   (eg next Wednesday
morning)   morning)

                         *... I will be lying on
                         a tropical beach*

We use the *future continuous* to talk about an action happening at a point in the future. (Compare this with the present continuous and the past continuous.)

We can also use *may* and *might* to talk about actions possibly happening at a point in the future.

> Don't call at one o'clock tomorrow because I **may/might** be having my lunch. (possibly)

Future perfect continuous: will + have been + -ing

We use the future perfect continuous to talk about actions that are in progress up to a point in the future.

> I**'ll have been living** here for ten years at the end of June.

I started   now   the end of June
living here

10 years

At the end of June, I can say: *I have been living here for 10 years.*

So, now I can say: *I will have been living here for 10 years at the end of June.*

✅ QUICK CHECK

1 *I'll have finished by 6 o'clock.* When will I finish?
   before 6/after 6

2 Can we use other modals instead of *will* in the future perfect?
   yes/no

3 What tense is used to talk about an action happening at a point in the future?

Transferred negation

> I **don't think** Laura is coming to the party.
> I **don't suppose** we'll have the picnic because it's raining.

When we want to express a negative idea using *think, suppose, believe* or *imagine*, we normally make these verbs negative and not the second verb.

> ~~I think I can't come on Saturday.~~ (✗) (not natural)
> I **don't think** I can come on Saturday. (✓) (more natural)
> ~~Sam says she thinks she doesn't have your book.~~ (✗) (not natural)
> Sam says she **doesn't think** she has your book. (✓) (more natural)

We don't do this with the verb *hope*.

> ~~I don't hope we lose the match tomorrow.~~ (✗)
> I hope we **don't** lose the match tomorrow. (✓)

✅ QUICK CHECK

1 Which is better?
   I think he's not coming./I don't think he's coming.

2 *I don't hope my mum has forgotten my birthday!* Is this correct?
   yes/no

16 Conditionals (2): third

We can't change the past. When we want to **imagine** the past being different, we can talk about it using the third conditional.

hypothetical (unreal) possibility, past

Third conditional: *if … past perfect … would have … past participle*

> If I **had known** about the party, I **would have gone.**
> (I didn't know about the party. I didn't go.)
> We **wouldn't have been** on time if we **hadn't run.**
> (We ran. We were on time.)

Instead of *would*, we can also use these other modals.

> If I had known about the party, I **might** have gone. (I'm not sure.)
> If we had had enough money last night, we **could** have gone to the cinema. (It would have been possible.)

✅ QUICK CHECK

1 Does the third conditional refer to a real possibility?
yes/no

2 What does the third conditional refer to?
the past/the present/the future

3 Can we use other modals, apart from *would*?
yes/no

Wishes and regrets

The tenses we use with *wish* are like the tenses we use in hypothetical conditional sentences (past to talk about the present, past perfect to talk about the past). You can see this because we can use *If only …* as an emphatic form of *I wish … .*

Wishes about the present/future: *wish* + **past (simple or continuous) (or past modal)**

> I wish I **was/were** taller. (If only I **was/were** taller!)
> Don't you wish you **knew** more languages?
> I wish I **was having** German lessons.
> I wish I **could** come with you next week.

Wishes about the past (regrets): *wish* + **past perfect**

> We wish we **had seen** that film when we had the chance.
> I wish I **hadn't told** Hannah all my secrets.

Wishes about other people's behaviour: *wish* + *would*

We can use *wish* to talk about things that other people do that annoy or irritate us.

> I wish you **wouldn't** speak when I'm speaking.
> I wish you **would** stop making that noise.

❗ BE CAREFUL!

We don't say: *I wish I would …* (✗)

We only use *wish* to talk about **hypothetical** situations. When we want to talk about **real** possibilities in the past, present or future, we usually use *hope*.

> I **hope** we have a good time next Saturday.
> I **hope** you enjoyed the party last night.

✅ QUICK CHECK

1 *I wish I was still in bed!* What does this refer to?
the past/the present/the future

2 *I wish I would stop smoking.* Is this correct?
yes/no

3 *I wish I pass the exam next week.* Is this correct?
yes/no

Alphabetical index of Grammar database points

Articles	172
Causative (The)	193
Comparatives and superlatives	175
Conditionals (1): zero, first, second	185
Conditionals (2): third	196
Countable and uncountable nouns	177
Future (1) (The)	178
Future (2) (The)	195
Gradable and ungradable adjectives and adverbs	193
Indirect questions	182
Full infinitives (with *to*) and *-ing* forms after verbs	183
Infinitives of purpose	192
Modals (1)	187
Modals (2): modal perfect	194
Passive (The)	176
Past continuous	168
Past perfect continuous	174
Past perfect	174
Past simple	168
Prefer, would rather, had better	184
Present continuous	166
Present perfect continuous	171
Present perfect	171
Present simple	166
Question tags	180
Relative clauses	189
Relative pronouns and prepositions	190
Reported speech	181
Result clauses: *so, such, too, enough*	191
Stative verbs	167
Transferred negation	195
Unless, in case, as long as	186
Unreal past (The)	194
Wishes and regrets	196
Would, used to, be used to	170

Webquests

Units 1–2

1 Find the answers online!

1. In what year did Facebook go online? _____

2. What was the plane called that the Wright brothers made their first successful flight in? _____

3. Which state is Brisbane in? _____

4. Who was the main founder of Facebook? _____

5. What did Frank Whittle invent in 1928? _____

6. What is the busiest airport in New York called? _____

7. Who was the first man to step onto the Moon? _____

8. What is another name for the London Underground? The T_____

9. In what year did the Space Shuttle stop flying? _____

10. In which year did the first modern helicopter take off? _____

Units 3–4

1 Find the answers online!

1. A philatelist collects stamps. What does a deltiologist collect? _____

2. What does an arctophile collect? _____

3. What's the formal word (like the words in questions 1 and 2) for someone who collects coins? _____

4. What's the formal word for someone who collects wild birds' eggs? _____

5. If someone's an amateur vexillologist, what are they interested in? _____

6. The Prime Minister of the UK works at 10 Downing Street in London. Who works at number 11? (clue: the answer is in the form *the C… of the E…*) _____

7. PAYE in Britain stands for 'pay as you earn'. Pay what? _____

8. If someone describes him/herself as a 'tonsorial artist', what do they cut? _____

9. In Britain, the letters NI stand for 'Northern Ireland'. They also stand for something that workers pay. What? _____

10. If a shop sells something 'retail', it sells it to a customer who's a member of the public. What's the word for when a business sells something to a shop, so the shop can later sell it retail? _____

Units 5–6

1 Find the answers online!

1. What did the first text message ever sent say? _____

2. What was the hottest temperature ever recorded in Europe? _____

3. In which country could you watch CBS and NBC? _____

4. What are the seven colours of the rainbow? _____

5. There used to be a show called *Dallas* on TV. Was it a game show, a chat show or a soap opera? _____

6. What do meteorologists measure with the Beaufort scale? _____

7. The title of the show *Big Brother* comes from which book? _____

8. Large storms in the Atlantic Ocean are called hurricanes. What are they called in the Pacific Ocean? _____

9. When talking about the internet, what does *www* stand for? _____

10. June is usually a sunny month in London. What was unusual about 2nd June 1975? _____

Units 7–8

1 Find the answers online!

1. Chinese food is often eaten using thin pieces of wood or plastic rather than knives and forks. What are they called in English? _____

2. In January 2012, the cruise ship *Costa Concordia* had a very serious accident when it hit a rock off which Italian island? _____

3. Jamie Oliver, a famous chef, made a TV series for people who need to cook very quickly. What was the programme called? _____

4. Which city has these airports: Newark and LaGuardia? _____

5. If you're eating *Bombay Duck*, what kind of meat are you eating? _____

6. In which city is Waverley train station? _____

7. Which two men created Worcestershire sauce? _____

8. In Britain, if you order 'bangers and mash' at a café or restaurant, you'll receive a dish with mashed potato and what else? _____

9. Only one city in the world is in two continents. Which city? _____

10. The city in question 9 had two names in English before it got its modern name. One starts with B and the other starts with C. What are they? _____

Webquests

Webquests

Units 9–10

1 Find the answers online!

1. In which year did Apple® start selling apps through their App Store? _____

2. Which Australian soap opera did the actress Isla Fisher appear in? _____

3. In CD-ROM, what do the letters ROM stand for? _____

4. What was Justin Bieber's first album called? _____

5. What is Madonna's full name? _____

6. When was the iPhone® first released? _____

7. Which avenue in New York is famous for its theatres? _____

8. In which decade was the computer mouse invented? _____

9. The *Twilight* series of novels are popular children's books. Who is the writer? _____

10. When was Einstein born, and when did he die? _____

Units 11–12

1 Find the answers online!

1. The University of Warwick isn't actually in the town of Warwick. Which city is it in? _____

2. BA stands for Bachelor of Arts. MA stands for Master of Arts. PhD stands for a phrase in Latin. What is the most common English translation of this Latin phrase? _____

3. You hear these words in a lecture: *integer, prime, differentiation, complex, quadratic, imaginary*. Which subject is the lecture about? _____

4. The set of school exams that many British students take when they're 15 or 16 years old changed its name in 1988. What are the exams called now? _____

5. What were they called in 1987? _____

6. What's another word for a chemist? (clue: it starts with the letter 'p') _____

7. A famous writer gave a London children's hospital a great gift when he said the hospital could have all the money earned by a play and novel he had written. What was the name of the writer? _____

8. What was the name of the hospital? _____

9. What was the name of the main character in the play and novel? _____

10. What's the more common way to refer to the 'scapula' in the human body? _____

Units 13–14

1 Find the answers online!

1. Who painted the *Mona Lisa* and where is it? _____

2. Women first competed in the heptathlon at the Olympic Games™ in which year and in which city? _____

3. How many symphonies did Beethoven compose? _____

4. In which decade was the game of volleyball invented? _____

5. Which famous Spanish painter was born in 1881 and died in 1973? _____

6. Which of these is not a race in the Olympics®: 400m, 5,000m, 7,000m or 10,000m? _____

7. How did the painter Vincent van Gogh die? _____

8. Which country won the football World Cup in 1950? _____

9. Which story by Charles Dickens describes what happens to Mr Scrooge? _____

10. Which famous tennis tournament takes place in London each summer? _____

Units 15–16

1 Find the answers online!

1. What's the name for a garden with a number of fruit trees? (clue: it starts with the letter 'o') _____

2. CFCs can be harmful to the environment. What do the letters CFC stand for? _____

3. What's another noun from the word 'environment'? _____

4. If someone's good at making plants grow, we might say they have what kind of fingers? _____

5. A meteorologist would say that rain and snow are two different kinds of what? (clue: the word starts with the letters 'pre') _____

6. Policemen are sometimes known as 'bobbies'. This word refers to which UK politician from the 1800s? _____

7. The word 'jail' means 'prison'. There's another word with a very similar meaning and the same pronunciation. How is it spelled? _____

8. *Porridge* was the name of a very popular British sitcom set in a prison. What was the name of the fictional prison in the show? _____

9. 'Porridge' is a traditional dish eaten at breakfast. In British slang, though, if someone 'does porridge', what do they do? _____

10. A forest is bigger than a wood, and a wood is bigger than a what? (clue: it's five letters and starts with the letter 'c') _____

Webquests

Macmillan Education
4 Crinan Street
London N1 9XW
A division of Macmillan Publishers Limited
Companies and representatives throughout the world

ISBN 978-0-230-43366-3

Text, design and illustration © Macmillan Publishers Limited 2013
Written by Malcolm Mann & Steve Taylore-Knowles
The authors have asserted their rights to be identified as the authors of this work in accordance with the Copyright Designs and Patent Act 1988.

This edition published 2013
Second edition published 2008
First edition published 2004

All rights reserved; no part of this publication may be reproduced, stored in a retrieval system, transmitted in any form, or by any means, electronic, mechanical, photocopying, recording, or otherwise, without the prior written permission of the publishers.

Original design by Peter Burgess
Page make up by Red Giraffe
Illustrated by Red Giraffe and Oxford Designers and Illustrators
Cover design by Peter Burgess
Picture research by Susannah Jayes

Authors' acknowledgements
Malcolm and Steve would like to thank the staff at Macmillan for all their hard work bringing this project to fruition, and all the many people around the world – far too many to mention – who continue to support and provide feedback on the *Laser* series.

The authors and publishers would like to thank the following for permission to reproduce their photographs:

Alamy/allOver Photography p105(cl), Alamy/David Bagnall p74, Alamy/Corbis Bridge p106, Alamy/Corbis Super RF p100(bcr), Alamy/David Gee p17(cr), Alamy/GL Archive p83(cl), Alamy/Nick Hanna p126(tl), Alamy/Robert Harding Picture Library p17(cl), Alamy/D. Hurst p28(bcr), Alamy/Marmaduke St. John p104(bl), Alamy/Kacper Kida p7(cl), Alamy/Geoffrey Kidd p63(1), Alamy/Oleksiy Maksymenko p79, Alamy/Jeff Morgan 06 p20, Alamy/OJO Images Ltd p127, Alamy/Sean Pavone p84, Alamy/PhotoSpin Inc p83(bl), Alamy/Chris Rout pp6(tr),8, Alamy/Sergiy Serdyuk p136(bcl), Alamy/supershoot p105(tcl), Alamy/David Young-Wolff p134; **Bananastock** pp7(tl),86; **Brand X** p133(bc); **Corbis** p128(tcr), Corbis/Albright-Knox Art Galley p114, Corbis/James L. Amos p117(tr), Corbis/Ben Blankenburg p151, Corbis/Marcus Botzek p137, Corbis/Geoffrey Clements/© ADAGP, Paris and DACS, London 2012 p115, Corbis/Philip James Corwin p90(bc), Corbis/jf/cultura p18(cr), Corbis/Zero Creatives/cultura p17©, Corbis/Strauss/Curtis p39(cl), Corbis/Kerim Okten/epa p126(br), Corbis/Ales Fevzer p123, Corbis/Elmer Frederick Fischer p29, Corbis/Scott Gibson p140(cl), Corbis/Hulton-Deutsch Collection p117(tl), Corbis/Lawrence Manning p125(tr), Corbis/Ocean pp51,128(tcl), Corbis/Gabe Palmer p32(br), Corbis/PictureNet p125(br), Corbis/Radius Images pp132–133, Corbis/Chuck Savage p90(br), Corbis/Shannon Fagan/Spaces Images p28(bl), Corbis/Jean-Yves Ruszniewski/TempSport p126(bcr), Corbis/Rob Lewine/Tetra Images p101, Corbis/Brian Tolbert p140(tr), Corbis/Troy House p100(br); **Getty Images** p63(3,5), Getty Images/Altrendo Images p37, Getty Images/Asia Images p33(bl), Getty Images/Blue Jean Images pp78,100(bl), Getty Images/Josefine Bolander p32(cl), Getty Images/ColorBlind Images p100(bcl), Getty Images/Creative Crop p28(bcl), Getty Images/Nick David p44, Getty Images/Peter Dazeley p38, Getty Images/Erik Dreyer p47, Getty Images/Digital Vision p10, Getty Images/Echo p32(bl), Getty Images/Fuse p19, Getty Images/John Giustina p6(cr), Getty Images/Vladamir Godnik p6(br), Getty Images/Geri Lavrov p7(bl), Getty Images/Bernd Opitz p146, Getty Images/Kibae Park p136(bl), Getty Images/Caroline Purser p18(br), Getty Images/Jon Riley p33(cl), Getty Images/Ned Frisk/Spaces Images p136(br), Getty Images/SW Productions p11, Getty Images/Stockbyte p104(bcl); **Goodshot** p70; **Image Source** p32(cr); **Geoffrey Kidd** p63(4); **Photodisc** p136(bcr); **Press Association**/Rick Gargiulo/AP p104(cl), Press Association/Owen Humphreys p54; **Paul Bricknell/Dean Ryan** p63(2); © 2009 **Sony Computer Entertainment Inc**. All rights reserved p28(br); **Superstock** p56.

These materials may contain links for third party websites. We have no control over, and are not responsible for, the contents of such third party websites. Please use care when accessing them.

Although we have tried to trace and contact copyright holders before publication, in some cases this has not been possible. If contacted we will be pleased to rectify any errors or omissions at the earliest opportunity.

Printed and bound in Thailand
2017 2016 2015
13 12 11 10 9 8 7